89728

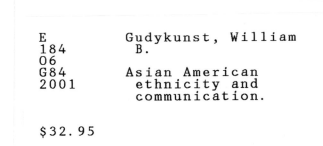

BAKER & TAYLOR

ASIAN AMERICAN ETHNICITY AND COMMUNICATION

ASIAN AMERICAN ETHNICITY AND COMMUNICATION

WILLIAM B. GUDYKUNST

Sage Publications, Inc.
International Educational and Professional Publisher
Thousand Oaks ▪ London ▪ New Delhi

For information:

Sage Publications, Inc.
2455 Teller Road
Thousand Oaks, California 91320
E-mail: order@sagepub.com

Sage Publications Ltd.
6 Bonhill Street
London EC2A 4PU
United Kingdom

Sage Publications India Pvt. Ltd.
M-32 Market
Greater Kailash I
New Delhi 110 048 India

Printed in the United States of America

Library of Congress Cataloging-in-Publication Data

Gudykunst, William B.
  Asian American ethnicity and communication / by William B. Gudykunst.
    p. cm.
Includes bibliographical references and index.
ISBN 0-7619-2041-2 (cloth: acid-free paper)
ISBN 0-7619-2042-0 (pbk.: acid-free paper)
  1. Asian Americans—Ethnic identity. 2. Asian
Americans—Communication. 3. Asian Americans—Cultural assimilation.
I. Title.
  E184.O6 .G84 2000
  305.895073—dc21   00-009515

01   02   03   04   05   10   9   8   7   6   5   4   3   2   1

Acquiring Editor: Margaret H. Seawell
Editorial Assistant: Heidi Van Middlesworth
Production Editor: Denise Santoyo
Editorial Assistant: Victoria Cheng
Typesetter/Designer: Marion Warren
Indexer: Teri Greenberg
Cover Designer: Michelle Lee

Contents

List of Tables and Figures	vii
Preface	ix
1. COMMUNICATION AND ETHNICITY	*1*
Asian American Communication	3
Plan for the Book	13
2. CULTURAL CHARACTERISTICS OF ASIAN CULTURES	*17*
Individualism-Collectivism	18
Hofstede's Dimensions of Cultural Variability	36
Confucianism	47
Conclusion	51
3. ASIAN AMERICAN ETHNIC GROUPS	*53*
General Immigration Patterns	53
Chinese Americans	59
Japanese Americans	63
Filipino Americans	71
Korean Americans	76
Vietnamese Americans	80
Individualism-Collectivism Across Ethnic Groups	85
Conclusion	87
4. ETHNIC AND CULTURAL IDENTITIES	*89*
Ethnicity and Ethnic Identity	90
Asian American Panethnicity	100

Models of Ethnic and Cultural Identities 105
Ethnic Identity, Generation, and Language Ability 117
Conclusion 129

5. ASIAN AMERICAN COMMUNICATION PATTERNS 131
Communication Expectations 132
Communication Styles 147
Conclusion 167

6. COMMUNICATION AND ACCULTURATION 169
The Acculturation Process 170
Communication Acculturation 174
Interethnic Dating and Marriage 187
Conclusion 192

APPENDIX
Survey of Asian American Communication 195
Respondents 195
Measurement 196

References 205

Index 227

About the Author 244

List of Tables and Figures

List of Figures

2.1 The Influence of Cultural Individualism-Collectivism
on Communication   27

List of Tables

2.1 Individualistic and Collectivistic Cultures   37

2.2 Low and High Uncertainty Avoidance Cultures   42

2.3 Low and High Power Distance Cultures   44

2.4 Masculine and Feminine Cultures   47

3.1 Asian American Immigration Patterns for Selected Years   58

3.2 Asian American Population in the United States
for Selected Years   58

3.3 Individualistic and Collectivistic Tendencies by Ethnicity   86

3.4 Individualistic and Collectivistic Tendencies by
Where Asian Americans Are Born and the Language
Spoken at Home When They Were Children   87

4.1 Strength of Ethnic and Cultural Identities by Ethnicity 98

4.2 Individualistic and Collectivistic Tendencies
and Language Usage by Ethnic/Cultural Identity Type   115

4.3   Individualistic and Collectivistic Tendencies
       and Language Usage by Strength of Ethnic and
       Cultural Identities   116

4.4   Generation and Language Usage of Children,
       Adolescents, and Young Adult Asian Americans   123

4.5   Language Usage by Ethnicity   125

4.6   Language Usage by Where Asian Americans Are
       Born and the Language Spoken at Home When
       They Were Children   127

4.7   Associations Among Individualistic and
       Collectivistic Tendencies, Language Usage,
       and Generation   128

5.1   Relational Expectations by Ethnicity   135

5.2   Relational Expectations by Strength of Ethnic and
       Cultural Identities   135

5.3   Politeness Rules for Asian Americans and
       European Americans   139

5.4   Stereotypes of Own Ethnic Group by Ethnicity   145

5.5   Stereotypes of Own Group by Strength of
       Ethnic and Cultural Identities   148

5.6   Communication Styles by Ethnicity   156

5.7   Communication Styles by Strength of Ethnic
       and Cultural Identities   157

5.8   Anxiety, Uncertainty, and Effectiveness by Ethnicity   166

5.9   Anxiety, Uncertainty, and Effectiveness by
       Strength of Ethnic and Cultural Identities   167

Preface

$\mathcal{M}$y purpose in writing this book is to summarize what we know about Asian American communication and the factors that influence it. I am interested in how communication is similar and/or different across Asian American ethnic groups. My focus is not on comparing Asian Americans' communication with European Americans' communication, but I do present this type of research where it is available.

It is impossible to examine communication in all Asian American ethnic groups in this book. I choose to limit my coverage to Chinese Americans, Filipino Americans, Japanese Americans, Korean Americans, and Vietnamese Americans. I selected these specific groups because they tend to be the largest Asian American ethnic groups (although Asian Indian Americans also are a large group). Also, it appeared at the outset that more research has been conducted on these five groups than on other Asian American ethnic groups.

As I started collecting information for the book, it became clear that there has not been a great deal of research conducted specifically on Asian American communication. Communication researchers have focused on understanding communication in Asian cultures more than on understanding Asian American communication. The research that has been conducted on communication in Asian cultures, nevertheless, is necessary background information for understanding Asian American communication (i.e., Asian Americans' communication is based on their Asian cultural heritages, at least to some extent).

The research that has been conducted on Asian American communication varies tremendously by ethnic group. The most research on Asian American interpersonal communication has been conducted on Japanese Americans and Chinese Americans. The most research on communication acculturation of immigrants, in contrast, has been conducted on Korean Americans and Vietnamese Americans. The differences in the focus of the research that has been conducted is due to the different ethnic groups' immigration experiences in the United States. There is, however, no research of which I am aware that has examined any aspect of communication across the five ethnic groups I discuss in this book.

To fill the void in the research, I conducted a Survey of Asian American Communication. In the study, I collected data on selected aspects of communication from Chinese Americans, Filipino Americans, Japanese Americans, Korean Americans, and Vietnamese Americans in southern California. This study was not designed to be a definitive study but rather a first attempt to compare communication across the five ethnic groups. I present data from the Survey where appropriate throughout the book. I present the results of the Survey in a non-statistical manner. Where differences across the five groups are presented, readers can assume that the statistical tests (e.g., analysis of variance) were significant. The correlations presented in the book also are significant correlations. The methods used in the Survey are presented in the appendix.

To further fill in gaps in research on Asian Americans, I re-analyzed data from several recent studies that I have conducted with colleagues that included Asian American and European American respondents. Unfortunately, these studies do not include sufficient respondents in each Asian American ethnic group to compare findings across ethnic groups, and panethnic analyses had to be conducted. I also asked a colleague (Min-Sun Kim) to provide similar analyses. These analyses are presented only to begin to fill in gaps in research, not as definitive results.

Before thanking the people who helped me prepare the book, I want to make a brief comment on spelling. The traditional spelling of *Filipino* is with an "F." There are, however, many people from the Philippines who prefer the spelling *Pilipino*. I used the Pilipino spelling on the Survey of Asian American Communication. About one-third of the respondents "corrected" my spelling. I debated switching back and forth in the spelling I used, but decided that this would be confusing. Since the vast majority of references I cited use the Filipino spelling, I decided to use it throughout the book.

I want to thank several people who helped in making this book possible. Peter Lee, Daryl Nagano, Linh Chau, and Belinda Wells helped me collect the data for the Survey of Asian American Communication (Peter and Daryl also assisted in coding the data). I would not have been able to complete the study without their help. I want to thank Min-Sun Kim for providing re-analyses of data from several of her studies in Hawaii that included Asian American re-spondents. These analyses were very helpful in filling in gaps in the research. Jeff Brody also made preliminary analyses available from his study of Vietnam-ese Americans in southern California. I also want to thank Young Yun Kim for providing information on the research she has conducted on Asian immigrants. Talking with Young also was very helpful in working through some of the ideas I present in the book.

I have been a member of the Asian American Studies Program Council at California State University, Fullerton since shortly after its inception. My col-leagues on the Council have been very supportive of my efforts to study Asian American communication (including allowing me to collect data in their classes). They also have been supportive of including Asian American commu-nication as part of the Asian American Studies curriculum.

Margaret Seawell, the Communication Editor at Sage, has supported my work on this book since I first proposed the book. The book would not exist without her efforts. Finally, writing the book was made possible by a sabbatical leave from California State University, Fullerton.

—*Bill Gudykunst*
Laguna Beach, California

Chapter One

Communication and Ethnicity

The first Asians arrived in the United States before the Declaration of Independence was signed (i.e., a small group of "Manila men" arrived in New Orleans in the 1760s). There was no significant Asian immigration to the United States, however, until after the California gold rush when Chinese workers arrived in the 1850s. Immigration policies restricted Asian immigration until the 1965 Immigration and Naturalization Act. Asian immigration increased significantly after the 1965 Act. Immigrants from Asia accounted for over 40% of the legal immigration to the United States in the 1990s (Kitano & Daniels, 1995).

The majority of Asians living in the United States were not born in the United States. The percentage of U.S.-born Asian Americans varies tremendously—ranging from 67.7% for Japanese Americans to 20.1% for Vietnamese Americans (U.S. Bureau of the Census, 1993). The population of Asian Americans in the United States was estimated at 10,480,000 (3.9% of the population) in 1998 (U.S. Bureau of the Census, 1998). Given the immigration patterns and birth rates, the Bureau of the Census estimates that the population of Asian Americans will double by 2040 (29,235,000; 7.9% of the population).

There are many Asian American ethnic groups in the United States. The largest groups include Chinese Americans, Filipino Americans, Japanese Americans, Korean Americans, Vietnamese Americans, Asian Indian Ameri-

1

cans, Cambodian Americans, Laotian Americans, Hmong Americans, and Thai Americans. Pacific Islanders (e.g., those from Guam, Samoa) also often are included in discussions of Asian Americans. I am not including them in this book because "Pacific Islanders, by definition, have different origins and different experiences from Asians" (Ancheta, 1998, p. 128).

Even omitting Pacific Islanders, there is not a clear boundary as to who is included under the category "Asian." The label Asian has replaced the use of labels such as "Mongolian," "Asiatic," and "Oriental." "Asian," nevertheless, is an imprecise term. "Does 'Asian' describe a geographical category or a biological/appearance-based category? If it is geographical, where does Asian begin and end?" (Ancheta, 1998, p. 129). There is no clear boundary marking Asia from other parts of the world. Using Asian as a biological/appearance-based category also is problematic. Individuals from one Asian country may look very different from individuals from other Asian countries.

There are many differences among individuals of Asian heritage, but there also are similarities. Ancheta (1998), for example, isolates several characteristics that Asian Americans tend to share in common. First, "What all these people have in common is outsider racialization: because of appearance, they are treated as if they are . . . outsiders and not really Americans" (p. 129). Second, with the exception of Japanese Americans, most Asian Americans are foreign-born (i.e., most are immigrants). Third, with the exception of Filipino Americans and Asian Indian Americans, a large percentage of the members of other Asian American ethnic groups speak little or no English. Fourth, Asian Americans tend to live in households that are larger than the national average. Fifth, Asian Americans' per capita income is below the national average, and poverty rates are higher than the national average. Despite these general tendencies, Ancheta claims that Asian Americans generally are "doing well" economically in the United States. There also are "cultural" similarities among Asian Americans, which are discussed below.

It is impossible to discuss all of the different Asian American ethnic groups in this book. I, therefore, have limited the ethnic groups examined to Chinese Americans, Filipino Americans, Japanese Americans, Korean Americans, and Vietnamese Americans. With the exception of Asian Indian Americans, the five groups I discuss are the largest Asian American ethnic groups. Also, there is more written about communication in these five ethnic groups than the other Asian American ethnic groups.

My purpose in this chapter is to overview the issues that are discussed throughout the book. I begin with an overview of Asian American communication and the factors that influence communication of members of specific Asian American ethnic groups. I conclude this chapter by outlining my plans for the remainder of the book.

ASIAN AMERICAN COMMUNICATION

Asian Americans' communication tends to be different from European Americans' communication, but there also are many similarities in communication patterns between Asian Americans and European Americans. Numerous factors must be taken into consideration to explain why there are differences in communication among Asian Americans and communication between Asian Americans and European Americans (e.g., ethnicity, ethnic and cultural identities, generation, language abilities, individualistic and collectivistic tendencies, shared ethnic networks). My goal in this section is to overview the most important factors that influence Asian Americans' communication. To place this discussion in context, I begin with a brief overview of what I mean when I use the term *communication.*

Communication

Language often is equated with speech and communication.[1] There are, however, important differences. Languages are systems of rules regarding how sentences are formed, about the meaning of words or combinations of words, and about how the languages are used. Languages are mediums of communication. When the rules of languages are translated into channels of communication (e.g., the spoken word) using symbols, messages are created.

Symbols are things used to represent something else. Virtually anything can be a symbol—words, nonverbal displays, flags, and so forth. Referents for symbols can include objects, ideas, or behaviors. There are no natural connections between specific symbols and their referents. The relationships between symbols and their referents are arbitrary and vary from culture to culture and from ethnic group to ethnic group.

Individuals combine symbols into messages that they encode to send to others. Encoding involves putting thoughts, feelings, emotions, and/or attitudes into forms recognizable by others (e.g., the spoken word). The encoded messages individuals create are transmitted to others who decode them. Decoding is the process of perceiving and interpreting the messages and other stimuli from the environment that individuals receive through their senses (i.e., seeing, hearing, feeling, touching, smelling, and tasting). How individuals encode and decode messages is influenced by their life experiences (e.g., their experiences with others, the emotions they have felt). Life experiences include unique individual experiences, as well as shared ethnic and cultural experiences. No two individuals have exactly the same life experiences. No two people, therefore, interpret messages in the same way.

There are several possible channels of communication through which messages can be transmitted. Individuals can transmit their messages through the spoken word, use nonverbal cues, or write them. If a person cannot speak or hear, sign language may be used. Alternatively, messages can be transmitted through mathematics or through artistic forms of expression such as painting, photography, or music. Only when the channel is the spoken word does speech occur.

The term communication refers to the exchange of messages and the creation of meanings (e.g., assigning significance or interpreting the messages). Meanings cannot be transmitted from one person to another; only messages can be transmitted. When individuals send messages, they attach certain meanings to the messages and choose the symbols and channel of communication accordingly. The people who receive messages, however, attach their own meanings to the messages they receive. The meanings attached to messages are a function of the messages, the channels used, the environments in which messages are transmitted, and the people who receive them. Communication is effective to the extent that "listeners" attach meanings to the messages that are similar to what "senders" intended.

Culture

Communication and culture are intertwined highly. In fact, Hall (1959) says that "culture is communication and communication is culture" (p. 169). Culture is created, transmitted, and changed through communication. The ways individuals communicate is influenced by the cultures in which they are raised and the cultures in which they live. Since ethnicity is based on cultural practices (see below), it is necessary to briefly discuss the concept of culture before we examine ethnicity.

There are many definitions of culture, but it is necessary to select one to guide our analysis. I find the following definition useful:

Culture, conceived as a system of competence shared in its broad design and deeper principles, and varying between individuals in its specificities, is then not all of what an individual knows and thinks and feels about his [or her] world. It is his [or her] theory of what his [or her] fellows know, believe, and mean, his [or her] theory of the code being followed, the game being played, in the society into which he [or she] was born. . . . It is this theory to which a native actor [or actress] refers in interpreting the unfamiliar or the ambiguous, in interacting with strangers (or supernaturals), and in other settings peripheral to the familiarity of mundane everyday life space; and with which he [or she] creates the stage on which the games of life are played. . . . But note that the actor's [or actress'] "theory" of his [or her] culture, like his [or her] theory of his [or her] language may be in large measure unconscious. Actors [or actresses] follow rules of which they are not consciously aware, and assume a world to be "out there" that they have in fact created with culturally shaped and shaded patterns of mind. We can recognize that not every individual shares precisely the same theory of the cultural code, that not every individual knows all the sectors of the culture . . . even though no one native actor [or actress] knows all the culture, and each has a variant version of the code. Culture in this view is ordered not simply as a collection of symbols fitted together by the analyst but as a system of knowledge, shaped and constrained by the way the human brain acquires, organizes, and processes information and creates "internal models of reality." (Keesing, 1974, p. 89)

Culture, therefore, involves individuals' theories of the games being played in their societies.

Individuals generally are not highly aware of the rules of the games being played, but they behave as though there is a general agreement on the rules (Keesing, 1974). Individuals use their theories of the games being played to interpret things they encounter. Individuals also use their theories in interacting with other people in their societies. Members of cultures do not all share the same views of their cultures. No one individual knows all aspects of a culture, and everyone has unique views of their cultures. The theories that members of cultures share, however, overlap sufficiently so that they can coordinate their behavior in everyday life.

There are numerous subdivisions within cultures (e.g., subcultures) in which members share similar theories. One of the major subdivisions is based on ethnicity (see next section). Others include but are not limited to, regional subcultures, social class subcultures, occupational subcultures, and so forth.

Children learn to be members of their cultures from their parents, from their teachers in schools, from their religious institutions, from their peers, and from the mass media. Originally, children learn about their cultures from their parents. Parents begin to teach their children the norms and communication rules that guide behavior in their cultures. Norms are guidelines of how individuals should behave or should not behave that have a basis in morality. Rules, in contrast, are guidelines for the ways individuals are expected to communicate. Rules are not based in morality (Olsen, 1978). Parents do not explicitly tell their children the norms and rules of their cultures. Parents in the United States, for example, do not tell their children that when they meet someone for the first time they should stick out their right hands and shake three times. Rather, parents teach their children the norms and rules by modeling how to behave and correcting their children when the children violate the norms or rules.

Once children are old enough to interact with others, their peers reinforce the norms and rules they learned from their parents. Children also learn additional norms and rules of their cultures from their peers. Children learn how to be cooperative and how to compete with others from their peers. When children attend religious services or school, they learn other norms and rules of their cultures. Another way children learn about their cultures is through the mass media, especially television. Television teaches children many of the day-to-day rules of their cultures and provides them with views of reality. Television has become the medium through which most children learn what others' expectations are for their behavior.

All cultures are unique, and at the same time, all cultures share similarities with other cultures. There are dimensions on which cultures are similar and different (these are discussed in detail in Chapter 2). One dimension on which Asian cultures are similar to and different from the mainstream U.S. culture is individualism-collectivism. The mainstream U.S. culture is individualistic, and Asian cultures are collectivistic. In individualistic cultures, individuals take precedence over groups (e.g., if there is a conflict between individuals' values and groups' values, individuals follow their values). In collectivistic cultures, in contrast, groups take precedence over individuals (e.g., if there is a conflict between individuals' values and groups' values, individuals follow the groups' values).

Individualism-collectivism influences how individuals view themselves and how they communicate. Members of individualistic cultures tend to view themselves as unique and separate from others. Members of collectivistic cultures, in contrast, tend to view themselves as interconnected with others in their ingroups (e.g., when collectivists think of themselves as family members, they also think of the other members of their family, not of themselves as separate from their family members). Because they are interconnected with others, collectivists tend to communicate in an indirect manner in order to preserve harmony in their ingroups. Individualists, on the other hand, tend to communicate in a direct manner.

Asian immigrants are raised in collectivist cultures, but they are living in the individualistic culture of the United States. Asian immigrants tend to teach their children collectivistic tendencies, but the children learn individualistic tendencies in the schools and from their interactions with European American children.

Ethnicity

Ethnicity involves the cultural characteristics associated with individuals' races, religions, national backgrounds, or a combination of these factors (Gordon, 1964). Ethnicity differs from race, which is based on socially constructed biological traits (e.g., skin color). Ethnicity involves cultural practices and communication patterns associated with specific ethnic groups.

With respect to Asian Americans, ethnicity involves the cultural practices and communication patterns that Asian Americans learned about the cultures of the countries to which their families trace their heritages. Ethnic cultural practices and communication patterns, however, are not necessarily the same as those in the culture to which Asian American families trace their heritages. Roosens (1989) points out that members of ethnic groups recreate their ethnic cultures. Lowe (1991) suggests that "culture may be a much 'messier' process than unmediated vertical transmission from one generation to another, including practices that are partly inherited, partly modified, as well as partly invented" (p. 27).

Immigrant groups modify and adapt the cultural practices of their native cultures. Japanese Americans' ethnicity, for example, involves the cultural practices and communication patterns that Japanese Americans learned when they were socialized that can be traced to Japan. Japanese immigrants, however, modified and adapted Japanese cultural practices and communication patterns based on their experiences in the United States. These changes are not based on conscious decisions. Rather, the changes are a function of the experiences immigrants have living in the United States. Japanese Americans' ethnicity, therefore, is similar to and different from Japanese Peruvians' ethnicity (i.e., people of Japanese ancestry born and raised in Peru).

Ethnicity and communication clearly are interrelated. Ethnicity, however, does not influence all Asian Americans' communication equally. The extent to which ethnicity influences Asian Americans' communication depends, at least in part, on the extent to which individual Asian Americans identify with their ethnic groups (see the discussion of ethnic and cultural identities below). Ethnicity should influence Asian Americans' communication for those who strongly identify with their ethnic groups, but ethnicity might not influence Asian Americans' communication for those who weakly identify with their ethnic groups.

The extent to which ethnicity influences Asian Americans' communication also is a function of the extent to which they maintain the cultural practices of the cultures to which they trace their heritage. I refer to this as the "content" of ethnic and cultural identities (see below). As indicated earlier, Asian cultures are collectivistic. If individual Asian Americans do not maintain collectivistic values and behaviors, their ethnicities probably will not influence their communication to a great extent (see the discussion of self construals below).

Ancheta (1998) points out that "the tendency among many Asian Americans, particularly among recent immigrants, is not to identify along racial lines but along ethnic lines" (p. 129). He goes on to argue that "race remains relevant, however, because it operates as the primary determinant of panethnicity. Externally defined concepts of 'Asian'—that is, how non-Asians view Asians—typically ignore the multiplicity of ethnic groups" (p. 130).

Understanding Asian Americans' communication requires examining the aspects of ethnicity associated with specific Asian American ethnic groups (e.g., Japanese Americans, Vietnamese Americans). Understanding Asian Americans' communication also requires examining Asian American panethnicity (e.g., ethnicity associated with being Asian Americans, not members of specific Asian American ethnic groups). Espiritu (1992) points out that Asian American panethnicity emerged from European Americans' categorizing Asian Americans in a panethnic category (i.e., Asian American) and ignoring Asian Americans memberships in specific ethnic groups. Panethnic similarities exist and influence Asian Americans' communication.

Generation in the United States

Asian Americans' generation in the United States can influence their communication, either directly or indirectly. First-generation Asian Americans (e.g., Asian Americans who moved to the United States after age 13) and 1.5-generation Asian Americans (e.g., Asian Americans who moved to the United States before age 13) have experiences in the United States that are different from other generations of Asian Americans; they are immigrants. Second and later generations of Asian Americans are not immigrants; they are born in the United States.

Whether Asian Americans are immigrants or not tends to influence their communication. Immigrants, for example, may acculturate to the United States, but they never totally loose the cultural values and communication patterns of their cultures of birth. Non-immigrants, in contrast, are born in the United States. Non-immigrants may be taught the cultural values and communication patterns of their parents' native cultures, but they also learn U.S. cultural values and communication patterns at school, from their mainstream cultural peers, from the U.S. mass media, and so forth. The different experiences that immigrants and non-immigrants have in the United States influence their communication. One of the major factors that generation in the United States influences is Asian Americans' language abilities.

Language Abilities

Asian immigrants to the United States obviously are competent in their native languages when they arrive in the United States (e.g., Chinese immigrants speak a dialect of Chinese; Korean immigrants speak Korean). Asian immigrants generally are not competent speakers of English when they arrive. Whether or not Asian immigrants become competent in English depends in large part on where they live, what they do to earn a living, and their motivation to acculturate to the United States. Immigrants who live and work in ethnic enclaves (e.g., Chinatown, Little Saigon) may not have to learn English to survive in the United States. Immigrants who live and work in areas with very low concentrations of their coethnics, in contrast, are forced to learn English to survive.

Second and later generations of Asian Americans learn English from their parents or when they attend school in the United States. Whether these Asian

Americans learn the languages of their heritages initially depends on their parents. Parents, for example, might choose to speak the ethnic language to their children or to send their children to ethnic language schools on the weekends. Asian Americans who strongly identify with their ethnic groups but did not learn their ethnic languages as children also may choose to study these languages in college.

Language abilities influence Asian Americans' communication. Having an Asian language as the only language spoken, for example, obviously limits Asian Americans' abilities to communicate with European Americans. Having Asian languages as first languages also tends to be associated with communicating in a more indirect fashion when speaking English than having English as a first language (indirectness of communication is discussed in detail in Chapter 2). Knowing Asian Americans' language abilities, therefore, is important to understanding their communication in the United States.

Strength of Ethnic and Cultural Identities

Individuals have identities (e.g., senses of themselves) that guide their behavior. Individuals' identities emerge from their experiences. J. Turner (1987) isolates three types of identities that individuals develop: (1) human identities, (2) social identities, and (3) personal identities. Human identities are those identities that separate humans from non-humans (e.g., animals). Human identities are based on those things that humans have in common. Social identities are based on individuals' memberships in social groups (e.g., culture, ethnicity, gender) or the roles that individuals fill (e.g., physician, professor). Social identities are based on things that individuals sharing the identities have in common—things that separate them from people having other social identities. Personal identities are based on how individuals are different from others who share their social identities. Individuals' personality characteristics, for example, can be viewed as their personal identities.

Stryker (1987) argues that individuals' identities are arranged in hierarchies of importance and that individuals have master identities that influence how they view their other identities. Stryker suggests that individuals' age, gender, and ethnic identities generally serve as master identities and influence how they view their other identities. To illustrate, individuals' gender identities influence how they perform their professional identities (e.g., account executive, engineer). Deaux (1991) generally agrees with Styker's conceptualization of identities, but she points out that everyone does not necessarily have hierarchies of identities. Deaux contends that some individuals' identities are arranged at the same level of inclusiveness. That is, these individuals give equal importance to all of their identities and do not see some identities as more important (e.g., master identities) than others.

No matter whether individuals' identities are arranged in hierarchies or are viewed as equally important, individuals integrate their identities into a coherent sense of who they are. My physician, for example, might view herself as a Japanese American, a woman, a physician, a mother, a wife, a daughter, and a chief of staff of her hospital, among her other social identities. My physician's ethnicity may be a master identity for her (e.g., an identity that influences how she views her other identities). Her ethnicity, in contrast, may be equally important to her other identities. Alternatively, her ethnicity may be less important than one or more of her other social identities (e.g., being a physician). These various identities can be distinguished conceptually, but my physician, nevertheless, integrates all of her identities into a coherent sense of who she is.

Two of the most important identities influencing Asian Americans' communication are their ethnic and cultural identities. Ethnic and cultural identities are social identities. Ethnic identities involve Asian Americans' views of themselves as members of their specific ethnic groups (e.g., Vietnamese Americans). Asian Americans also may have panethnic identities associated with being Asian Americans (e.g., as opposed to being Japanese Americans or Filipino Americans; see Chapter 4). Cultural identities involve Asian Americans' views of themselves as members of the mainstream U.S. culture. I discuss these identities separately throughout the remainder of this book. They are being separated only for purpose of discussion. All are part of Asian Americans coherent senses of themselves.

The degree to which Asian Americans identify with their ethnic groups (i.e., the strength of ethnic identities) influences their communication. Asian Americans who strongly identify with their ethnic groups, for example, tend to think and communicate in ways that are consistent with their ethnic heritages in some situations and possibly in all situations. Asian Americans who do not strongly identify with their ethnic groups, in contrast, may not tend to think or communicate in ways based on their cultural heritages in very many situations. These issues are discussed in detail in Chapter 4.

The degree to which Asian Americans identify with the U.S. culture (i.e., the strength of their cultural identities) also should influence their communication. Asian Americans who identify strongly with the U.S. culture, for example, may tend to communicate in ways that are similar to European Americans. Asian Americans who do not identify strongly with the U.S. culture, in contrast, may not have learned U.S. communication patterns and may communicate differently than European Americans.

Asian Americans who strongly identify with their ethnic groups do not always maintain ethnic cultural practices, and Asian Americans who strongly identify with the U.S. culture do not always engage in U.S. cultural practices. In addition to the strength of Asian Americans' ethnic and cultural identities, the "content" of their identities also needs to be considered. The content of identities involves the meanings associated with their identities. The meanings are developed from the cultural practices of their ethnic heritages and the cultures in which they live.

Content of Ethnic and Cultural Identities

The meanings associated with Asian Americans' identities are derived from the cultural practices they learned. These can be described based on dimensions of cultural variability (see Chapter 2). The most important dimension of cultural variability that needs to be taken into consideration to understand the content of Asian Americans' ethnic and cultural identities is individualism-collectivism. The major reason for this is that Asian cultures are all collectivistic cultures and the United States is an individualistic culture.

Collectivism involves an emphasis on the groups over individuals (Triandis, 1995).[2] Individualism and collectivism both exist in all cultures, but one tends to be predominate. Individualism and collectivism influence many aspects of communication (see Chapter 2). Asian immigrants tend to be collectivists. That is, Asian immigrants tend to learn collectivistic values and ways of viewing themselves when they are raised in their native Asian cultures.

Not all Asian immigrants are highly collectivistic. Recall from the earlier discussion of culture that not all members of cultures learn the same theories of their cultures. Some Asian immigrants may have learned to be individualists in their native Asian cultures. In order to understand how Asian Americans' ethnicities influence their communication, it is necessary to know the extent to which they are collectivists. Ethnicity should influence Asian Americans' communication if they strongly identify with their ethnic groups and they are collectivists.

Cultural-level individualism and collectivism influence individuals' personalities, their individual values, and how they perceive themselves (see Chapter 2 for a detailed discussion). Individualists, for example, tend to view themselves as unique and separate from others; they use independent self construals

(Markus & Kitayama, 1991). Collectivists, in contrast, tend to view themselves as interconnected to others; they use interdependent self construals. Everyone has both independent and interdependent self construals, but people tend to use one more than the other to guide their behavior. Knowing whether Asian Americans emphasize independent or interdependent self construals or both is important in understanding their communication.

Throughout the book I examine how Asian Americans' independent and interdependent self construals influence their communication where possible. I do not use the label "content" of ethnic and cultural identities when self construals are examined. Self construals, however, are examined because they are important aspects of the content of Asian Americans' ethnic and cultural identities.

Additional Factors

Numerous other factors might influence Asian Americans' communication. The extent to which Asian Americans are connected to other Asian Americans clearly influences their communication. Asian Americans who are raised in ethnic enclaves, for example, learn different ethnic and cultural identities than Asian Americans raised in predominately European American neighborhoods.

Regardless of where they are born, Asian Americans' networks with other Asian Americans should influence their communication. Asian Americans who interact mostly with other Asian Americans and who have mostly Asian Americans as friends and best friends will communicate differently than do Asian Americans who interact mostly with European Americans and have mostly European Americans as friends and best friends.

PLAN FOR THE BOOK

My goal for the book is to summarize what we know about the similarities and differences in communication among Chinese Americans, Filipino Americans, Japanese Americans, Korean Americans, and Vietnamese Americans. I also look at how European Americans' communication is similar to and/or different from Asian Americans' communication in general and communication in specific Asian American ethnic groups in particular. I focus on summarizing the state of existing research.

Research that has been conducted on Asian American communication does not include all five ethnic groups I am discussing. The amount of information available on the five different ethnic groups varies tremendously. There is more research on Chinese Americans and Japanese Americans than on Filipino Americans, Korean Americans, and Vietnamese Americans. The differences in the research that has been conducted leads to differences in my coverage of the various groups throughout the book.

The focus of the book is on communication within Asian American ethnic groups (e.g., how Vietnamese Americans communicate with other Vietnamese Americans). I do not examine Asian Americans' interethnic communication (e.g., Vietnamese Americans communication with European Americans). The major reason for this is that there is very little research on Asian Americans' interethnic communication (e.g., there is insufficient research to write a chapter on the topic, even a short chapter).

As I collected the information I needed to write the book, it became apparent that there were numerous areas where no research had been conducted. It also became apparent that there were no studies that had compared communication across the five ethnic groups on which I am focusing (there were a few studies comparing communication across three or four groups). To fill the voids where no research had been conducted, I collected data using the Survey of Asian American Communication (the methods I used are discussed in the appendix).

I present results from the Survey of Asian American Communication in a non-statistical manner. The Survey of Asian American Communication includes responses from members of all five ethnic groups being examined. It was designed to begin to fill in the gaps in our knowledge of Asian American communication. I also re-analyze data from other studies that I have conducted with colleagues in recent years that include Asian American respondents.

I do not constantly qualify the trends I isolate by using terms like *most* or *many*. This would make the writing very awkward. Please keep in mind as you read the book that I am presenting general trends that emerge from the research. None of the trends presented apply to all members of specific Asian American ethnic groups or to all Asian Americans in general.

Given this brief overview of my general purpose in writing the book, I will overview what is covered in each of the chapters. In Chapter 2, I focus on the cultural characteristics that can be used to describe Asian cultures. I isolate dimensions (e.g., individualism-collectivism) on which Asian cultures are both similar and different (e.g., these are referred to as dimensions of cultural variability). I examine the general cultural characteristics and also how the various dimensions of cultural variability are manifested in China, Japan, Korea, the Philippines, and Vietnam. The cultural characteristics and communication patterns isolated provide the foundation for Asian American ethnicity and communication in the United States.

In Chapter 3, I examine general patterns of Asian immigration to the United States and the five Asian American ethnic groups discussed throughout the book. For each group, I summarize their immigration history, the ethnic institutions that provide support for maintaining ethnicity, and ethnic family patterns. The material I present in this chapter helps to isolate similarities and differences among the members of the various groups and their experiences in the United States.

In Chapter 4, I examine issues related to ethnicity and Asian Americans' communication. I look at issues of ethnicity, ethnic and cultural identities, generation, language abilities, and panethnicity. These factors clearly are interrelated, and each is an important factor that influences how Asian Americans communicate. Also in this chapter, I examine the various models of Asian American ethnic identities and test predictions based on two of these models.

In Chapter 5, I summarize the research that has been conducted on Asian Americans' communication. Specifically, I examine Asian Americans' expectations for communicating with members of their own ethnic groups, including their ingroup stereotypes. I also summarize research on Asian Americans' communication styles in this chapter. I examine research on communication styles within specific ethnic groups when it is available (e.g., *Nisei*, second-generation Japanese Americans, communication style has been discussed extensively).

In Chapter 6, I examine the role of communication in the acculturation (e.g., learning U.S. culture) of immigrants. I look at the role the adaptation process plays, issues of assimilation versus pluralism, immigrants' communication with coethnics and European Americans, and the role of "Americans'" attitudes toward immigrants in immigrants' acculturation. In this chapter, I also examine Asian Americans' interethnic dating and marriage. This material is included in this chapter because interethnic marriage is one indicator of ethnic assimilation.

NOTES

1. This section is adapted from Gudykunst (1998, Chapter 1).

2. I am focusing on individualism-collectivism because Asian cultures share a collectivistic orientation and the U.S. culture is individualistic. Other dimensions of cultural variability are discussed in Chapter 2.

Chapter Two

Cultural Characteristics of Asian Cultures

$\mathcal{J}$t is not possible to understand Asian American communication without understanding the cultural characteristics of the cultures to which Asian Americans trace their heritages. Unless Asian Americans are assimilated totally in the mainstream U.S. culture (e.g., give up their Asian values and behaviors and totally adopt the values and behaviors of the mainstream U.S. culture, which is almost impossible), the cultures to which they trace their heritages influence their communication in some way.

One way that we could examine the cultural characteristics of Asian cultures is to isolate the characteristics of each culture independent of the others. In so doing, however, we would ignore the cultural characteristics that Asian cultures share in common. Communication is unique within each Asian culture, and at the same time, there are systematic similarities and differences across Asian cultures. Understanding both the similarities and differences in the cultural characteristics of Asian cultures is necessary to explain Asian American communication.

Similarities and differences in the cultural characteristics of Asian cultures can be explained and predicted theoretically using dimensions of cultural vari-

17

ability (e.g., dimensions on which cultures vary, such as individualism-collectivism). In individualistic cultures, for example, individuals take precedence over groups. Groups, in contrast, take precedence over individuals in collectivistic cultures (Triandis, 1988). There are systematic variations in communication that can be explained by cultural differences in individualism and collectivism. To illustrate, members of individualistic cultures emphasize person-based information to predict one anothers' behavior, and members of collectivistic cultures emphasize group-based information to predict one anothers' behavior (Gudykunst & Nishida, 1986).

As indicated earlier, there are general patterns of behavior that are consistent in individualistic and collectivistic cultures. Individualism and collectivism, however, are manifested in unique ways in each culture. In the Japanese culture, for example, collectivism involves a focus on the concepts of *wa* (harmony), *amae* (dependency), and *enryo* (reserve or restraint) (Gudykunst & Nishida, 1994). Other Asian collectivistic cultures emphasize different cultural constructs as part of their collectivistic tendencies. Understanding communication in Asian cultures, therefore, requires culture-general information (i.e., where the cultures fall on the various dimensions of cultural variability) and culture-specific information (i.e., the specific cultural constructs associated with the dimension of cultural variability). My purpose in this chapter is to explain the general patterns and illustrate how the dimensions of cultural variability can be used to explain communication in Asian cultures.

There are many dimensions on which cultures differ. I begin with individualism-collectivism, the dimension that is used most frequently to differentiate Asian cultures from Western cultures like the United States, and the one dimension on which all Asian cultures are similar (i.e., they are all collectivistic). Following this, I look at three dimensions of cultural variability isolated by Hofstede (1980): uncertainty avoidance, power distance, and masculinity-femininity. I conclude this chapter with a discussion of Confucianism. In each section, I discuss the general dimension of cultural variability, and how that dimension is manifested in China, Japan, Korea, the Philippines, and Vietnam (where information is available).[1]

INDIVIDUALISM-COLLECTIVISM

Individualism-collectivism is the major dimension of cultural variability used to explain differences and similarities in communication across cultures. Individualism-collectivism exists at the cultural level (e.g., cultural norms/rules) and at the individual level (e.g., individual values). I begin with cultural-level individualism-collectivism.

Cultural-Level Individualism-Collectivism

Individuals' goals are emphasized more than groups' goals in individualistic cultures. Groups' goals, in contrast, take precedence over individuals' goals in collectivistic cultures. In individualistic cultures, "people are supposed to look after themselves and their immediate family only," and in collectivistic cultures, "people belong to ingroups or collectivities which are supposed to look after them in exchange for loyalty" (Hofstede & Bond, 1984, p. 419).

Importance of Ingroups. Triandis (1988) argues that the relative importance of ingroups is the major factor that differentiates individualistic and collectivistic cultures. Ingroups are groups that are important to their members and groups for which individuals will make sacrifices. Individualistic cultures have many specific ingroups (e.g., families, religions, social clubs, and professions, to name only a few) that might influence individuals' behavior in any particular social situation. Since there are many ingroups, individual ingroups exert relatively little influence on individuals' behavior. In collectivistic cultures, there are only a few general ingroups (e.g., work groups, universities, families, to name the major ingroups that influence behavior in Asian collectivistic cultures) that have a major influence on individuals' behavior across situations. People in individualistic cultures tend to be universalistic and apply the same value standards to everyone. People in collectivistic cultures, in contrast, tend to be particularistic and apply different value standards for members of their ingroups and members of outgroups.

Ingroups may be the same in individualistic and collectivistic cultures, but their spheres of influence are different. The spheres of ingroups' influence in individualistic cultures are very specific (e.g., ingroups affect behavior in very specific circumstances). The spheres of ingroups' influence in collectivistic cultures are very general (e.g., ingroups affect behavior in many different aspects of individuals' lives). To illustrate, in the individualistic culture of the United States, the universities individuals attend generally influence their behavior only when they are at their universities or at alumni events. In collectivistic cultures like Japan and Korea, in contrast, the universities individuals attend influence their behavior throughout their adult lives, including situations that do not directly involve their universities. If Japanese meet strangers and discover that they attended the same universities, for example, the strangers' behavior will be generally predictable because of the shared ingroup membership.

Collectivistic cultures emphasize the goals, needs, and views of ingroups over those of individuals—the social norms/rules of ingroups, rather than individuals' pleasure; shared ingroup beliefs, rather than unique individual beliefs; and cooperation with ingroup members, rather than maximizing individual outcomes. Ingroups have different rank-orders of importance in collectivistic cultures; some, for example, put families ahead of all other ingroups, and others put their companies ahead of other ingroups (Triandis, 1988). To illustrate, the company often is considered the primary ingroup in Japan (Nakane, 1970), but the family tends to be the primary ingroup in other Asian collectivistic cultures.

Individualism-collectivism is expected to affect communication mainly through its influence on group identities and the differentiation between ingroup and outgroup communication. Cultures tend to be predominantly either individualistic or collectivistic, but both tendencies exist in all cultures. Parsons (1951), for example, suggests that a self-orientation involves the "pursuit of private interests" (p. 60) and a collectivity orientation involves the "pursuit of the common interests of the collectivity" (p. 60). He claims that the same behavior can be simultaneously self- and collectivity-oriented. To illustrate this position, Parsons points to department heads in organizations whose actions may be aimed toward their own welfare, their departments' welfare, their firms' welfare, and even their society's welfare at the same time.

Horizontal Versus Vertical Cultures. Triandis (1995) argues that individualistic and collectivistic cultures can differ in whether relations among individuals in the culture are horizontal or vertical. Individuals are not expected to stand out from other members of their ingroups in horizontal cultures. In horizontal cultures, individuals tend to see themselves as the same as others, and there is an emphasis on valuing equality. Individuals are expected to stand out from other members of their ingroups in vertical cultures. In vertical cultures, individuals tend to see themselves as different from others, and equality is not valued highly.

In the horizontal, collectivistic cultures high value is placed on equality, but little value is placed on freedom (Triandis, 1995). To illustrate, in Japan there is a saying, "The nail that sticks out, gets hammered down," which illustrates that members of the culture are not expected to stand out from other ingroup members. In vertical, collectivistic cultures (e.g., Philippines, Korea), individuals are expected to fit into their ingroups, and at the same time, they are allowed or expected to stand out from their ingroups. Individuals in vertical, collectivistic cultures do not value equality or freedom. In vertical, individualistic cultures (e.g., the United States), individuals are expected to act as individuals and try to stand out from others. Individuals in these cultures place a low value on equality and a high value on freedom. In horizontal, individualistic cultures (e.g., Sweden, Norway), individuals are expected to act as individuals but, at the same time, not stand out from others. People in these cultures place a high value on equality and freedom.

Culture-Specific Aspects of Individualism-Collectivism

As indicated earlier, there are culture-specific aspects of all dimensions of cultural variability. In this section, I examine culture-specific aspects of individualism-collectivism for China, Japan, Korea, Philippines, and Vietnam.

Japanese Collectivism. Japanese draw a clear distinction between insiders (ingroup) and outsiders (outgroups). Lebra (1976), for example, points out that the Japanese "differentiate their behavior by whether the situation is defined as *uchi* or *soto*. . . . Where the demarcation line is drawn varies widely; it may be inside versus outside . . . a family, a group of playmates, a school, a company, a village, or a nation" (p. 112). Who is an insider or an outsider depends on the situation. Japanese have a "warm feeling of *ittaikan* ('feeling of oneness') with fellow members of one's group" (p. 25).

Japanese strive for *wa* ("harmony") in their ingroups. The importance of *wa* can be traced back to Prince Shootoku and the first article of the constitution written in the seventh-century: "Above all else esteem concord" (Nakamura, 1968, p. 633). Concord is the translation used for *wa*. Kawashima (1967) points out that when divergent viewpoints are integrated into a unity, *wa* emerges.

Wierzbica (1991) points out that *wa* is something that "is desired or aimed for" in Japanese groups. Wierzbica contends that this explains why *wa* is frequently used as a slogan or motto in Japan by companies and people responsible for the success of different groups (e.g., baseball coaches). She claims that *wa* generally is not discussed in conjunction with naturally cohesive groups like families.

Wa is possible, in part, because Japanese draw a clear distinction between *tatemae* and *honne. Tatemae* refers to the principles or standards by which individuals are bound, at least outwardly (it is a public presentation). *Honne,* in contrast, refers to individuals' "real" or inner wishes (Lebra, 1976). *Wa* is developed and maintained through *tatemae,* not *honne.*

The second Japanese concept related to collectivism is *amae* ("dependence"). Doi (1973) defines *amae* as "the noun form of *amaeru,* an intransitive verb which means 'to depend and presume upon another's benevolence' . . . [it involves] helplessness and the desire to be loved" (p. 22). He contends that *amae* is "a thread that runs through all of the various activities in Japanese society" (p. 26).

Doi (1973) argues that *amae* is based on infants' relationships with their mothers. *Amae* is not limited to family relationships, but when it occurs in other relationships it is perceived in terms of the relationship between parents and children. *Amae* involves a "trustful dependence" that nothing bad will happen if individuals are dependent on others who have good feelings for them. Doi also points out that *amae* involves conscious awareness; that is, Japanese are consciously aware of those on whom they depend.

The third Japanese concept directly related to collectivism is *enryo* ("reserve or restraint"). Lebra (1976) points out that *enryo* is a response to group pressure for conformity. In the presence of this pressure, Japanese may refrain from expressing opinions that go against the majority. Wierzbica (1991) contends that *enryo* is not limited to personal opinions, it also involves restraint from expressing desires, wishes, or preferences. It also includes sidestepping choices when they are offered (R. Smith, 1983). This extends to declining to state what is convenient or even desired when asked (Mizutani & Mizutani, 1987).

Lebra (1976) links *enryo* to collectivism in Japan. She points out that it

> is a product of the suppression of individuality under the pressure of group solidarity and conformity, empathetic considerations for [others'] convenience or comfort, concern to prevent . . . embarrassment, and the wish to maintain . . . freedom by avoiding social involvement without hurting [others]. (p. 252)

Wierzbica (1991) believes that *enryo* is a conscious or semiconscious attitude and that it is expressed verbally and nonverbally to others.

Chinese Collectivism.   Gao (1998) argues that the Chinese concept of the self is other oriented. "The Chinese self involves multiple layers of relationships with others" (p. 164). *Zuo ren* ("conducting oneself") is a life goal in China and crucial to individuals' being aware of their relationships with others. In developing their other-oriented construals of the self, Chinese draw clear distinctions between *zi ji ren* (insiders) and *wai ren* (outsiders). *Zi ji ren* (insiders) and *wai ren* (outsiders) are treated differently. Insiders are expected to be "nice, trustworthy, caring, helpful, and empathetic" (Gao, 1996, p. 87). *Zi ji ren* (insiders), the focus of Chinese social relationships, include families, friends, and established relationships. *Bu fu hori wang* ("to live up to others' expectations") "is aspired to and cherished in Chinese culture" (Gao, 1998, p. 165).

Gao (1996) argues that the other-oriented self construal in China is reflected in cultural rules regarding modesty and humility. "To be modest is to treat oneself strictly and others leniently" (p. 85). Gao suggests that Chinese values such as *tuan jie* ("solidarity with others"), *sui he* ("harmony with others"), *rong ren* ("tolerance of others") reflect the other-oriented self construal in China. *Gan qing* ("mutual good feelings") is the basis of personal relationships and requires interdependency.

Chinese communication patterns are guided by their other-oriented self construals (Gao, 1998). Chinese do not spell everything out for the people with whom they are communicating. Rather, they leave the "unspoken" for the listeners to figure out (this is referred to as *han xu,* "implicit communication"). For Chinese, the meaning of what is said lies beyond the words that are spoken (*yi zai yan wai*). Listeners must use *ti hui* ("to apprehend or to experience") and *zuo mo* ("to contemplate or to ponder") to figure out the meanings speakers intended.

Korean Collectivism. Cha (1994) isolates several concepts associated with Korean collectivism. *Woori* ("we") refers to the ingroup, which tends to be closed and exclusionary. The major ingroup is the *kamun* ("family, clan"). *Cheong* ("affection") and *uichi* ("dependence") are the "glue" that hold ingroups together. Choi, Kim, and Choi (1993) point out that

> *cheong* is shared among members of a primary group. The family is a prototypical example. . . . Within a family, members are encouraged to share with, to care for, and to trust in one another. The family serves as a model for all future relationships. Children are encouraged to develop similar relationships in other contexts, in school and later in life in the workplace. *Cheong* reflects relationship centeredness rather than person centeredness. (p. 205)

Koreans are expected to follow *ch'ung-hyo* ("the dual principles of loyalty to country and filial piety"), *bunsu* ("one's station in life"), and *ye* ("courtesy") in their ingroups (Cha, 1994).

Communication in Korea requires *noon-chi* ("other awareness, or situation sensitivity") (Lim & Choi, 1996). Lim and Choi argue that Koreans

> who decide not to express their meanings explicitly do not necessarily want the other to figure out their meanings, or do not necessarily assume that the other will be able to figure out their intentions. In addition, the parties who have to use *noon-chi* to figure out the intention of the other do not necessarily have concrete clues about the intentions. They have to go through the *noon-chi* operation, which makes use of all kinds of world knowledge, the knowledge of the other, the knowledge of the context, the history of their interaction, and verbal and nonverbal messages, if any. (p. 131)

The ability to use *noon-chi* in Korea is related to communication competence. Koreans who cannot use *noon-chi* are considered as incompetent.

Cha (1994) reports that the vast majority of both younger (75%) and older (86%) Koreans value loyalty and filial piety. Younger and older Koreans accept ingroup obligations. Cha concludes that younger Koreans are more individualistic than older Koreans, but both groups are still collectivistic.

Filipino Collectivism. Filipinos draw a distinction between *hindi ibang-tao* ("insider, one of us") and *ibang-tao* ("outsider") (Enriquez, 1978). Enriquez contends that *kapwa* ("fellow being") is a central concept necessary to understand Filipino behavior. *Kapwa* involves a unity of self and others; it does not recognize the self as separate from others.

The family is the primary ingroup in the Philippines (Pido, 1986). The family extends through marriage to the children's families. Parents do not "lose" their children when the children in their families marry; rather, they gain sons and daughters and alliances with the in-law families. Filipino social life revolves around the family, and "it demands an almost absolute loyalty and allegiance throughout a person's lifetime" (p. 18). The family "offers material and emotional support and the individual expects it as a matter of right" (p. 18). Any status or power that family members gain is shared by others in their families. "Interaction within the family is governed by norms, often accompanied by rituals which are determined by one's genealogical and social position in the family" (p. 24). Threats to individual Filipinos' self-esteem also threaten their families' collective self-esteem and visa versa.

Lynch (1973) suggests that social acceptance motivates Filipino behavior. Social acceptance occurs "when one is not rejected or improperly criticized by others" (p. 8). Smooth interpersonal relations are necessary for social acceptance in Filipino families and other groups as well. Lynch points out that smooth interpersonal relations involve

> a facility at getting along with others in such a way as to avoid outward signs of conflict: glum or sour looks, harsh words, open disagreement, or physical violence. . . . It means being agreeable, even under difficult circumstances. . . . It means a sensitivity to what people feel at any given moment. (p. 10)

Maintaining smooth interpersonal relations requires *pakikiramdam*, "being sensitive to and feeling one's way toward another person" (Mataragon, 1988, p. 252). Filipinos will feel *hiya* ("shame") if they are not socially accepted.

Vietnamese Collectivism. The family is the primary ingroup in Vietnam. There are two conceptions of the family: *nha* and *ho* (Rutledge, 1992). The *nha* is the extended family, which includes the nuclear family, the husband's parents, and the sons' families. The *ho* also includes family members living in close proximity.

Vietnamese draw a clear boundary between family members and non-family members. "Everyone is expected to work for the well being of the family, since the group takes precedence over the individual" (Rutledge, 1992, p. 116). All blood relatives are to be treated with respect, and Vietnamese are expected to assist any family member when they can. Rutledge points out that "awards or reprimands received by any one member [reflect] on the family unit as a whole. In the broadest sense, all members [are] responsible for all other members" (p. 118). Individual Vietnamese's self-esteem is tied to the family (i.e., it is based on how the family does, not on how individual members do).

Individual Factors That Mediate the Influence of Cultural Individualism-Collectivism on Individuals' Behavior

Cultural individualism-collectivism influences communication in a culture through the cultural norms and rules associated with the major cultural tendency (e.g., the United States tends to have individualistic norms/rules; Asian cultures tend to have collectivistic norms/rules). In addition to cultural norms/rules, individualism-collectivism also influences the ways individuals are socialized in their cultures. Individuals in a culture generally are socialized in ways consistent with the cultural-level tendencies, but some individuals in every culture learn different tendencies (e.g., most individuals in the United States learn individualistic tendencies, but some learn collectivistic tendencies). Cultural individualism-collectivism, therefore, indirectly influences communication through the characteristics individuals learn when they are socialized.

Three different individual characteristics mediate the influence of cultural individualism-collectivism on individuals' communication: their personalities, their individual values, and their self construals. Figure 2.1 schematically illustrates how the influence of cultural individualism-collectivism on communication is mediated by these factors.

Personality Orientations. Triandis et al. (1985) propose idiocentrism and allocentrism as the personality orientations individuals learn as a function of individualism and collectivism, respectively. Allocentrism is associated positively with social support and negatively with alienation and anomie (e.g., feelings of normlessness) in the United States. Idiocentrism, in contrast, is associated positively with an emphasis on achievement and perceived loneliness in the United States.

Gudykunst et al. (1992) report that the more idiocentric people are in the United States, the less sensitive they are to others' behavior. The more idiocentric Japanese are, the less sensitive they are to others' behavior, the less they pay attention to others' status characteristics, and the less concern they have for behaving in a socially appropriate fashion. Gudykunst, Gao, and Franklyn-Stokes (1996) note that the more idiocentric Chinese and English are, the less they pay attention to others' status characteristics and the less concerned they are with behaving in a socially appropriate fashion.

Idiocentric individuals in individualistic cultures see it as natural to "do their own thing" and disregard needs of their ingroups, but allocentric individuals in individualistic cultures are concerned about their ingroups (Triandis et al., 1988). Allocentric individuals in collectivistic cultures "feel positive about accepting ingroup norms and do not even raise the question of whether or not to accept them," but idiocentric individuals in collectivistic cultures "feel ambivalent and even bitter about acceptance of ingroup norms" (Triandis et al., 1988, p. 325).

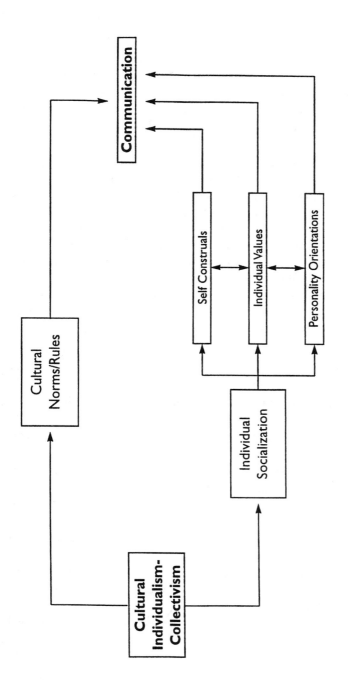

Figure 2.1. The Influence of Cultural Individualism-Collectivism on Communication

Source: Gudykunst (1998).

Yamaguchi (1994) argues that collectivism at the individual level involves the tendency to give priority to the collective self over the private self, especially when the two are in conflict. He reports that the more collectivistic Japanese are, the more sensitive they are to others and the less they have a tendency to want to be unique. Yamaguchi, Kuhlman, and Sugimori (1995) note that these tendencies extend to people in Korea and the United States.

Individual Values. Ball-Rokeach, Rokeach, and Grube (1984) argue that values serve as the major component of individuals' personalities and that values help individuals maintain and enhance their self-esteem. Feather (1995) reports that the type of values individuals hold influences the valences (positiveness/negativeness) they attach to different behaviors (e.g., if individuals value self-direction, they will view making decisions alone positively). Feather (1990) points out that individuals' values influence the way they define situations, but values are not tied to specific situations.

Schwartz (1992) isolates 11 value domains. Value domains specify the structure of values and consist of specific values. Specific values fall in each of the domains [example values are given in brackets below]:

1. *Self-direction.* "Independent thought and action—choosing, creating, and exploring" (p. 5). [independent, freedom, curious]
2. *Stimulation.* "Excitement, novelty, and challenge in life" (p. 8). [exciting life, daring]
3. *Hedonism.* "Pleasure or sensuous gratification for oneself" (p. 8). [pleasure, enjoy life]
4. *Achievement.* "Personal success through demonstrated competence" (p. 8). [social recognition, capable, ambitious]
5. *Power.* "attainment of social status and prestige, and control or dominance over people" (p. 9). [authority, wealth, social recognition]
6. *Security.* "Safety, harmony, and stability of society, of relationships, and of self" (p. 9). [family security, social order, healthy]
7. *Conformity.* "Restraint of actions, inclinations, and impulses likely to upset or harm others and to violate social expectations or norms" (p. 9). [obedient, politeness, self-discipline]
8. *Tradition.* "Respect, commitment and acceptance of the customs and ideas that one's culture or religion impose on the individual" (p. 10). [respect for tradition, humble, moderate]

9. *Spirituality.* "Endow life with meaning and coherence in the face of seeming meaninglessness of everyday existence" (p. 10). [meaning in life, inner harmony, devout]

10. *Benevolence.* "Preservation and enhancement of the welfare of people with whom one is in frequent social contact" (p. 11). [helpful, loyal, responsible]

11. *Universalism.* "Understanding, appreciation, tolerance, and protection for the welfare of *all* people and for nature" (p. 12). [equality, world at peace, social justice]

Schwartz argues that value domains can serve individualistic, collectivistic, or mixed interests. Stimulation, hedonism, power, achievement, and self-direction serve individual interests; tradition, conformity, and benevolence serve collective interests; and security, universalism, and spirituality serve mixed interests.

Schwartz (1990) contends that individualistic and collectivistic values do not necessarily conflict. With respect to individualistic values, he points out that

> hedonism (enjoyment), achievement, self-direction, social power, and stimulation values all serve self interests of the individual, but not necessarily at the expense of any collectivity. . . . These same values might be promoted by leaders or members of collectivities as goals for their ingroup. (p. 143)

With respect to collectivistic tendencies, Schwartz indicates that

> prosocial, restrictive conformity, security, and tradition values all focus on promoting the interests of others. It is other people, constituting a collective, who benefit from the actor's [or actress'] concern for them, self-restraint, care for their security, and respect for shared traditions. But this does not necessarily occur at the expense of the actor [or actress]. (p. 143)

Individuals, therefore, can hold both individualistic and collectivistic tendencies, but one tends to predominate. In the mainstream U.S. culture, for example, there are collective tendencies, and some subcultures tend to be collectivistic, but most people hold individualistic values.

Self Construals. Triandis (1989) argues that cultural variations in individual-ism-collectivism can be linked directly to the ways members of cultures con-ceive of themselves. Markus and Kitayama (1991) contend that people use two different construals of the self: the independent and the interdependent construals of the self. Emphasizing independent self construals *predominates* in individualistic cultures, and emphasizing interdependent self construals *predominates* in Asian collectivistic cultures (Gudykunst, Matsumoto et al., 1996; Singelis & Brown, 1995).

The independent construal of self involves the view that individuals' selves are unique, independent entities. Geertz (1975), for example, describes the self "as a bounded, unique, more or less integrated motivational and cognitive universe, a dynamic center of awareness, emotion, judgment, and action organized into a distinctive whole and set contrastively both against other such wholes and against a social and natural background" (p. 48). Individualists' cultural "goal of independence requires construing oneself as an individual whose behavior is organized and made meaningful primarily by reference to one's own internal repertoire of thoughts, feelings, and action, rather than by reference to the thoughts, feelings, and actions of others" (Markus & Kitayama, 1991, p. 226).

The important tasks for individuals who emphasize independent self construals are to be unique, strive for their own goals, express themselves, and be direct (e.g., "say what you mean"; Markus & Kitayama, 1991). The self-esteem of individuals who emphasize independent self construals is based on their abilities to express themselves and their abilities to validate their internal attributes (Markus & Kitayama, 1991).

Markus and Kitayama (1991) point out that

> experiencing interdependence entails seeing oneself as part of an encom-passing social relationship and recognizing that one's behavior is deter-mined, contingent on, and, to a large extent organized by what the actor [actress] perceives to be the thoughts, feelings, and actions of *others* in the relationship. (p. 227)

The self-in-relation to specific others guides behavior in specific social situa-tions. Depending on the situation, different aspects of the interdependent self will guide individuals' behavior. If the behavior is taking place at home, the family interdependent self guides behavior; if the behavior is taking place on the job, the co-worker interdependent self guides behavior.

The important tasks for individuals who emphasize interdependent self construals are to fit in with their ingroups, act in an appropriate fashion, promote their ingroups' goals, occupy their proper places, be indirect, and read other people's minds (Markus & Kitayama, 1991). Markus and Kitayama also point out that "giving in is not a sign of weakness, rather it reflects tolerance, self-control, flexibility, and maturity" (p. 229). The self-esteem of individuals who emphasize an interdependent self construal is based on individuals' abilities to adjust to others and their abilities to maintain harmony in the social context when an interdependent self construal predominates (Markus & Kitayama, 1991).

Everyone has both an independent and interdependent construal of the self, but individuals tend to use one more than the other. Individuals with predominately interdependent self construals exist in individualistic cultures like the United States, and individuals with predominately independent self construals exist in Asian collectivistic cultures. The critical issue is which self construal predominates to influence individuals' behavior and which self construal individuals use in guiding their behavior in particular situations.

Low- and High-Context Communication

Individualism-collectivism provides an explanatory framework for understanding cultural similarities and differences in interpersonal communication. There are cultural differences in the communication process that predominate in individualistic and collectivistic cultures.

Characteristics of Low- and High-Context Communication. Hall (1976) differentiates between low- and high-context communication. High-context communication occurs when "most of the information is either in the physical context or internalized in the person, while very little is in the coded, explicit, transmitted part of the message (Hall, 1976, p. 79). Low-context communication, in contrast, occurs when "the mass of information is vested in the explicit code" (p. 70). Hall points out that

> people raised in high-context systems expect more of others than do the participants in low-context systems. When talking about something that they have on their minds, a high-context individual will expect his [or her] inter-

locutor to know what's bothering him [or her], so that he [or she] doesn't have to be specific. The result is that he [or she] will talk around and around the point, in effect putting all the pieces in place except the crucial one. Placing it properly—this keystone—is the role of his [or her] interlocutor. (p. 98)

These expectations clearly are different from those used in low-context communication where information is embedded mainly in the messages transmitted.

Members of individualistic cultures tend to use low-context communication and communicate in a direct fashion. Members of collectivistic cultures, in contrast, tend to use high-context messages when maintaining ingroup harmony is important and, therefore, communicate in an indirect fashion. The characteristics of low- and high-context communication influence the conversational maxims used to guide everyday communication.

Many people in individualistic cultures where low-context communication predominates assume that indirect, high-context communication is unclear and ineffective. This, however, is not necessarily the case. Some high-context communication can be ineffective like some low-context communication. Most high-context is clear and effective. The clarity and effectiveness comes from listeners' knowing how to interpret indirect messages in specific contexts.

Conversational Maxims. Grice (1975) isolates four maxims regarding coordinated social interaction that are characteristic of low-context communication in the mainstream U.S. culture. First, individuals should not give others more or less information than necessary (quantity maxim). Second, individuals should state only that which they believe to be true with sufficient evidence (quality maxim). Third, what individuals say should be pertinent to the context of conversations (relevancy maxim). Fourth, individuals should avoid obscure expressions, ambiguity, excessive verbosity, and disorganization (manner maxim). These conversational maxims are not characteristic of high-context communication in Asian cultures.

Direct communication (Grice's, 1975, manner maxim) involves transmitting verbal messages that "embody and invoke speakers' true intentions," and indirect communication involves transmitting verbal messages that "camouflage and conceal speakers' true intentions" (Gudykunst & Ting-Toomey, 1988, p. 100). Indirect communication emphasizes listeners' abilities to infer speakers' intentions, and direct communication emphasizes speakers' abilities to express their intentions (Okabe, 1987; Okabe, 1983; Yum, 1988b). To illustrate, Okabe (1987) points out that someone being direct might say "The door is open" when asking someone to close the door, and someone being indirect might say "It is somewhat cold today."

Okabe (1983) suggests that low-context communication involves the use of categorical words such as "certainly," "absolutely," and "positively." High-context communication, in contrast, is expressed through the use of qualifiers such as "maybe," "perhaps," and "probably" (Okabe, 1983, p. 34). Qualifier words are used to avoid leaving an assertive impression with listeners.

High-context communication involves the use of indirect, implicit, and often ambiguous messages. When individuals' responses to others' messages are indirect and ambiguous, the responses may not appear to be relevant to what others said (e.g., they appear to violate Grice's, 1975, relevancy maxim). In order to communicate effectively using high-context communication, listeners must infer how what speakers say is relevant to what they said. Listeners also must infer speakers' intentions accurately to understand utterances correctly. Yum (1988b) contends that to be a competent high-context communicator, individuals must "hear one and understand ten" (p. 384). This saying emphasizes the importance of receivers' sensitivity and abilities to capture the nonverbal aspect of indirect communication.

Consistent with Grice's (1975) quality maxim, speaking one's mind and telling the truth are "characteristic of a sincere and honest person" using low-context communication (Hofstede, 1991). Individuals using low-context communication are expected to communicate in ways that are consistent with their feelings (Hall, 1976). Individuals using high-context communication, in contrast, are expected to communicate in ways that maintain harmony in their ingroups. This may require that individuals transmit messages that are inconsistent with their true feelings (Hall, 1976).

Speaking one's mind and telling the truth in low-context communication requires that individuals be open with others. Openness involves revealing "personal information about the self in communicative interactions" (Norton, 1978, p. 101). Personal information is necessary to predict behavior when low-context communication is being used (Gudykunst & Ting-Toomey, 1988). When individuals are open, they are not reserved. Open communicators also are not secretive, and they are relatively frank with others (Norton, 1978).

Openness is not characteristic of high-context communication in Asian cultures. In high-context communication, individuals do not reveal large amounts of personal information about themselves. Personal information is not used to predict behavior in high-context communication. Rather, group-based information (e.g., background, group memberships, status, age) is needed

(Gudykunst & Nishida, 1986). Communicators perceived as competent high-context communicators are not open but tend to be reserved (Okabe, 1983). Being reserved is considered an active, not a passive, behavior in Asian collectivistic cultures.

Low-context communication also involves being precise (Grice's, 1975, quantity maxim), and high-context communication involves the use of understatements. As indicated earlier, Grice's (1975) quantity maxim states that individuals' contributions to conversations should provide neither more nor less information than is required. High-context communication, in contrast, is not precise. Rather, high-context communication involves using understatements, or providing the least amount of information possible to allow listeners' to infer speakers' intentions, and using pauses and silences in everyday conversation. Okabe (1983) argues that high-context communication requires transmitting messages through understatement and hesitation rather than through superlative expression (the opposite of Grice's, 1975, quantity maxim). In high-context communication, there is a negative association between the amount of spoken words individuals use and the images others have of them, especially in terms of their trustworthiness. Individuals who use few words, for example, are viewed as more trustworthy than those who use many words in Japan (Lebra, 1987).

Closely related to the lack of emphasis on spoken words is the use of silence. In low-context communication, silence is space to be filled (Mare, 1990). Individuals using low-context communication tend to experience a general discomfort with silence because it interrupts the flow of conversations. Silence often is interpreted by individuals using low-context communication as violating the quantity maxim. Silence also can be viewed as violating the relevancy maxim when individuals are using low-context communication. In high-context communication, in contrast, "silence is a communicative act rather than mere void in communicational space" (Lebra, 1987, p. 343). Lebra argues that silence can be used to indicate truthfulness, disapproval, embarrassment, and disagreement in Japan.

Hasegawa and Gudykunst (1998) examine silence in Japan and the United States. They report that Japanese have a more negative view of silence when communicating with strangers than with close friends, but there is no difference for U.S. Americans. Japanese also have a more negative view of using silence when communicating with strangers than do U.S. Americans, but there are no cultural differences for using silence with close friends. Finally, Hasegawa and Gudykunst observe that U.S. Americans use silence more strategically than Japanese.

Individualism-Collectivism and Low- and High-Context Communication

High-context communication can be characterized as being indirect, ambiguous, and understated with speakers being reserved and sensitive to listeners. Low-context communication, in contrast, can be characterized as being direct, explicit, open, precise, and being consistent with one's feelings. As indicated earlier, these patterns of communication are compatible with collectivism and individualism, respectively.

Individuals use low- and high-context messages depending on their relationship with the person with whom they are communicating. To illustrate, European Americans in the mainstream individualistic culture of the United States use low-context communication in the vast majority of their relationships (Hall, 1976). They may, however, use high-context messages when communicating with a twin or their spouse of 20 years. In these relationships, it is unnecessary to be direct and precise to be clearly understood. Individuals in Asian collectivistic cultures, in contrast, tend to use high-context messages when they communicate and must maintain ingroup harmony. They, nevertheless, also use low-context messages in some relationships (e.g., close friendships).

European Americans are more affect oriented (i.e., base their behavior on their feelings; Frymier, Klopf, & Ishii, 1990) and more inclined to talk (Gaetz, Klopf, & Ishii, 1990) than members of Asian collectivistic cultures. Members of collectivistic cultures like Japan pay more attention to others' behavior and more attention to others' status characteristics than do members of individualistic cultures like the United States (Gudykunst et al., 1992). Members of collectivistic cultures like Korea are more concerned with avoiding hurting others and imposing on them than are members of individualistic cultures like the United States (Kim, 1994). Members of individualistic cultures like the United States are more concerned with clarity in conversations (Kim, 1994) and view clarity as necessary for effective communication (Kim & Wilson, 1994) more than do members of collectivistic cultures like Korea. Members of individualistic cultures perceive direct requests as the most effective strategy for accomplishing their goals, and members of Asian collective cultures perceive direct requests as the least effective (Kim & Wilson, 1994).

As indicated earlier, not all members of individualistic cultures are individualists, and not all members of collectivistic cultures are collectivists (Triandis et al., 1985). Individuals' communication styles are dependent on the degree to which they have internalized the values of the culture in which they are socialized, and the way they see themselves is dependent on the way their culture socializes people to see themselves (e.g., as independent, unique individuals or as individuals embedded in social groups).

Gudykunst and Nishida (1994) point out that "when a person's goal is to assert him or herself as a unique person (individualism), he or she must be direct so that others will know where he or she stands" (p. 40). Kim, Sharkey, and Singelis (1994) observe that using interdependent self construals is associated with concern for others' feelings and using independent self construals is associated with a concern for clarity in conversations. Singelis and Brown (1995) report that using an interdependent self construal is related to using high-context communication styles. Singelis and Sharkey (1995) note that using an independent self construal is associated negatively with embarrassability. Sharkey and Singelis (1993) observe that using an independent self construal is associated negatively with social anxiety.

Gudykunst, Matsumoto et al. (1996) report that independent self construals and individualistic values positively influence the use of dramatic communication, use of feelings to guide behavior, openness of communication, and preciseness of communication in the United States, Australia, Korea, and Japan. Interdependent self construals and collectivistic values positively influence the tendency to use indirect communication and be interpersonally sensitive.

Summary. To summarize, members of individualistic cultures like the United States predominately use low-context communication, but they also use high-context communication at times. Members of collectivistic cultures, in contrast, predominately use high-context communication, but they also use low-context communication at times. Table 2.1 summarizes the characteristics of individualistic and collectivistic cultures. All Asian cultures tend to be collectivistic.

HOFSTEDE'S DIMENSIONS OF CULTURAL VARIABILITY

Hofstede (1980, 1983) empirically derives four dimensions of cultural variability in his large-scale study of a multinational corporation. The first dimension isolated in his study, individualism, already has been discussed. The other three dimensions are uncertainty avoidance, power distance, and masculinity-femininity.

TABLE 2.1 Individualistic and Collectivistic Cultures

Individualism	*Collectivism*
Major Characteristics	
Focus on individuals' goals	Focus on group's goals
Self-realization	Fitting into ingroups
Many ingroups	Few ingroups
Little difference between ingroup and outgroup communication	Large difference between ingroup and outgroup communication
"I" Identity emphasized	"We" identity emphasized
Universalistic	Particularistic
Individual Level	
Idiocentrism	Allocentrism
Value stimulation, hedonism, power, self-direction	Value traditions, conformity, benevolence
Independent self construals	Interdependent self construals
Communication	
Low-context messages: direct, precise, clear, and absolute	High-context messages: indirect, often ambiguous, implicit, and probabilistic

SOURCE: Adapted from Gudykunst (1998).

Uncertainty Avoidance

Uncertainty avoidance deals with the degree to which members of a culture try to avoid uncertainty. I begin with cultural-level uncertainty avoidance.

Cultural Uncertainty Avoidance. In comparison to members of cultures low in uncertainty avoidance, members of cultures high in uncertainty avoidance have a lower tolerance "for uncertainty and ambiguity, which expresses itself in higher levels of anxiety and energy release, greater need for formal rules and absolute truth, and less tolerance for people or groups with deviant ideas or behavior" (Hofstede, 1979, p. 395).

In high uncertainty avoidance cultures, aggressive behavior of self and others is acceptable, but individuals prefer to contain aggression by avoiding conflict and competition. There is a strong desire for consensus in cultures high in uncertainty avoidance, and deviant behavior is not acceptable. Members of high uncertainty avoidance cultures tend to display emotions more than do members of low uncertainty avoidance cultures. Members of low uncertainty avoidance cultures have lower stress levels, weaker superegos, and accept dissent and taking risks more than members of high uncertainty avoidance cultures.

Hofstede (1991) points out that uncertainty avoidance should not be equated with risk avoidance. Individuals in

> uncertainty avoiding cultures shun ambiguous situations. People in such cultures look for a structure in their organizations, institutions, and relationships which makes events clearly interpretable and predictable. Paradoxically, they are often prepared to engage in risky behavior to reduce ambiguities, like starting a fight with a potential opponent rather than sitting back and waiting. (p. 116)

Hofstede summarizes the view of members of high uncertainty avoidance cultures as "what is different, is dangerous," (p. 119) and the credo of members of low uncertainty avoidance cultures as "what is different, is curious" (p. 119).

Hofstede (1980) reports that members of high uncertainty avoidance cultures resist change, have high levels of anxiety, have high levels of intolerance for ambiguity, worry about the future, see loyalty to their employers as a virtue, have low motivation for achievement, and take few risks. Members of low uncertainty avoidance cultures tend to have the opposite tendencies. In organizations, workers in high uncertainty avoidance cultures prefer specialist careers, prefer clear instructions, avoid conflict, and disapprove of competition between employees more than workers in low uncertainty avoidance cultures.

Uncertainty avoidance is especially useful in understanding differences in how strangers are treated. Members of high uncertainty avoidance cultures try to avoid ambiguity and, therefore, develop rules and rituals for virtually every possible situation in which they might find themselves, including interacting with strangers. Interaction with strangers in cultures high in uncertainty avoidance may be highly ritualistic and/or very polite. If members of high uncertainty avoidance cultures interact with strangers in a situation where there are not clear rules, they may ignore the strangers or treat the strangers as though they do not exist.

Culture-Specific Uncertainty Avoidance.   There are rules to guide behavior in different situations in high uncertainty avoidance cultures. One culture-specific aspect of uncertainty avoidance is the importance of rules in Japan. Edgerton

(1985), for example, points out that outsiders often view Japan as "regimented," "rigid," "closely ordered," and "oppressively controlled." He argues that in Japan, individuals "gained virtue by following the rules and lost it by failing to do so" (p. 176). Edgerton goes on to suggest that "there are legitimate exceptions to rules in Japan today based on age, gender, intoxication, ceremony, and various settings. These exceptions are as clearly understood as the rules that they exempt one from following" (p. 177).

One area where there are clear rules in Japan is with respect to meeting obligations: *on* and *giri*. *On* involves one person's doing a favor for another, resulting in the person for whom the favor was done owing a debt to the person who did the favor (Lebra, 1974). Lebra (1974) points out that "an *on* must be accepted with gratitude since it is evidence of a giver's benevolence or generosity; at the same time it must be carried as a burden, because the *on,* once granted, makes the receiver a debtor and compels him [or her] to repay" (p. 194). *On* imposes an obligation on the person receiving the favor, and *on* occurs in vertical relationships.

Lebra (1976) indicates that the person receiving the *on* does not externally demonstrate gratitude to the person granting the favor but, rather, maintains an awareness of being in debt to and recognizing the person granting the favor as a benefactor. Not all debts, however, create *on,* only those perceived to be "unpayable" (Wierzbica, 1991). Lebra (1974) contends that the relationship between the individuals involved is "asymmetrical in that the *on* is considered limitless and unpayable and that the receiver feels urged to return at least 'one-ten-thousandth' of the received sum through total, sometimes life-long, devotion to the donor" (p. 195).

Closely related to *on* in Japan is *giri* ("duty or obligation"). *Giri* clearly involves a sense of obligation, but it is an obligation to a particular person with whom one interacts. Lebra (1976) indicates that *giri* encompasses all aspects of a person's life. *Giri* is a moral imperative to perform one's duties toward other members of one's group" (Befu, 1986, p. 162). It provides a special bond between individuals and can strengthen existing relationships that are viewed as more or less permanent (Wierzbica, 1991).

Giri may be based on a particular relationship between individuals or it might arise because of a favor one person does for another. Dore (1958) points out that

> *giri*-relationships may be "ascribed" in the sense that they are implied in the very nature of the position occupied by two parties . . . relations between relatives not of the same household group, relations between employer and

employee, between landlord and tenant, between neighbors, or between
fellow-employees. They may also arise as the result of a particular favor
conferred, for example, relations between marriage go-between and married
pair, or between employee and the [person] who found [the] job. (p. 254)

A person who violates the obligations in a *giri* relationship will be labeled as
lacking integrity or honor (R. Smith, 1983).

Chinese, Koreans, Vietnamese, and Filipinos have concepts similar to Japanese *on*. In China, *bao* ("to respond," "to repay") is considered a relational bond
(Gao, 1996). Chinese are expected to repay debts they have to others. *Xiao* ("filial piety") is a special form of *bao*. In Korea, *uye-ri* is a long-term obligatory relationship (Yum, 1987). *Uye-ri* requires that Koreans in a relationship meet
their obligations to one another. Yum (1988b) points out that *uye-ri* "is the bind-
ing rule of social interaction" in Korea (p. 377). In the Philippines, *utang na
loob* ("debt of gratitude") regulates interpersonal behavior (Kaut, 1961). Filipinos comply with *utang na loob* obligations because failure to do so would be insulting to the other person. Insulting others destroys the smoothness of relationships. Vietnamese have a proverb that states "*Am man tra dao*," which translates
as "If one receives a plum, one must return a peach" (Rutledge, 1992, p. vi).

Individual-Level Uncertainty Avoidance. The individual-level factor that mediates the influence of cultural uncertainty avoidance on communication is the
uncertainty-certainty orientation (Gudykunst, 1995).

There are many people who simply are not interested in finding out information about themselves or the world, who do not conduct causal searches,
who could not care less about comparing themselves with others, and who
"don't give a hoot" for resolving discrepancies or inconsistencies about the
self. Indeed, such people (we call them certainty oriented) will go out of
their way not to perform activities such as these (we call people who *do* go
out of their way to do such things uncertainty oriented). (Sorrentino &
Short, 1986, pp. 379-380)

Uncertainty-oriented individuals are interested in reducing uncertainty, and
certainty-oriented individuals try to avoid looking at uncertainty when it is
present.

Uncertainty-oriented individuals integrate new and old ideas and change
their belief systems accordingly (Sorrentino & Short, 1986). They evaluate

ideas and thoughts on their own merit and do not necessarily compare them with others. Uncertainty-oriented individuals want to understand themselves and their environment. The more uncertainty oriented individuals are, the more likely they are willing to question their own behavior and its appropriateness when communicating with others. Certainty-oriented individuals, in contrast, like to hold on to traditional beliefs and have a tendency to reject ideas that are different. Certainty-oriented individuals maintain a sense of self by not examining themselves or their behavior. A certainty orientation at the individual level predominates in high uncertainty avoidance cultures, and an uncertainty orientation predominates in low uncertainty avoidance cultures.

Summary. Table 2.2 summarizes the characteristics of low and high uncertainty avoidance cultures. Different degrees of uncertainty avoidance exist in every culture, but one tends to predominate. Japan and Korea have high uncertainty avoidance cultures, and the Philippines has a low uncertainty avoidance culture like the United States. Taiwan has a high uncertainty avoidance culture, but Hong Kong and Singapore have low uncertainty avoidance cultures.

Power Distance

Power distance is "the extent to which the less powerful members of institutions and organizations accept that power is distributed unequally" (Hofstede & Bond, 1984, p. 419). I begin with cultural-level power distance.

Cultural Power Distance. Individuals from high power distance cultures accept power as part of society. As such, superiors consider their subordinates to be different from themselves and vice versa. Members of high power distance cultures see power as a basic fact in society and stress coercive or referent power. Members of low power distance cultures, in contrast, believe power should be used only when it is legitimate and prefer expert or legitimate power.

In summarizing the differences between cultures low in power distance and cultures high in power distance, Hofstede (1991) points out that

> in small power distance countries there is limited dependence of subordinates on bosses, and a preference for consultation, that is, *interdependence* between boss and subordinate. The emotional distance between them is relatively small: subordinates will quite readily approach and contradict their

TABLE 2.2 Low and High Uncertainty Avoidance Cultures

Low Uncertainty Avoidance	High Uncertainty Avoidance
Major Characteristics	
Low stress and anxiety	High stress and anxiety
Dissent accepted	Strong desire for consensus
Comfortable in ambiguous situations	Fear of ambiguous situations
High level of risk taking	Low level of risk taking
Deviant behavior tolerated	Deviant behavior is suppressed
Few rituals	Many rituals
"What is different is curious"	"What is different is dangerous"
Individual Level	
Uncertainty orientation	Certainty orientation

SOURCE: Adapted from Gudykunst (1998).

bosses. In large power distance countries there is considerable dependence of subordinates on bosses. Subordinates respond by either *preferring* such dependence (in the form of autocratic or paternalistic boss), or rejecting it entirely, which in psychology is known as *counterdependence*: that is dependence, but with a negative sign. (p. 27)

The power distance dimension focuses on the relationships between people of different statuses (e.g., superiors and subordinates in organization).

Hofstede (1980) reports that parents in high power distance cultures value obedience in their children, and students value conformity and display authoritarian attitudes more than those in low power distance cultures. In organizations, close supervision, fear of disagreement with supervisors, lack of trust among co-workers, and directed supervision are all manifested more in high power distance cultures than in low power distance cultures.

Power distance is useful in understanding behavior in role relationships, particularly those involving different degrees of power or authority. Members of high power distance cultures, for example, do not question their superiors' orders. They expect to be told what to do. Members of low power distance cultures, in contrast, do not necessarily accept superiors' orders at face value; they want to know why they should follow them.

Culture-Specific Power Distance. The Philippine culture is a high power distance culture. Pido (1986) points out that the Spaniards instituted a stratification system based on race in the Philippines. The power differences ranged from the Spaniards born in Spain at the top to pure Indians at the bottom. "Access to economic opportunities, education and prestige depended on where one was in the complex stratification which cut across the native social structure" (p. 22). The Spaniards set up their headquarters in Manila in the Tagalog speaking region. This "historical accident" gave individuals in Manila more power, which continued in the post-colonial era. "Being exposed to or part of the urbanization process which was going on in Manila, rather than being a Tagalog, became important for individual or organizational upward mobility" (p. 22).

Power in the Philippines "is based on factions or alliances of factions" (Pido, 1986, p. 20). Once in a position of power, factions maintain power by the support of the "masses" who are allied with them. Pido points out that the elite have a paternalistic concern toward those who serve them. Individual Filipinos support those in power because their chance of surviving or "getting ahead" is better than if they are "independent nobodies."

Power distance in China, Japan, Korea, and Vietnam is influenced by Confucianism. Confucianism is a Chinese philosophy developed over 2,500 years ago that has permeated the cultures of China, Japan, Korea, and Vietnam. One of the major components of Confucian philosophy is ordering relationships in a hierarchical fashion (e.g., father-son, employer-employee) and behaving based on this order. These relationships, therefore, are examined when Confucian dynamism is discussed later in this chapter.

Individual-Level Power Distance. The individual-level factor that mediates the influence of cultural power distance on communication is egalitarianism (Gudykunst, 1995). Egalitarianism involves viewing others as equals. High egalitarianism is related to low power distance and low egalitarianism is related to high power distance.

Summary. Table 2.3 summarizes the characteristics of low and high power distance cultures. Low and high power distance tendencies exist in all cultures, but one tends to predominate. Japan and Korea tend to be moderate power distance cultures, and the Philippines, Hong Kong, and Singapore tend to be high power distance. Taiwan tends to be a low power distance culture like the United States.

TABLE 2.3 Low and High Power Distance Cultures

Low Power Distance	High Power Distance
Major Characteristics	
Individuals viewed as equals	Individuals viewed as unequal
Emphasis on legitimate power	Emphasis on coercive/referent power
Superiors and subordinates are interdependent	Subordinates are dependent on superiors
Obedience of children to parents is not valued highly	Obedience of children to parents is valued highly
Individual Level	
High egalitarianism	Low egalitarianism

SOURCE: Adapted from Gudykunst (1998).

Masculinity-Femininity

Masculinity-femininity focuses on gender issues at the cultural and individual levels. I begin with cultural-level masculinity-femininity.

Cultural Masculinity-Femininity. The major differentiation between masculine and feminine cultures is how gender roles are distributed in a culture.

> *Masculinity* pertains to societies in which social gender roles are clearly distinct (i.e., men are supposed to be assertive, tough, and focused on material success whereas women are supposed to be more modest, tender, and concerned with the quality of life); *femininity* pertains to societies in which social gender roles overlap (i.e., both men and women are supposed to be modest, tender, and concerned with the quality of life). (Hofstede, 1991, pp. 82-83)

Members of cultures high in masculinity value performance, ambition, things, power, and assertiveness (Hofstede, 1980). Members of cultures high in femininity value quality of life, service, caring for others, and being nurturing.

Hofstede (1980) reports that members of masculine cultures have a strong motivation for achievement, view work as central to their lives, accept their company's "interference" in their private lives, have high job stress, and view recognition, advancement, or challenge as important to their satisfaction with their work. Members of feminine cultures tend to have the opposite tendencies.

Hofstede (1998) points out that in masculine cultures, women are assigned the role of being tender and taking care of relationships. In feminine cultures, in contrast, both men and women are allowed to engage in these behaviors. In masculine cultures, fathers are expected to deal with facts with the children and mothers should deal with feelings with children. Both parents engage in both behaviors in feminine cultures. In masculine cultures, employees "live in order to work," and in feminine cultures employees "work in order to live" (p. 16). Masculine cultures focus on ego enhancement, and feminine cultures focus on relationship enhancement, regardless of group ties.

Masculinity-femininity is useful in understanding cultural differences and similarities in opposite-sex and same-sex relationships. People from highly masculine cultures, for example, tend to have little contact with members of the opposite sex when they are growing up. They tend to see same-sex relationships as more intimate than opposite-sex relationships.

Culture-Specific Masculinity-Femininity. As indicated earlier, masculinity-femininity influences same- versus opposite-sex relationships. White's (1993) research on teenagers in Japan and the United States illustrates masculinity in Japan. She points out that Japanese teenagers form three types of relationships: (1) best friends (*shinyuu*) who provide intimate relationships (a typical student will have two or three best friends); (2) "*group friends* provide standards for peer acceptance, a testing ground for the tensions between a newly emerging sense of self and the demands of the group" (p. 142; a group is an even number, usually six or eight); and (3) *sempai-kohai* (senior-junior) relationships, which occur in formal and informal student clubs. White contends that both best friends and group friends are members of the same sex. She points out that group friends spend so much time together that it makes it difficult for either boys or girls to spend time with members of the opposite sex. "When a girl actually does go steady, she may be seen as remote, even unavailable, to her friends, who feel betrayed" (p. 155). Teenagers in the United States, in contrast, do not experience the same pressure to interact with members of the same sex, and they develop friendships with members of the opposite sex.

Masculinity in Japan influences all opposite-sex relationships. Gorer (1962) argues that "the male world gives orders and expects obedience; the female world threatens and pleads, but can always be made to yield if the male is sufficiently strong and persistent in his aggression" (p. 320). Lebra (1976) points out that masculinity in Japan is asserted against the opposite sex. In public (outside the house), *fushoo-fugui* ("the husband initiates, the wife follows") pre-dominates. The wife, in contrast, is in charge at home, including being in charge of the family finances. The ideal wife in Japan is a *sewa nyobi* ("caretaker wife").

Vietnam was not part of Hofstede's (1980, 1991) study, so its position on masculinity-femininity is not clear-cut. The husband-wife relationship in Vietnam, nevertheless, appears to reflect cultural masculinity. Rutledge (1992), for example, points out that "the roles within the family have been traditionally well defined. The father is the head of the family unit, and is responsible for maintaining family traditions" (p. 117). Women in Vietnam are expected to follow the "three obediences": "Submit to her father while under his care, obey her husband following marriage, follow the authority of the eldest son if widowed" (p. 117). The wife, however, is not expected to simply follow the husband in the home. Rather, she is expected to be *moi tuong* ("home minister"). The wife is responsible for maintaining harmony in the *nha* (nuclear family, husband's parents, sons' families) and in the *ho* (extended family), and she is responsible for maintaining the family's finances.

Individual-Level Masculinity-Femininity. The individual-level factor that mediates the influence of cultural masculinity-femininity on communication is psychological sex roles (Gudykunst, 1995). Individuals have masculine gender identities if they exhibit high degrees of stereotypical masculine traits and behaviors (e.g., aggressive, competitive, dominant) and low degrees of stereotypical feminine traits and behaviors (e.g., compassionate, sensitive, warm) (Bem, 1974). Individuals have feminine gender identities if they exhibit high degrees of stereotypical feminine traits and behaviors and low degrees of stereotypical masculine traits and behaviors. Individuals have androgynous gender identities if they exhibit high degrees of stereotypical masculine *and* feminine traits and behaviors. They have undifferentiated gender identities if they exhibit low degrees of stereotypical masculine and feminine traits and behaviors.

Traditional gender-oriented individuals (high-masculine men, high-feminine women) tend to organize and recall information about others on the basis of their genders (Bem, 1993). Also, traditional gender-oriented individuals tend to follow cultural definitions of appropriate behavior. To illustrate, "conventionally masculine men [are] independent but not nurturant, and conventionally feminine women [are] nurturant but not independent" in mainstream U.S. culture (Bem, 1993, p. 157). Androgyny predominates in feminine cultures, and high masculinity and high femininity predominate in masculine cultures.

TABLE 2.4 Masculine and Feminine Cultures

Masculine	*Feminine*
Major Characteristics	
Differentiated gender roles	Overlapping gender roles
Assertiveness, performance, things, and power are valued	Quality of life, service, being nurturing, and caring for others are valued
Sympathy for the strong	Sympathy for the weak
"Live in order to work"	"Work in order to live"
Ego enhancement	Relationship enhancement
Individual Level	
Masculine/feminine sex roles	Androgyny

SOURCE: Adapted from Gudykunst (1998).

Summary. Table 2.4 summarizes the characteristics of masculine and feminine cultures. Both masculinity and femininity tendencies exist in all cultures. One tendency, however, tends to predominate. Japan and the Philippines tend to be masculine cultures, and South Korea is a feminine culture. Taiwan and Singapore tend to have feminine cultures, but Hong Kong tends to have a masculine culture.

CONFUCIANISM

Confucianism is a philosophical system developed by the Chinese philosopher Confucius about 2,500 years ago. Weber points out that "Confucianism is extremely rationalistic since it is bereft of any form of metaphysics . . . it lacks and excludes all measures that are not utilitarian" (cited by Nakamura, 1964, p. 16).

Cultural-Level Confucianism

Hofstede (1980) isolates the four dimensions of cultural variability I have discussed so far in this chapter (individualism-collectivism, power distance, uncertainty avoidance, masculinity-femininity) in his study of a large multinational company. The dimensions, however, may have a Western bias because of the methods Hofstede used in collecting the data. The Chinese Culture Connection (1987) look at Hofstede's conclusions using a methodology with a Chinese bias.[2] They isolate four dimensions of cultural variability: Confucian dynamism (e.g., "ordering relationships by status and observing this order," "having a sense of shame"), integration (e.g., "harmony with others," "solidarity with others"), human-heartedness (e.g., "patience," "courtesy," "kindness"), and moral discipline (e.g., "having few desires," "moderation"). Three of these dimensions correlate with dimensions in Hofstede's study: integration correlates with individualism, moral discipline correlates with power distance, and human-heartedness correlates with masculinity-femininity. The only dimension in the Chinese Culture Connection's study that does not correlate with one of Hofstede's dimensions is Confucian dynamism.

The Confucian dynamism dimension involves eight values. Four values are associated positively with the dimension: ordering relationships, thrift, persistence, and having a sense of shame; four are associated negatively with the dimension: protecting one's face, personal steadiness, respect for tradition, and reciprocation. The Chinese Culture Connection (1987) argues that the four positively loaded items reflect a hierarchical dynamism present in Chinese society, and the four negatively loaded items reflect "checks and distractions" to this dynamism.

The Confucian dynamism dimension is consistent with Confucianism. Hofstede (1991) summarizes four tenets of Confucianism:

1. The stability of society is based on unequal relationships between people. The *wu lun,* or five basic relationships . . . are ruler-subject, father-son, older brother-younger brother, husband-wife, and senior friend-junior friend. . . . The junior partner owes the senior partner respect and obedience. The senior partner owes the junior partner protection and consideration.
2. The family is the prototype for all social organizations. A person is not primarily an individual, he or she is a member of a family . . .
3. Virtuous behavior towards others consists of not treating others as one would not like to be treated oneself . . .
4. Virtue with regard to one's task in life consists of trying to acquire skills and education, working hard, not spending more than necessary, being patient, and persevering. (p. 165, italics omitted)

These four tenets influence behavior in China (and other Chinese cultures such as Singapore), Japan, Korea, and Vietnam, but not in the Philippines.

Yum (1988b) suggests that in Confucianism "right conduct" emerges from "*jen* (humanism), *i* (faithfulness), [and] *li* (propriety)" (p. 377). *Jen* ("humanism") "means warm human feelings between people" (p. 377). The practice of *jen* involves engaging in virtuous behavior toward others (see Tenet 3). Central to *jen* ("humanism") is *shu* ("reciprocity" or "like heartedness") (McNaughton, 1974). The second principle, *i* ("faithfulness"), suggests that "human relationships are not based on individual profit, but rather on betterment of the common good" (Yum, 1988b, p. 377). *Li* ("ritual propriety") is the "fundamental regulatory etiquette of human behavior" (p. 378), or behaving in ways that demonstrate respect for the proper social forms.

Confucianism directly influences several different aspects of behavior in China, Japan, Korea, and Vietnam. Confucianism, for example, leads Asians to see themselves in webs of reciprocal obligation; individuals are obligated to others who in turn are obligated to them (Yum, 1988b). The obligations exist in the *wu lun* (five basic relationships, see Tenet 1 above) and other ingroup relationships. *Li* ("ritual propriety") requires that individuals meet these obligations in the proper ways. The principle of *i* ("faithfulness") is limited to ingroups. "Confucianism provides an elaborate moral code for relationships among known members, but it does not provide any universal rules for others because Confucianism is a situation- and context-centered philosophy" (Yum, 1988b, pp. 379-380). The primary function of communication in Confucianism is to develop and maintain social relationships.

All of the *wu lun* (five basic relationships) in Confucianism are vertical relationships. These vertical relationships seem similar to the inequalities in power distance. Confucian dynamism, however, is not correlated with power distance in the Chinese Culture Connection's (1987) study; moral discipline is. It could be argued that the Chinese Culture Connection's moral discipline dimension includes values that are inherent in Confucianism (e.g., "having few desires," "moderation," "prudence") and that Confucian dynamism and moral discipline are part of the same higher-order dimension. Whether this is the case does not matter here. What does matter is that Confucianism involves unequal relationships, similar to those characteristic of high power distance.

Culture-Specific Confucianism

In the Chinese hierarchical structure, statuses are defined clearly and behaviors are guided by *li* ("ritual propriety") or engaging in the proper behavior in relationships. The proper behavior depends on whether the individuals communicating are the seniors or the juniors in the relationships. This leads to an asymmetrical style of communication. "The adoption of an asymmetrical style of communication, reflecting core Confucian values, serves to maintain the existing status and role relationships" (Gao & Ting-Toomey, 1998, p. 43). Chinese believe that not everyone is entitled to speak in all situations. Subordinates are supposed to engage in *ting hui* ("listens talk"). Obedient children, for example, listen to their parents and do not voice their opinions. Similarly, good employees are expected to listen to their employers and do what they are told. "Respect for authority and status differences are reflected not only in the focus on listening but also in the use of a deferential style of communication" (Gao & Ting-Toomey, 1998, p. 44). Subordinates (e.g., children, employees) should be hesitant when they talk and be restrained (e.g., do not express their opinions).

Nakane (1970) refers to Japan as a *tateshakai* ("vertical society"). *Bun* ("status") is central to Japanese behavior. *Bun* ("status") refers to individuals' positions in status hierarchies. Lebra (1976) points out that "status orientation first involves sensitivity to the rank order [*joretsu ishiki*] according to which behavior must be differentiated" (p. 69). Japanese can only decide how to behave when they know where they fit in status hierarchies. They must always know whether they are *sempai* ("seniors") or *kohai* ("juniors") in relationships. Their positions determine not only their behavior but also the language they use (i.e., there are different forms of the Japanese for communicating with people superior to you, equal to you, and inferior to you).

Vietnamese behavior also is based on Confucianism. Liem (1980), for example, points out that employer-employee relationships are vertical in Vietnam.

> The Vietnamese employee considers his [or her] employer as his [or her] mentor. As such, the latter is expected to give guidance, advice, and encouragement, and the former is supposed to execute orders, to perform his [or her] task quietly, and not to ask questions or have doubt about the orders. Because of his [or her] concept of the relationship, the Vietnamese employee does not voice his [or her] opinion to the boss, he [or she] just listens to his [or her] orders. (p. 16)

Employer-employee relationships in Vietnam, therefore, are highly structured and involve clear vertical relationships with reciprocal obligations.

CONCLUSION

All Asian cultures are collectivistic. Asian Americans tend to learn these shared cultural characteristics when they are socialized in the United States. Asian Americans, therefore, share a common basis for much of their communication. Asian Americans, for example, tend to be allocentric, emphasize interdependent self construals, and hold collectivistic individual values. Of course, not all Asian Americans fit these patterns, but these are the general tendencies based on their cultural heritages.

Asian cultures differ somewhat with respect to cultural-level uncertainty avoidance, power distance, and masculinity-femininity. The differences in the cultural heritages among the Asian American ethnic groups leads to differences in their communication styles in the United States. To illustrate, high power distance in the Philippines leads Filipino Americans to view individuals as unequal. Low power distance in Taiwan, in contrast, leads Chinese Americans who trace their heritage to Taiwan to view individuals as equals.

Understanding where the Asian cultures to which Asian Americans trace their heritage fall on the dimensions of cultural variability discussed in this chapter provides a framework for explaining their behavior. The specific experiences of the Asian American ethnic groups in the United States, however, also must be taken into consideration. This is the topic of the next chapter.

NOTES

1. The general material on the dimensions of cultural variability presented in this chapter are adapted from Gudykunst (1998, Chapter 2).
2. The Chinese Culture Connection is a group of researchers organized by Michael Bond at the Chinese University of Hong Kong.

Chapter Three

Asian American Ethnic Groups

$\mathcal{J}$n the previous chapter, I examined the cultural factors that influence Asian American communication. Explaining the similarities and differences in communication for members of Asian American ethnic groups also requires understanding similarities and differences among the various ethnic groups and their experiences in the United States.

I begin this chapter with a general overview of Asian American immigration to the United States. Following this, I examine the immigration patterns, institutional support, and family patterns for Chinese Americans, Japanese Americans, Filipino Americans, Korean Americans, and Vietnamese Americans.[1] I conclude this chapter by looking at the individualistic and collectivistic tendencies for members of the five ethnic groups.

GENERAL IMMIGRATION PATTERNS

In this section, I provide a broad overview of Asian immigration to the United States.[2] I examine patterns for each ethnic group in more detail in the sections that follow.[3]

The first Asians to arrive in the United States appear to be Filipinos. The early Filipinos were the "Manila men" who were forced to build and work as crew members on Spanish galleys. Some of these Filipinos crew members jumped ship in Mexico and Louisiana. Those who jumped ship in Louisiana established a village outside New Orleans in 1763 (Agbayani-Siewert & Revilla, 1995). Descendents of these early settlers are in their eighth generation in the United States (Cordova, 1983). These early immigrants, however, had little to do with later waves of Filipino immigrants.

There was no apparent Asian immigration after the "Manila men" until a few Chinese arrived in the United States just before the California Gold Rush of 1849. A large number of Chinese immigrated just after the gold rush began, and there were more than 30,000 Chinese residing in California by 1860, nearly all men. The vast majority of these Chinese saw themselves as sojourners (e.g., they came to the United States to "get rich" and then return to China). A small number of Japanese men arrived in Hawaii (an independent Kingdom) about the same time that the first large group of Chinese immigrated to California (e.g., around 1850). In the middle to late 1800s, a large number of Chinese and Japanese women were brought to the United States, "often under brutally coercive conditions to labor as prostitutes in California and on the east coast" (Lee, 1999, p. 89).

The small number of Chinese to arrive before the California gold rush settled mostly on the East Coast and "were viewed primarily as curiosities embodying the exotic difference of the Orient" (Lee, 1999, p. 28). The large number of Chinese in California, however, were not viewed as curiosities. Because of the large numbers, "they could no longer be imagined as simply foreign, made strange by their distance. Chinese in America were now alien and threatening through their very presence" (Lee, 1999, p. 28).

The first U.S. government legislation that affected Asians occurred in 1870 when American-born children of non-citizens were declared to be citizens. The Page Act of 1870 was the first to limit Asian immigration to the United States. This Act prohibited Chinese, Japanese, and "Mongolian" women from entering the United States to engage in "immoral" behavior (e.g., prostitution).

In 1870, there were about 60,000 Chinese in the United States, with 50,000 in California. Anti-Chinese sentiment increased in the 1870s. "Irish immigrants who were in the process of consolidating their own claim to Americanness and a white identity led the popular anti-Chinese movement" (Lee, 1999, p. 9). There were about 100,000 Chinese in the United States and 95,000 in California by 1880. The anti-Chinese sentiment led to the Chinese

Exclusion Act of 1882, which suspended the immigration of Chinese for 10 years.

Shortly after the Chinese Exclusion Act, a few Korean exiles moved to the United States around 1885. The attitudes toward the Chinese did not improve, and the Geary Act of 1892 extended the exclusion of Chinese for another 10 years. Shortly after this, the United States took possession of the 7,000+ Philippine Islands and annexed Hawaii at the end of the Spanish-American War of 1898. This made Filipinos U.S. nationals (which lasted until the Philippines became semi-independent in 1935). When the United States annexed Hawaii, many of the Japanese living in Hawaii moved to the West Coast, and there were about 25,000 Japanese in the United States by 1890.

The Chinese Exclusion Act was extended indefinitely in 1902. Shortly after this, the first large group of Filipino students arrived in the United States between 1903 and 1910 as part of a U.S. government-sponsored education program. Most of these students returned to the Philippines and became leaders of the country. Small numbers of Koreans also moved to Hawaii (about 7,300) in the 1903 to 1905 period. Anti-Japanese sentiment began about the same time, and by 1907-1908 a "gentleman's agreement" was reached between the U.S. and Japanese governments. Based on this agreement, the Japanese government agreed to limit the number of laborers coming to the United States to work.

The Alien Land Acts of 1913-1920 in California and other western states prohibited marriage between Asians and whites. About the same time, Congress created a "barred zone" (in 1917) whereby people from China, South and Southeast Asia, and the Pacific and Southeast Asian Islands not owned by the United States were barred from admission to the United States. Japanese, however, were not included in those being barred. Legislation was passed in 1921 that denied alien women their husbands' U.S. citizenship. Since others were barred and the number of Japanese was limited, Filipino men began to move to Hawaii in the 1920s and 1930s to work in sugar fields.

The exclusions of Asians from U.S. citizenship was challenged in 1922 when a Japanese immigrant, Takeo Ozawa living in Hawaii, petitioned to become a citizen (see Lee, 1999, pp. 140-142, for a discussion of the case). His petition was turned down by all of the lower federal courts, and he appealed to the U.S. Supreme Court with the support of the Japanese American community, but not the Japanese consulate. Ozawa wrote his own brief in which he asserted that he was totally assimilated into the U.S. society (e.g., he had no connection with Japanese churches, schools, or organizations; he was educated in American schools; and he spoke English at home so his children would not be able to speak Japanese). The Supreme Court ruled unanimously that no matter how assimilated he was, Ozawa could not become a U.S. citizen (*Takeo Ozawa v. the United States*). The court ruled that only members of the "Caucasian race" could be U.S. citizens.

The Immigration Act of 1924 added Japanese to those barred from immigration to the United States, and it also barred aliens ineligible for citizenship from coming to the United States. This Act also established quotas for European countries (e.g., Great Britain's was about 65,000; Germany's was about 26,000). People of Asian decent born in European countries could be part of these quotas, but they were still barred from U.S. citizenship. Asian countries were given token quotas of 100, but only "whites" who happened to be born in these countries could use the quotas. The 1924 Immigration Act was modified in 1930 to allow women married to U.S. citizens prior to 1924 to enter the United States.

Ten years after the 1924 Immigration Act there were about 120,000 Filipino laborers in Hawaii (87% men) in 1934. These laborers signed three-year contracts. After their contracts were completed, some renewed their contracts, some went to the West Coast (there were 30,000 in California in 1930, mostly men), and some returned to the Philippines. The Tydings-McDuffe Act of 1934 promised the Philippines independence in 1945 (it was delayed until after World War II) and gave the Philippines a quota of 50 people per year who could come to the United States. As a result of the 1934 Act, the Philippines became semi-independent in 1935, and at that time Filipinos were no longer considered U.S. nationals.

There were about 250,000 Asians living in the continental United States and about the same number in Hawaii by 1940. About this time, Chinese and Japanese citizens began to outnumber the aliens, but most of the citizens were young children. The Japanese attack on Pearl Harbor and the U.S. entry into World War II led to the "relocation" of people of Japanese ancestry (i.e., anyone with one-eighth Japanese blood; about 120,000 people) on the West Coast to concentration camps in six western states and Arkansas.

During World War II, the Chinese Exclusion Act was repealed by the Magnuson Act in 1943, and the Chinese were given a quota of 105 per year. The War Brides Act of 1945 made naturalization for Filipino wives of American soldiers possible. The Act was amended in 1947 to include Japanese and Chinese wives of U.S. citizens. Between 1947 and 1952 (when the Act was amended) about 6,000 Chinese wives came to the United States. The Displaced Person Act of 1948 gave permanent-resident status to about 3,500 Chinese in the United States when the Chinese civil war began.

Congress passed the Emergency Detention Act in 1950 when the Korean War broke out. This Act gave the U.S. Attorney General the authority to establish concentration camps for anyone who might be considered a threat during a national emergency. "The mere authorization of such sweeping powers of detention served as stark warning to Chinese Americans that what had been done to Japanese Americans a decade earlier could also be done to them without effort" (Lee, 1999, p. 152).

The McCarren-Walter Act of 1952 was the first general immigration Act since the 1924 law. This Act removed racial bias in immigration and naturalization, and allowed for family reunification (e.g., parents, children, and siblings of U.S. residents could immigrate outside their country's quota). The 1952 Act also allowed female U.S. citizens to bring their husbands to the United States outside the quota system. Japan was given a quota of 185 per year. Korean immigration to the United States started in large numbers about the same time the Korean War ended. The Refugee Relief Act of 1953 allowed about 2,800 Chinese refugees of the Chinese civil war to enter the United States.

Lee (1999) contends that the "Cold War" in the 1950s led to viewing Asian Americans as "model minorities." He suggests that Asian Americans were a racial minority "whose successful *ethnic* assimilation was a result of stoic patience, political obedience, and self-improvement" (p. 145). Lee goes on to argue that this vision of Asian Americans "simultaneously promoted racial equality and sought to contain demands for social transformation" (p. 145). This view of Asian Americans carried over into the 1960s (e.g., there was an article in the *New York Times Magazine* in January 1966 titled "Success Story: Japanese-American Style"; see Osajima, 1988).

The 1965 Immigration and Naturalization Act substituted a hemispheric system for the national quotas. The Western Hemisphere was given a quota of 120,000 with no country quotas. The Eastern Hemisphere quota was 170,000 with a maximum quota of 20,000 per country. The 1965 Act gave priority to immigrants with occupational skills needed in the United States, family reunification, and immigrants suffering from religious or political persecution. The entry of occupational immigrants, however, was limited when the 1965 Act was revised in 1976. The 1965 Act was further revised in 1981 to give the People's Republic of China the same quota as Taiwan.

Asians were the primary beneficiaries of the 1965 Immigration Act. There were about 900,000 Asians in the United States (including Hawaii) in 1960. Vietnamese began to immigrate to the United States in the early 1970s toward the end of the Vietnam War. By 1980, there were 3.5 million Asians in the United States and about 7.3 million by 1990. Table 3.1 presents immigration

TABLE 3.1 Asian American Immigration Patterns for Selected Years

	Chinese[a]	Filipino	Japanese	Korean	Vietnamese
1960	3,687	2,954	5,471	1,507	—
1970	14,093	31,203	4,485	9,314	1,450
1980	27,651	42,316	4,225	33,320	43,483
1990	31,815	63,756	5,734	32,301	48,792

SOURCE: Immigration and Naturalization Service, 1960-1978, 1979-1992.
a. The 1990 data for China does not include Taiwan; other years do.

TABLE 3.2 Asian American Population in the United States for Selected Years

	Chinese American	Filipino American	Japanese American	Korean American	Vietnamese American
1960	237,292	181,614	464,368	—	—
1970	436,062	336,731	591,290	69,155	—
1980	806,040	774,652	700,974	354,974	261,729
1990	1,645,472	1,460,770	847,562	798,849	614,547

SOURCE: U.S. Bureau of the Census (1993).
NOTE: Koreans became a separate census category in 1970; Vietnamese in 1980.

numbers for the various Asian American ethnic groups for 1960 to 1990. Table 3.2 presents the total population for the various groups 1960 to 1990.

The U.S. Bureau of the Census estimated that the total population of people of Asian descent was 10,480,000 (3.9% of the population) in 1998 (U.S. Bureau of the Census, 1998). The Bureau estimates that by 2040 the population will be about 29,235,000 (7.9% of the population).

The percentage of each Asian American ethnic group that was born in the United States varied tremendously in 1990. Japanese Americans had the largest percentage of its population born in the United States (67.7%). Filipino Americans (35.6%), Chinese Americans (30.7%; figure does not include Taiwan), and Korean Americans (27.3%) were about equal. Vietnamese Americans had the smallest percentage of its population born in the United States (20.1%) (U.S. Bureau of the Census, 1993). These differences have clear implications for the experiences of members of the various groups in the United States. These issues are discussed in the following sections where I examine each group separately. I begin with Chinese Americans.

CHINESE AMERICANS

Chinese were the first Asian group to arrive in the United States in large numbers. Today, Chinese Americans are the largest Asian American ethnic group. I begin this section with a discussion of their immigration patterns.

Chinese Immigration Patterns

As indicated earlier, the first Chinese (about 50) arrived in San Francisco before the California Gold Rush of 1849, and most moved to the East Coast. The discovery of gold initiated a large influx of Chinese immigrants. More than 30,000 Chinese were in California by 1860, and nearly all were males. The initial arrivals were all sojourners who planned to get rich in the United States and return to China. The initial immigration pattern for Chinese was similar to that of European immigrants who planned to return home and were mostly male (Archdeacon, 1983). The Chinese, nevertheless, were different from the Europeans for three reasons: "(1) their race, (2) the region to which they came, and (3) the fact that in 1882 they became the first group of voluntary immigrants to be shut out by the American government" (Kitano & Daniels, 1995, p. 22).

By 1870, there were about 60,000 Chinese in the United States, with 50,000 in California. The initial Chinese immigrants worked at gold mining, various urban occupations, agriculture, and building the western part of the transcontinental railroad. In the 1870s, anti-Chinese sentiment developed in California and the other western states because the Chinese were perceived to be taking jobs from other immigrants (e.g., the Irish). Whites viewed the racial differences between themselves and the Chinese as threatening (Lee, 1999). Lee claims that the Chinese were seen as "pollutants." "Pollutants are anomalies in the symbolic structure of society, things that are out of place and create a sense of disorder. A mere presence in the wrong place, the intentional or unintentional crossing of a boundary, gives offense" (p. 31).

By 1880, there were 100,000 Chinese in the United States, with about 95,000 in California centered around San Francisco. When the Chinese Exclusion Act of 1882 was passed, there were about 125,000 in the United States. The

Scott Act of 1888 prohibited the return of Chinese who temporarily departed the United States.

The 1906 San Francisco earthquake destroyed many municipal records, including Chinese citizenship and immigration records. This allowed for the possibility of "paper sons" (Wong, 1995). Since children of American-born fathers became citizens, Chinese could claim American citizenship, and the U.S. authorities could not disprove their claims. Some of the Chinese who claimed U.S. citizenship after the earthquake returned to China and reported the birth of sons. This created immigration slots that could be used later by relatives or sold to other Chinese who wanted to immigrate to the United States. The Chinese who came to the United States filling these quotas assumed the identities of the sons who were reported born, and they were called "paper sons."

There are no solid estimates of how many Chinese men entered the United States as "paper sons." The Refugee Escape Act of 1957 allowed "paper sons" to become legal permanent residents under certain conditions. About 8,000 "confessions" were made during the 1959 to 1969 amnesty period (Wong, 1995). The confessions were used by the government to try to deport Chinese who supported China (as opposed to Taiwan) and domestic troublemakers (Lee, 1999).

The population of Chinese declined after the Chinese Exclusion Act of 1882 until around 1920 (about 61,000) because the number of males was so much larger than the number of females. The population of Chinese began to rise after 1920 (in 1930 there were about 75,000). Attitudes toward the Chinese began to change in the 1930s. One of the reasons for this is that Pearl Buck's novels (e.g., *The Good Earth* in 1931) and the movies made from them portrayed Chinese peasants in a positive light (e.g., admirable people who are hardworking) (Kitano & Daniels, 1995).

The total Chinese population was around 77,500 in 1940, and the number of Chinese citizens outnumbered the number of Chinese aliens, but most of the citizens were young children. In 1943, the Chinese Exclusion Act was repealed, and the Chinese were given a quota of 105 per year. There were about 20,000 Chinese babies born in the 1940s (all U.S. citizens). After the Japanese attack on Pearl Harbor, China and the United States became allies. Chinese were then seen as heroic resisters of Japanese aggression.

There were 237,292 Chinese in the United States in 1960, with about 38,000 in Hawaii. The 1965 Immigration Act opened the door for new immigrants. In 1970, there were 436,062 Chinese in the United States. The number of Chinese almost doubled in each of the next two decades so that by 1980 there were

806,040 and by 1990 there were almost 1.65 million people of Chinese heritage in the United States.[4] Much of the increase between 1980 and 1990 was due to immigration. These immigrants are becoming naturalized citizens and not planning on returning to China (Yang, 1999).

Chinese American Institutions

Chinatowns throughout the United States provide strong institutional support for maintaining Chinese ethnicity. There are urban Chinatowns in large cities like New York, Los Angeles, San Francisco, and Chicago, among others. Many of these Chinatowns are quite large. The New York Chinatown, for example, has about 150,000 inhabitants and another 150,000 live in surrounding areas (Kinkead, 1992).[5]

Chinatowns tend to contain all of the things found in small cities in China or Taiwan. There are Chinese stores of all kinds (e.g., groceries, clothing), churches, and social organizations; books, magazines, and newspapers in Chinese also are available. In the larger Chinatowns, Chinese immigrants can do everything they would do in China or Taiwan speaking Chinese. This clearly supports maintaining Chinese ethnicity in the United States.

Recently there has been an increase in the number of Chinese living in suburban areas. The 1990 population of Chinese in Alhambra and Monterey Park, California, for example, was almost 10% (Li, 1999). Some writers refer to these new areas as suburban Chinatowns (e.g., Fong, 1994, refers to Monterey Park, California, as the first suburban Chinatown). Other writers (e.g., Li, 1999) point out that this label may be misleading. Li contends that there are sufficient differences in how the concentrations of Chinese occurred to view urban and suburban concentrations as being different. He calls the suburban concentrations like that in Monterey Park "ethnoburbs." Li argues that the Chinese ethnoburbs share characteristics with other ethnic concentrations in the suburbs.

Regardless of what they are called, the suburban concentrations of Chinese provide virtually the same level of institutional support for maintaining Chinese culture that urban Chinatowns do. When asked why Chinese people choose to live in Monterey Park, one respondent that Li (1999) interviewed said:

Because of living here we feel like home. There are so many Chinese people and Chinese stores, restaurants, banks, newspapers, radios and TV, almost everything you need. Nowhere else can provide us such [a] comfortable living environment and so many kinds of services in such a compact geographical area. (p. 14)

Another respondent said that "we who live in Monterey Park feel no difference from living back in Taiwan" (pp. 14-15).

Chinese American Families

Chinese American families in the United States are based on the traditional Chinese families in China.[6] Traditional Chinese families are male dominated with the father and oldest son having the primary roles (Hsu, 1971). Women are relegated to subordinate positions within the family. Ideally, the extended family (e.g., the father, his parents, the sons and their families) live in the same household. All members of the families are expected to obey the fathers and oldest sons (see Tsui & Schultz, 1988). Confucianism values influence Chinese families. Filial piety, for example, requires that Chinese be reverent and obedient to their elders and make sacrifices for them.

Huang (1981) argues that first- and second-generation Chinese in the United States form nuclear families, with grandparents tending to live apart from the nuclear families. There is still extensive interaction between members of nuclear families and extended families, even if they do not live in the same household. Huang goes on to suggest that women in first- and second-generation families tend to be helpers to their husbands, not totally equal. Chinese American children grow up in the adult world (e.g., parents take them with them to business and social gatherings). In this way, children learn how to behave in socially appropriate ways. Tam and Detzner (1995) suggest that grandparents are critical resources for Chinese American families. They provide child care, serve as mentors, and serve as role models. Tam and Detzner claim that acculturated Chinese American parents do not want to impose on their parents and think that their parents will not teach their children things that are useful in the United States.

Wong (1995) argues that Chinese American families fall into one of two types (see Glenn, 1983, for an alternative typology of Chinese American families). The first type involves those families living in or near Chinatowns. In these families, both the husband and the wife tend to work, often in ethnic businesses. Wong contends that these families tend to segregate work and family life. The second type of Chinese families involves those who have moved to the suburbs. Wong claims that these families tend to be more "American" than Chinese. Both types of families, however, have "more conservative sexual values, fewer out-of-wedlock births, and more conservative or traditional attitudes toward women than the white population" (Wong, 1995, p. 72).

Uba (1994) contends that Chinese Americans believe that raising children is the mother's responsibility and that children are supervised closely. Conformity is emphasized, and children are controlled through "guilt and shame." Also, Uba points out that Chinese Americans "think communication styles and emotion expression should be restrained and indirect" (p. 50).

Cooper et al. (1993) report that first- and second-generation Chinese American adolescents rely on their families for social support and guidance more than do European American adolescents.[7] Chinese American adolescents, however, rely on their peers to discuss dating, sex, and marriage. Feldman and Rosenthal (1990) also observe that first- and second-generation Chinese American adolescents expect to be older when they date than do European American adolescents.

JAPANESE AMERICANS

Japanese were the second Asian group to arrive in the United States in large numbers. Today, they are the third largest group of Asian Americans in the United States. I begin this section with Japanese Americans' immigration patterns.

Japanese Immigration Patterns

Japanese sojourners began to arrive in the United States around 1850, but Japanese immigrants did not arrive in significant numbers until the late 1800s. The initial group of Japanese laborers went to Hawaii, and then many moved to the West Coast after the United States annexed Hawaii in 1898. The laborers in Hawaii and on the West Coast worked in low-paying jobs requiring physical labor. Those on the West Coast tended to work in agriculture or agriculture-related jobs. These immigrants were almost all men.

Japanese immigration to the United States began about the time that the Chinese were excluded. There were 25,000 Japanese in the United States in 1900. Anti-Japanese sentiment began in the early 1900s. This led to the gentleman's agreement between the United States and Japan that limited Japanese immigration starting in 1908. This agreement, however, allowed Japanese women to immigrate.

The Japanese government tried to exert social control over the Japanese in the United States because the government thought that how Japanese behaved in the United States would influence Americans' attitudes toward Japan. In 1909, for example, the Japanese Counselor General in San Francisco formed the Japan Association of America. All Japanese in the United States were expected to join this association. To give the association power, it controlled issuing travel certificates, the ability to bring wives to the United States, and other activities of Japanese in the United States.

In 1920, there were about 110,000 Japanese living in the United States, with about 30,000 of these being born in the United States. The Japanese community on the West Coast was mostly lower middle class by 1930. In 1940, there were about 125,000 Japanese in the United States with about 80,000 of these born in the United States (and, therefore, citizens), and the number of males and females was relatively balanced (55% male). The Japanese American Citizens League was formed in 1940 (discussed below under institutions).

There was no Japanese immigration during World War II. Japanese immigration resumed after the passage of the McCarran-Walter Immigration Act in 1952. After the passage of this Act, Japanese "war brides" began to immigrate in large numbers. Of the 45,500 Japanese immigrants who came to the United States during the 1950s, about 86% were women, and about three-quarters of the women were wives of U.S. citizens (Nishi, 1995).

The 1965 Immigration Act led to a large influx of Asian immigrants, but Japanese were a relatively small percentage. Between 1965 and 1970, about 22,500 Japanese immigrants came to the United States. The Japanese population in the United States was 591,290 in 1970. In the 1970s, there were about 44,500 Japanese immigrants, and there were 700,974 Japanese in the United States in 1980. There were about 43,250 Japanese immigrants in the 1980s, and the total population was 847,562 in 1990.

Japanese American Internment and Redress

Following the Japanese attack on Pearl Harbor on December 7, 1941, Franklin D. Roosevelt's Executive Order 9066 on February 19, 1942, required that all people of Japanese ancestry (i.e., anyone who had one-eighth Japanese blood) on the West Coast be put in "internment camps" (really concentration camps located in six western states and Arkansas). Over 120,000 individuals were placed in the camps, and two-thirds were U.S. citizens. The camps were surrounded by barbed wire and patrolled by armed soldiers. About 10,000 people of Japanese ancestry living on the East Coast and those of Japanese ancestry living in Hawaii were not included in the Executive Order. The U.S. Supreme Court ruled that the internment camps were constitutional on June 21, 1943.

The Japanese American internment is the central event in the history of the Japanese in the United States.[8] Daniels and Kitano (1970) point out that the majority of Americans living in the United States at the time supported the internment. They go on to argue that the European Americans' view of the internment was different from their view of the German's action during the war. European Americans tended to view the German treatment of the Jews as due to a few "sick individuals," but the Japanese were viewed as a "sick race."

The Japanese internment ended on January 2, 1945, when the U.S. Supreme Court ruled that it was no longer constitutional since the "military necessity" was over (*Mitsuye Endo v. United States*). After World War II, about 5,000 Japanese Americans were so embittered by the internment that they repatriated to Japan.

Japanese Americans who were in the internment camps and remained in the United States generally did not talk about their experiences (including with their children). Takezawa (1995) quotes a *Nisei* (second-generation Japanese) as saying, "It was something you buried under the carpet and hoped the dust would never show up again" (p. 195). Kashima (1980) refers to this as "social amnesia."

Takezawa (1995) argues that the internment led *Nisei* to perceive being Japanese American as a stigma (e.g., being Japanese American was a disadvantage in the United States). Many *Nisei*, "whether they now admit it or not, identified as American at the expense of their Japanese cultural heritage. They ceased speaking Japanese and didn't encourage their children to learn it" (p. 195). The *Nisei* transmitted their stigmatized image of Japanese Americans to their children (the *Sansei*). Japanese Americans eventually overcame the stigmatized image through the redress movement.

The redress movement began in the 1970s, and a resolution to seek redress was passed at the Japanese American Citizen League convention in 1972. Initially there was not a lot of support for seeking redress.[9] One of the major factors that led to support for the movement was a "Day of Remembrance" held on November 25, 1978, in Seattle. On this day, Japanese Americans in Seattle re-enacted the relocation that had occurred in 1942.

The re-enactment had a profound effect on the participants (Takezawa, 1995). Those who had been in the internment camps remembered repressed feelings of shame and injustice. The *Nisei* talked about their experiences, many for the first time. The young Japanese Americans became aware of what their parents or grandparents had experienced. The Seattle Day of Remembrance received wide media coverage and led to similar observances in other cities.

The redress movement gained momentum when the Commission on Wartime Relocation and Internment issued its report in 1982. The report, *Personal Justice Denied,* concludes that the internment was based on racial prejudice. Kitano and Daniels (1995) argue that "the Japanese American experience should trouble all Americans, for it demonstrates how fragile their constitutional protections can be in a time of crisis" (p. 68). The Civil Liberties Act of 1988 provided for Japanese Americans who had been in the internment camps to receive an apology from the President and a one-time, tax-free payment of $20,000.

Takezawa (1995) argues that redress influenced how Japanese Americans view their ethnicity. "Many *Nisei* declare that redress has freed them from shame and endowed them with high ethnic pride. Others maintain that they will always feel like second-class citizens, that the psychological wounds are too deep to heal" (p. 197). Takezawa contends that even those who will continue to feel like second-class citizens moved from feeling shame to pride in being Japanese American. She goes on to point out that the redress movement required that Japanese Americans become more "American" as well; they had to give up the "quiet American" stereotype and publicly fight for their rights. Takezawa concludes that "the redress campaign and its victory have strengthened the identification of Japanese Americans as Americans and has furthered assimilation in behavioral patterns, norms, values, and ideologies. At the same time, it reawoke and enhanced their senses of themselves as Japanese Americans" (p. 210).

Japanese American Institutions

The majority of the initial Japanese immigrants lived in a *Nihonmachi* ("Japantown"). The first Japantowns were in San Francisco and Seattle.[10] By

1940, Los Angeles' Little Tokyo (see Lyman, 1986, for a study of Little Tokyo) had the largest population (about 37,000), with Seattle and its surrounding area second (about 11,700) and San Francisco and its surrounding area third (about 6,000). Other cities with 1,000 or more Japanese included New York, Portland, Sacramento, and Stockton. Even though Los Angeles had the largest Japanese population, San Francisco served as the headquarters for formal organizations, such as the Japanese American Citizens League (JACL; see below).

Many of the early Japantowns still exist today (e.g., "Little Tokyo" in Los Angeles), but the percentage of Japanese living in these areas is much smaller than prior to World War II. There are, however, other cities with large portions of Japanese Americans that provide institutional support for the continuation of the Japanese traditions. Gardena, California, for example, is a city with about one-quarter Japanese Americans. Gardena has a Japanese cable television station, numerous ethnic churches, ethnic stores, newspapers, and social organizations. The concentration of Japanese Americans living in cities like this allows them to maintain strong ethnic ties and traditions.

Japanese churches in areas where there was not a large concentration of Japanese provide institutional support for maintaining ethnicity. Most *Issei* (first-generation Japanese) were Buddhists. Buddhist temples in Japan are different from churches in the United States (e.g., they do not hold Sunday services). When the *Issei* moved to the United States, they adapted the Buddhist religion. Initially, the church services were held in Japanese, but later there was a transition to English as the number of *Nisei* and *Sansei* who could speak Japanese declined. Buddhist churches hold Sunday services and provide a place where Japanese Americans can congregate and socially interact. Many of the Buddhist churches also sponsor Japanese language and culture schools and other ethnic activities (e.g., *Obon* celebrations). The churches, therefore, facilitate the continuation of Japanese ethnicity even in areas without large Japanese populations.

In addition to churches, Japanese American social organizations help Japanese Americans maintain their ethnicity. Fugita and O'Brien (1991), for example, report that over 50% of the Japanese Americans in California are members of ethnic organizations. These organizations include the JACL, as well as neighborhood associations, bowling leagues, basketball leagues, and professional associations. O'Brien and Fugita (1991) point out that membership in voluntary associations is higher in areas where there are small numbers of Japanese Americans than in areas where there are large numbers. They go on to argue that "even though they generally live and work in a 'white world,' much of their meaningful interaction takes place within the ethnic community" (pp. 102-103).

Japanese generation in the United States influences their experiences with ethnic institutions. The first generation, the *Issei,* were the original immigrants. Most *Issei* felt that assimilation into the mainstream U.S. culture was not possible for them because of the cultural differences and the discrimination they experienced. The *Issei* tended to obtain the services they needed within the ethnic community. *Issei* generally lived *kodomo no tame ni* ("for the sake of the children"). They were the major force in the Japanese community until World War II. Their power in the community, however, diminished after the war.

The second-generation are *Nisei.* The *Nisei* generally worked in ethnic communities or at ethnic jobs (e.g., agriculture, gardening). It was not uncommon for college-educated *Nisei* to work in the family business. The *Nisei* tended to value many of the same things that the *Issei* did (e.g., *amae,* "dependence"; *enryo,* "reserve or restraint"). The *Nisei* generally accepted their position in the U.S. society (e.g., they held the attitude of *shikataganai,* "it can't be helped") and used indirect communication like their parents.

The *Nisei* started the Japanese American Assistance League (JACL) in 1940, and it continues today. The JACL is open only to U.S. citizens (so it excludes the *Issei*), and it is dedicated to helping Japanese Americans fit into the mainstream U.S. culture. Its creed recognizes that Japanese Americans will experience discrimination but that they must persevere to overcome it.

The *Sansei* (third-generation) came of age in the 1970s (e.g., many were born just after World War II). Takahashi (cited in Kitano & Daniels, 1995) found that *Sansei* hold many values similar to *Issei* and *Nisei* (e.g., good education, hard work, community solidarity, perseverance). Generational differences among *Sansei* and subsequent generations are not as meaningful as in earlier times (e.g., between *Issei* and *Nisei*). One reason for this was the new immigration that occurred after the 1965 Immigration Act. The new immigrants form different identities than Japanese Americans whose families have been in the United States for a longer period of time (see the discussion of ethnic identity in Chapter 4). All Japanese Americans, however, share one thing in common. No matter how much they acculturate to the mainstream U.S. culture, their physical features will always identify them as Japanese Americans (or Asian Americans more broadly) (Kitano & Daniels, 1995); in other words, their ethnicity is racialized.

Some *Sansei* and most *Yonsei* (fourth-generation) and *Gosei* (fifth-generation) do not have a lot of close ethnic ties and may not have experienced the overt discrimination that the *Issei* and *Nisei* did. Many of the subsequent generations, however, still maintain ethnic contacts through Japanese American athletic leagues in cities with large populations (e.g., basketball leagues) or community youth councils and ethnic activities such as *Nisei* Week, Cherry Blossom Festivals, or *Obon* (celebrations held for dead ancestors).

Nisei Weeks and Cherry Blossom Festivals involve ethnic celebrations and other activities such as holding pageants to select the queen of the celebration. One of the interesting controversies that often emerges in the pageants for queens is whether or not the queens have to be "full-blooded" Japanese (who often do not know much about Japan or speak the language) or can they be of mixed heritage (e.g., offspring of European Americans and Japanese Americans, some of whom take an interest in Japan and may be fluent in Japanese) (see King, 1997, for one case study).

Japanese American Families

Japanese American families are based on Japanese families.[11] The family is the basic unit of Japanese society (Nakane, 1970). Japanese learn how to behave, their values, and their codes of ethics in the family. In Japanese families, children learn the importance of duty and social obligations to other family members. The ethical system they learn is one of "collective obligations" to other family members (Miyamoto, 1984). The *ie* (family, household) is "a continuous entity which included all past, present, and future members of the family" (Kitano, 1993a, p. 117). Japanese collective obligations, therefore, extend to their families through time. This leads to strong feelings of solidarity with family members.

Yanagisako (1985) argues that *Issei* families generally followed the Japanese model. That is, there usually were arranged marriages, members of these families based much of their interaction on obligations, filial bonds were considered important, the males dominated the families, and there were clear sex roles within the families. She goes on to point out that *Issei* families tended to be characterized by emotional restraint and little verbal communication between husbands and wives. Kikumura and Kitano (1981) point out that in *Issei* families, family members "were encouraged and often socially pressured into behaving in a way that would benefit the reputation of the family" (p. 48).

Nisei families differed from *Issei* families because *Nisei* were exposed to the U.S. family model as well. Yanagisako (1985) suggests that in comparison with

Issei families, *Nisei* families involve more romantic love, more emphasis on conjugal bonds, more equality between the sexes, more flexible sex roles, and more communication between parents and children. In other words, the patterns of behavior in *Nissei* families is somewhere between the *Issei* and European American models. Kitano (1993b), however, points out that there is a lot of variability in *Nisei* families; some are closer to the *Issei,* some are closer to European Americans, and some are a mixture of the two.

The families of *Sansei* and subsequent generations appear to have moved more toward the mainstream U.S. model than the *Issei* model (Kitano, 1993b). This does not, however, mean that Japanese influences have disappeared. Many families that live in areas with large concentrations of Japanese Americans, for example, still maintain many Japanese behaviors. Some traditional Japanese behaviors and values may be maintained no matter where the families live. To illustrate, the importance placed on the family and *amae* ("dependency") needs appear to survive across generations (Connor, 1974).

Johnson (1977) examines solidarity in Japanese American families in Hawaii. She contends that Japanese Americans maintain relations with members of their families out of obligation rather than choice as European Americans do. The exchange of services (e.g., grandparents caring for grandchildren and receiving care in return), advice, and reciprocity among family members leads to high levels of interpersonal contact among the family members and feelings of solidarity with the family. Johnson reports that the Japanese values of obligations, interdependence, and reciprocity survive for at least three generations past the first generation born in Hawaii. Johnson concludes that Japanese family patterns continue in an altered state long after the members of the family acculturate to superficial aspects of the mainstream U.S. culture.

McDermott et al. (1983) point out that Japanese Americans in Hawaii endorse the family as a reference group, meeting family obligations, and clear lines of authority. Japanese American adolescents endorse the need for privacy of thoughts and feelings. McDermott et al. (1983) contend that Japanese Americans are taught to limit their emotional expressiveness in the family more than European Americans. Johnson, Marsella, and Johnson (1974) report that Japanese Americans use more indirect communication in their families than European Americans. Similarly, Hsu et al. (1985) find that Japanese American spouses are more reticent in communication and less comfortable discussing personal feelings than European American spouses. Overall, Japanese American spouses are more restrained and display emotions less than European American spouses.

Ching et al. (1995) note that Japanese American families are more likely to involve hierarchical status and role differentiation focusing on the males than are European American families. They also observe that Japanese American families emphasize collective harmony, cooperation, acceptance, and positive interactions in the family. Arkoff, Meridith, and Iwahara (1964) suggest that only Japanese American males prefer male-dominant and patriarchal attitudes regarding the roles of husbands and wives. Japanese American women prefer egalitarian marriages similar to European American women. Regardless of their attitudes toward sex roles, Japanese Americans emphasize positive family interactions, harmony in the family, and cooperation among family members more than do European Americans (Ching et al., 1995).

FILIPINO AMERICANS

Filipinos were technically the first Asians to arrive in the United States, but the initial numbers were very small. Today, they are the second largest group of Asian Americans. I begin this section with a discussion of Filipino immigration.

Filipino Immigration Patterns

As indicated earlier, Filipinos were the first Asians to enter the United States (i.e., the "Manila men" in Louisiana in 1763). These early immigrants, however, were not related to later waves of Filipino immigration. Filipino immigration differed from that of other Asian immigrants because of U.S. imperialism. After the Spanish-American War of 1898, the United States took possession of the Philippines. Until the Philippines became semi-independent in 1935, Filipino immigrants were not aliens, but U.S. nationals. In addition to the "Manila men," there were some wives of U.S. soldiers who fought in the Spanish-American War who immigrated to the United States, but no firm numbers are available.

The first large wave of Filipinos to come to the United States were the *pensionados,* student sojourners. These students came to the United States during the period 1903 to 1910 as part of a U.S. government-sponsored program to obtain an education and return to the Philippines. Many of these students returned to the Philippines and many became leaders of the country.

The second wave of immigrants started in the 1920s and 1930s. There were about 5,600 Filipinos in the United States in 1920 before this wave began. This wave of immigration was motivated by the economic conditions in the Philippines, and most Filipinos went to Hawaii to work in the sugar fields for the Hawaii Sugar Planters' Association (HSPA) (remember, Japanese could no longer do this work after the gentleman's agreement of 1907-1908). About 120,000 Filipinos arrived in Hawaii between 1906 and 1934 (87% were men). These laborers went to Hawaii on three-year contracts. After their contracts were completed, some laborers renewed their contracts, some moved to the West Coast, and some returned to the Philippines. The shortage of Filipino women caused problems, and in the 1920s the HSPA realized that family men would be better workers than single men. This allowed a stable Filipino community to be formed in Hawaii (Agbayani-Siewert & Revilla, 1995).

The Filipino immigrants who moved to the West Coast worked mostly in agriculture, and some worked for Japanese immigrants. Others performed menial jobs such as dishwasher or worked in the canneries in Alaska. There were about 45,000 Filipinos in the United States in 1930, with 30,000 in California (94% male). The Tydings-McDuffe Act of 1934 promised the Philippines its independence in 1945 (which was delayed until 1946 after World War II). When the Philippines became semi-independent in 1935, Filipinos were no longer considered U.S. nationals. In 1940, the number of Filipino immigrants increased only slightly (about 46,000 in the United States), but there was a modest increase by 1950 (about 62,000 in the United States, 40,000 in California).

Unlike the Chinese and the Japanese, the Filipino men who immigrated to the United States associated with white females (e.g., they went to dance halls). This caused problems with the white men, and anti-Filipino sentiment developed (see Parreñas, 1998). This culminated in the 1930 riot in Watsonville, California, where a group of white vigilantes rioted at a dance hall leased by a Filipino. Even though there were problems, some of the relationships between Filipino males and white females led to marriage, but there is no firm data on how many marriages occurred.

There were 181,614 Filipinos in the United States in 1960 (63% men). Since the 1965 Immigration Act, most of the Filipino immigrants have been professionals, especially health professionals. The largest single group was nurses. In 1970, there were 336,731 Filipinos in the United States. The majority of immigrants since 1976 when occupational immigration was halted have been admitted for family reunification. By 1980, there were 774,652 Filipinos in the United States. In 1990, there were over 1.4 million Filipinos in the

United States with concentrations in California and Hawaii, where about two-thirds live.

Filipino American Institutions

Before the last wave of Filipino immigration (post-1965), most Filipino communities on the West Coast involved distinct neighborhoods defined by residential segregation (Cordova, 1983).[12] In Seattle, for example, there were distinct communities of Beacon Hill, Central District, and Rainer Valley. Filipinos remained separate

> by choice as well as by necessity. For the most part, they have often found this to be the easier course because immigrants need not strain to change their ways and manners or eliminate their accents. Staying within the Filipino American community was part of survival. The community provided a relative "safe place" where new cultural acquisitions could be tried out and where, at the same time, traditional practices could be maintained and passed on to the next generation. (Bergano & Bergano-Kinney, 1997, p. 203)

These ethnic enclaves support ethnic activities such as picnics, queen pageants, and induction balls, as well as other resources that Filipinos could find in the Philippines.

Filipino Americans on the East Coast tend to be those who immigrated after 1965 and who hold professional degrees (Pido, 1986). This makes their acceptance in the mainstream U.S. culture easier than their West Coast counterparts. Filipinos on the East Coast generally do not live in ethnic communities "out of necessity." East coast Filipinos have been more successful economically than those on the West Coast. This upward mobility "may mean detachment from ethnicity, community ownership, and participation" (Bergano & Bergano-Kinney, 1997, p. 207).

Even though the Filipino ethnic enclaves today are not as strong as they once were, there are numerous Filipino fraternal organizations. In the Los Angeles area, for example, there are over 300 fraternal organizations (Agbayani-Siewert & Revilla, 1995). These fraternal organizations often are based on sharing a common place of origin in the Philippines and a common language. These organizations provide support for Filipino identities.

Language and place of origin are the major ways that Filipinos differentiate themselves (Pido, 1986). Pido, for example, points out that

> there are some covert differences among the major groups in terms of food, customs, traditions, and mode of dress, but the major discriminating differences are in the languages and ways they identify themselves. If a person spoke Tagalog and identified him/herself as Tagalog, then he/she is accepted as Tagalog. There is a strong linguistic consciousness. (p. 17)

These differences carry over to Filipino Americans in the United States.

If Filipino Americans claim membership in a linguistic group (e.g., Tagalog, Ilocano) by speaking that language, they are accepted as members of the group. Failure to do so would threaten the Filipino Americans claiming the identities with *hiya* ("shame"), and this is to be avoided if at all possible.

Filipino shops also contribute to Filipinos' maintaining their ethnicity whether they live in ethnic enclaves or not (see Bonus, 2000). Bonus (1997) argues that Filipino stores are "different worlds" from the mainstream U.S. culture that surrounds them. They are pieces of the Filipino culture in the United States; they contain most of the things Filipinos could buy in the Philippines, things they cannot buy in U.S. markets. Shopping at the Filipino stores also means a place to speak Filipino and engage in Filipino behaviors. One respondent in Bonus' study said, "It's fun here because what you can buy in the Philippines, you can buy here. It's like being in the Philippines" (p. 655). Bonus contends that the commodities in Filipino stores are affirmations of Filipino identities. "Looking at these products and shopping for them becomes an exercise in nostalgia, so that a specific identity is built on a kind of longing for what is missing and the attempt to fill that absence by consumption" (p. 655).

Okamura (1998) points out that focusing on Filipino enclaves may be misleading in understanding Filipinos' experiences in the United States. He contends that "Filipino Americans should be viewed as a diaspora, rather than only as an ethnic minority" (p. ix). Connor (1986) defines a diaspora as "that segment of people living outside the homeland" (p. 16). Okamura contends that to understand Filipino Americans, the diaspora must be viewed internationally, including relations among Filipino Americans, Filipinos in the Philippines, and Filipinos in other countries. Members of these groups are intertwined through letters, phone calls, monetary and other forms of assistance, and occasional visits. Institutional support for maintaining ethnicity, therefore, can come from many sources, not just the local community of Filipino Americans.

Filipino American Families

Filipino American families are based on Filipino families (see discussion of Filipino collectivism in Chapter 2).[13] Agbayani-Siewert and Revilla (1995) argue that

> the Filipino family structure is built on cultural values that reflect a system of cooperation; it provides a supportive and protective system that members can depend on for a sense of belonging and help when needed. The Filipino family's value of smooth interpersonal relationships discourages outward displays of behavior that might lead to conflict and instead encourages passive nonconfrontation. (p. 159)

Being loyal to the family, depending on it, and having solidarity with family members are of the highest priority for Filipinos.

Smooth interpersonal relationships are critical in Filipino families (Agbayani-Siewert & Revilla, 1995). Smooth interpersonal relationships within families bind the members of families together. Smooth interpersonal relationships are maintained through *utang ng loob* ("reciprocal obligations"), *pakikisama* ("going along with others"), *hiya* ("shame"), and *amor proprio* ("protecting self-esteem"). All of these values contribute to Filipino family members' subordinating themselves and their self-interests to their families.

Filipino American families often reflect Filipino values. Filipino Americans in the United States tend to have larger numbers of nonnuclear family members living with them than do all other Asian American ethnic groups except Vietnamese Americans. Filipino Americans have close ties with the people with whom they live and other family members, but not necessarily with nonkin members of the ethnic community (Agbayani-Siewert & Revilla, 1995). Cooper et al. (1993) report that first- and second-generation Filipino adolescents rely on their families for social support and guidance more than do European American adolescents. Filipino American adolescents, however, rely on friends to discuss dating, sex, and marriage.

Uba (1994) argues that Filipino Americans "emphasize etiquette, getting along with others, and appropriate social behavior" more than do European Americans (p. 50). Filipino Americans also emphasize family cohesion. Uba suggests that Filipino American parents control their children through guilt and shame.

Living in the United States places strain on traditional Filipino family relationships. Card (1985), for example, reports that there is less verbal communication between Filipino husbands and wives in the United States than in the
Philippines. Filipino American parents tend to hold onto traditional family values more than their children (Agbayani-Siewert & Revilla, 1995), but Filipino
American children still tend to be more dependent and less autonomous with respect to the family than European American children (Keith & Barranda,
1969). Generational differences, nevertheless, cause problems in Filipino
American families.

Pido (1986) argues that Filipino American parents are concerned about
many of the same issues as European American parents (e.g., juvenile delin-
quency), but Filipino Americans have some unique concerns as well. Filipino
Americans, for example, are concerned about children's lack of respect for parents and elders, children's not paying enough attention to their social obligations, and children's not realizing that there are consequences of their behavior
for others (e.g., the family). In the Philippines, parents would be assisted by the
extended family and community in dealing with these issues. In the United
States, however, most Filipino American parents have to deal with the problems
alone. Pido suggests that many Filipino American parents "prefer to relinquish
some control, and direction of their children and count on the latter's reciprocal
individual attachments and loyalty to the family, rather than risk losing them
completely by insisting on strong family controls and direction" (p. 113).

KOREAN AMERICANS

Koreans are relatively new arrivals in the United States in large numbers. They
are, nevertheless, probably the fastest-growing Asian American ethnic group. I
begin this section with a discussion of immigration patterns.

Korean Immigration Patterns

As indicated earlier, about 100 Korean political exiles came to the United
States as early as 1885 after diplomatic relations were established between the
United States and Korea. The next group of Koreans (e.g., about 7,300) to come
to the United States arrived between 1903 and 1905. These immigrants went to
Hawaii to work in the sugar fields. Most tended to have weak Korean identities.
Because of living in a new land and the Japanese occupation of Korea, however,

they developed stronger Korean identities (e.g., they met at Korean churches, started Korean language and culture schools, imported "picture brides" from Korea). The immigration of Korean workers ended in 1905, but about 2,000 Koreans moved to Hawaii and California before Asian immigration was halted by the 1924 Immigration Act. Koreans that came between 1906 and 1923 were wives of workers, political refugees, and students.

The second wave of Korean immigrants immigrating to the United States started at the end of the Korean War and lasted until the 1965 Immigration Act. The second wave of immigrants was a mixed group. It included wives of U.S. soldiers (about 28,000), war orphans adopted in the United States (about 6,300), and students. Many of the war brides had difficulty fitting into the mainstream U.S. culture. These immigrants and those who followed (third wave) have come almost exclusively from South Korea.

The third wave began after the 1965 Immigration Act. Unlike the Chinese, Japanese, and Filipinos, this group of immigrants consisted mostly of families. The Koreans who immigrated were highly educated, and most moved to large cities such as Chicago, New York, and Los Angeles (each of these have Koreatowns). In 1970, there were 69,155 Koreans in the United States. The corresponding numbers for 1980 and 1990 are 354,974 and 798,849.

About 350,000 Koreans were located on the West Coast in 1990 (about 260,000 in California and 200,000 in the Los Angeles/Long Beach area), but Korean Americans are more geographically scattered than other Asian Americans (Min, 1995). Many of the male immigrants in the third wave had to take jobs of lower status than they held in Korea. Many of these immigrants opened small businesses, usually in ethnic neighborhoods. Min (1993) maintains that many of the third wave of Korean immigrants are more individualistic than their Chinese and Japanese counterparts.

The Los Angeles riot of 1992 marked an important point for Korean immigrants. Korean-owned stores were targeted, and this resulted in feelings of despair and tense intergroup relations in Los Angeles.

Korean American Institutions

Many Koreans live in Koreatowns in cities such as Los Angeles, Chicago, and New York (see Min, 1996, for discussions of the New York and Los Angeles Koreatowns). The Los Angeles Koreatown, for example, is 25 square miles in size and contains over 3,000 Korean-owned businesses. There are ethnic restaurants; grocery stores; physicians and dentists who speak Korean; books, magazines, and newspapers written in Korean; ethnic social organizations; and so forth. The signs for businesses in Koreatown are mostly in Korean. Koreatowns, therefore, provide the institutional support necessary to allow Koreans in the United States to maintain their ethnicity. Even Koreans who do not live in Koreatowns tend to maintain membership in ethnic organizations (Hurh & Kim, 1988; see also Lee, 1982) and churches (see below).

Min (1995) argues that Koreans maintain their ethnic attachments for three reasons: (1) the nature of Korean culture, (2) Korean churches, and (3) Korean small businesses. Min points out that Korea is a small, homogeneous culture where everyone speaks the same language. This facilitates ethnic attachment when Koreans meet in the United States because there are not cultural or language barriers separating them like there may be for Chinese or Filipinos (e.g., Chinese and Filipinos may speak different languages or dialects).

Over 75% of the Koreans in the United States are affiliated with one of the Korean immigrant churches (Min, 1995). These churches are Christian and almost all are Protestant. Korean churches sponsor Korean language and culture programs and provide a structured meeting place for Koreans to get together. "Korean immigrant churches contribute to maintaining Korean ethnicity by helping to stimulate social interaction among Koreans on the one hand and by helping to preserve Korean culture on the other" (Min, 1995, p. 215).

Korean businesses also contribute to maintaining ethnic attachments (see Light & Bonacich, 1988, for a general discussion). Min (1995) points out that Korean owners tend to hire other Koreans. This facilitates social interaction among the immigrant group. It allows them to speak Korean and maintain Korean customs at work. Often these patterns continue in Korean-owned businesses in other ethnic areas as well (e.g., Korean-owned businesses in African American areas). The Los Angeles riots of 1992 influenced the way Koreans do business in these neighborhoods (see Abelman & Lie, 1995, for a discussion of Korean Americans' responses to the riots).

Korean American Families

Korean families generally involve clear tasks and roles (Kitano & Daniels, 1995).[14] The husbands' task is to work outside the house and bring home the family income. The wives' task is to stay at home and take care of the house.

The husbands make decisions for the family. Children are expected to be obedient to their parents. All members of the family are expected to subordinate their interests to those of the family.

Traditional Korean family patterns do not appear to totally generalize to Korean American families. Hong (1982), for example, reports that Korean American families in Los Angeles tend to be more egalitarian than traditional Korean families. In Hong's study, only 22% of the families are husband dominant; 71% are egalitarian (e.g., joint husband-wife decision making). The changes appear to cause problems. To illustrate, Lee (1975) notes that Korean American husbands complain that they do not have the same control over their wives in the United States that they had in Korea. Korean American wives, in contrast, regard their husbands' traditional sex role expectations as a major problem in their relationships. These different role expectations may be responsible for Korean American spouses not being as happy as national samples (Hong, 1982). Korean American marriages, however, still tend to be happy: 80% in Hong's study report that they are "very happy" (31.4%) or "happy" (48.6%). (Note: 69.1% of national samples are "very happy" and 27.4% are "happy.")

Hurh and Kim (1988) report that 90% of the Korean Americans in Chicago speak Korean at home. Language usage reflects the tendency to maintain traditional Korean family values in Korean American homes. Yu and Kim (1983) observe that there is little verbal communication between Korean American mothers and their children; rather, they rely on nonverbal communication and implicit communication. B. Kim (1980) notes that many Korean American children maintain a strong identification with the Korean culture (e.g., prefer Korean food, want to visit Korea).

One of the factors that affects Korean families in the United States is the availability of work for the wives and children (Kitano & Daniels, 1995). Only the male heads of the households are expected to work in Korea. Many of the wives and children, however, have to work to help support their families in the United States (56% of the wives work; Min, 1995). A large portion of the husbands do not help with household chores even when their wives work outside the home (Hurh & Kim, 1984). These changes in family dynamics place stress on the Korean American families because the traditional role expectations often still operate. This often leads to marital conflict among Korean American husbands and wives (Min, 1995; see Song, 1996, for a discussion of wife beating among Korean American husbands). Mothers working outside the house may influence communication between mothers and adolescents. Han (1985) reports that Korean American adolescents disclose more information to same-sex friends than to their mothers. European American adolescents, in contrast, disclose more to their mothers than to their friends.

VIETNAMESE AMERICANS

Vietnamese are among the latest Asian groups to arrive in the United States in large numbers. They differ from Chinese, Japanese, Filipino, and Korean immigrants in that most Vietnamese coming to the United States were refugees. I begin this section with Vietnamese immigration patterns.

Vietnamese Immigration Patterns

The first Vietnamese immigration to the United States occurred in 1952 when eight immigrants arrived (Rumbaut, 1995; also see Do, 1999). Immigration did not increase significantly until close to the end of the Vietnam War. To illustrate, there were only about 3,000 Vietnamese in the United States in 1970.

The Vietnamese who came to the United States after 1970 are different from most of the other Asian immigrants because most of the Vietnamese were refugees. Refugees are a special type of immigrant—ones who have left their countries for safety. Most Asian immigrants were "pulled" to the United States in order to better their lives, but Vietnamese who came after 1970 were "pushed" out of their country.

There were three waves of Vietnamese refugees, and virtually all lived in South Vietnam. The first wave was prior to 1975. This group included Vietnamese civil servants, soldiers, teachers, farmers, and employees of the U.S. government in Vietnam. This group consisted mostly of family units. Most came from somewhat "advantaged" backgrounds (e.g., about 50% were college educated).

The second wave started after the end of the war in 1975. Most of these refugees did not come directly to the United States. Most went to midway stops such as the refugee processing centers run by the United Nations High Commission for Refugees where they took classes in English as a second language and received cultural orientations to the United States. There were about 125,000 refugees in 1975. The following two years (1976 and 1977) involved only about 5,000 refugees. There were about 11,000 in 1978 and about 44,500 in 1979; the post-1975 numbers peaked in 1980 with about 95,200 refugees.

The third wave of Vietnamese arrived in the United States through the Orderly Departure Program (ODP) beginning in 1980 when there were 261,729 Vietnamese in the United States. The ODP focused on Amerasian children and relocation camps internees (political refugees). By 1990, there were 614,547 Vietnamese in the United States. In 1992, "over 300,000 Vietnamese had immigrated to the United States through the ODP, including 161,400 in the regular family reunification program, 81,500 Amerasians and their accompanying relatives, and 61,000 former political prisoners and their families" (Rumbaut, 1995, p. 238).

The U.S. government policy was to assign the refugees sponsors (e.g., social service agencies, U.S. families) across the country. The idea was to not burden any specific U.S. community with a large number of Vietnamese refugees (Rumbaut, 1995). Despite the U.S. government efforts, by 1980 almost half of the refugees had moved from the location they were assigned originally. Centers of Vietnamese population in the United States emerged from these moves. In 1990, there were about 280,000 Vietnamese in California, 70,000 in Texas, 21,000 in Virginia, 15,000 in Massachusetts, 19,000 in Washington, and 10,000 in Minnesota. Orange County in California has the largest Vietnamese concentration, followed by Los Angeles, San Jose, San Diego, and Houston.

Vietnamese American Institutions

Like other Asian American ethnic groups, Vietnamese have formed ethnic enclaves. There are Vietnamese enclaves in California, Texas, Louisiana, Washington, and Virginia, with the largest being "Little Saigon" in Orange County, California. Others such as Versailles Village in New Orleans are not as large but still provide most, if not all, of the resources needed to maintain Vietnamese ethnicity. A Vietnamese social worker, for example, said, "We are survivors, grasping each other for support. A place like Little Saigon provided that support" (Gropp, 1992, p. 28).

Little Saigon contains a large number of ethnic businesses (about 2,000).

Its diverse establishments now include pagoda-like mini-malls, glittering jewelry booths, trendy fashion boutiques, fabric stores, hair salons, fancy restaurants, noodle shops, and cafes, bakeries, supermarkets, laser-karaoke outlets, music stores, and night clubs—all reminiscent of the fallen capital of the former South Vietnam. (Zhou & Bankston, 1998, p. 75)

Zhou and Bankston point out that Little Saigon is a "cultural mecca" that contains "all things Vietnamese." Vietnamese who go to Little Saigon never "feel out of place."

Little Saigon has many of the same institutional structures that were used in South Vietnam. The Chamber of Commerce, for example, has over 2,000 members and numerous service organizations (Zhou & Bankston, 1998). Over 30 schools have been established to teach young Vietnamese to speak, read, and write Vietnamese. In addition, there are ethnic newspapers, magazines, and two small cable TV stations in Vietnamese. The vast majority of the Vietnamese who live in or around Little Saigon are Buddhists (80%).

A recent study of Vietnamese Americans in southern California (where Little Saigon is located) supports the importance of the ethnic enclave to Vietnamese Americans. Brody, Rimmer, and Trotter (1999) asked Vietnamese Americans, "How important is Little Saigon as part of your life?" The vast majority of respondents indicate that it is either "very important" (54.7%) or "important" (18.0%).

Versailles Village in New Orleans shows similarities with Little Saigon, but there are differences as well (Zhou & Bankston, 1998). The Associated Catholic Charities were responsible for the original Vietnamese refugees in New Orleans. The Catholic Church continues to play an important role today. About 80% of the Vietnamese in New Orleans, for example, are Catholic. "By the 1990s, Versailles Village had become a miniature Little Saigon" (p. 82). It contains most of the services Vietnamese need to "feel at home." "The various formal organizations [e.g., Vietnamese Parent-Teachers Association], as well as the existing network of families and friends, furnished coethnic members with both intangible (emotional, cultural, and spiritual) support and tangible support in the form of jobs, education, and housing" (p. 82).

Vietnamese American Families

Traditional Vietnamese families share many characteristics with traditional Chinese families (see the culture-specific discussion of collectivism in Chapter 2). Vietnamese families provide the major source of social identities for their members (Zhou & Bankston, 1998). They are headed by the fathers, and there are strict roles based on age and sex (Rutledge, 1992). Vietnamese fathers, however, do not share the absolute authority that Chinese fathers have. Vietnamese fathers involve other family members in decisions, delegate authority, and generally share responsibility for the family. All members of Vietnamese families are expected to work for the benefit of the family.

Vietnamese American families have the largest number of nonnuclear family members living in the same household of any of the Asian American ethnic groups (Rutledge, 1992). Rutledge contends that many of the traditional Vietnamese family values continue to be held among members of Vietnamese American families (see also Caplan, Whitmore, & Choy, 1989). Cooper et al. (1993) report that first- and second-generation Vietnamese American adolescents rely on their families for social support and guidance more than do European American adolescents. Vietnamese American adolescents rely on their friends to discuss sex, dating, and marriage. Rutledge argues that Vietnamese American parents tend to encourage their children to learn the customs of the mainstream U.S. culture, but many find it uncomfortable to see their children becoming "American." Uba points out that Vietnamese Americans tend to "avoid frank, verbal communication between parent and child" (p. 51).

Dinh, Sarason, and Sarason (1994) note that parent-child conflicts center around children perceiving that parents are overprotective and controlling. They also observe that Vietnamese American children born in Vietnam perceive that the quality of their relationships with their parents is not as good as Vietnamese American children born in the United States perceive their relationships to be. The father-son relationship is affected the most negatively by the sons' acculturation.

There are changes in "gender roles, family expectations, generational perspectives, and family relationships" taking place in Vietnamese American families (Rutledge, 1992, p. 125). In Vietnam, wives and children do not work outside the home. In the United States, many Vietnamese American wives and children must work to support the family, and the husbands sometimes help with the family chores, which they would not do in Vietnam. The changing roles in Vietnamese American families create conflicts and tensions in the families (Kibria, 1993; Tran, 1988).

Many Vietnamese American husbands and fathers may feel that they are losing their position in their families. One Vietnamese American woman that Rutledge interviewed said:

> Most of the time, my husband sits in his big chair and relaxes when he comes home from work. He helps me with some of the housework and sometimes

cooking, but he is not very good. This is hard for him. It is also hard for me. I try to show him that he is still the head of the family and that his helping does not change that. (p. 125)

Vietnamese American women perceive that they have fewer people from whom they can receive social support than European American women (Dinh et al., 1994).

Children working outside the home also can create problems. Earning their "own" money outside the home allows the Vietnamese American children to have a degree of independence from their families that children in Vietnam would not have.

Role conflicts emerge in Vietnamese American families because the children have acculturated to the mainstream U.S. culture more and speak better English than their parents. One parent in Rutledge's (1992) study said, "My son speaks English better [than I] and he does not speak Vietnamese good. Sometimes I have to get him for understanding [translating] and this I don't like. It makes him think he is better [than I]" (p. 127).

The mainstream U.S. culture dating practices also cause problems for Vietnamese Americans. In Vietnam, children are not free to select the people they will marry (Rutledge, 1992). Rather, the extended families select their spouses (i.e., there are arranged marriages). Many young people follow Vietnamese traditions, but other Vietnamese American young people see people in the United States marrying the people they love, and they want to do the same.

Not all Vietnamese American families have major problems in the United States. Zhou and Bankston (1998) point out that

in the best-adjusted families, members begin to practice a new form of family collectivism that [combines] the traditional belief in mutual protection and support with the American ideal of equality in family relations. Although at times the greater equality among family members [leads] to weakened power of men over women and parents over children, it [does] not always cause men or women to reject the traditional Vietnamese family system. Instead, the struggle to adjust to the new environment frequently [produces] attempts to preserve and adapt images of traditional families. (p. 87)

The principal of the family's coming first still dominates in well-adjusted families.

INDIVIDUALISM-COLLECTIVISM
ACROSS ETHNIC GROUPS

In Chapter 2, I pointed out that Chinese Americans, Filipino Americans, Japanese Americans, Korean Americans, and Vietnamese Americans share the common cultural heritage of coming from collectivistic cultures. As you may recall from Chapter 2, three individual-level factors that reflect individualism-collectivism can be isolated: personality orientations (idiocentrism vs. allocentrism), individual values, and self construals (independent vs. interdependent).

Several studies compare Asian Americans (as a group) with European Americans on one or more of these factors. Some studies, for example, find that Asian Americans emphasize interdependent self construals more than do European Americans (e.g., Gaines et al., 1997; Kim & Kitani, 1998; Singelis & Sharkey, 1995; unreported data from Gudykunst et al., 1996). Some studies also report that Asian Americans emphasize independent self construals less than do European Americans (e.g., Singelis & Sharkey, 1995; unreported data from Gudykunst et al., 1996) or that Asian Americans are less idiocentric than European Americans (e.g., Doherty et al., 1994). Other studies find no differences in independent self construals for European Americans and Asian Americans (e.g., Gaines et al., 1997). Nathan et al. (1999) also observe that there are no differences in how European Americans and Japanese Americans rate the concepts "individual" and "self." Japanese Americans, however, rate the term "group" as more "good" than do European Americans.

Rhee et al. (1995) report that some Asian Americans do not list their ethnicity when asked to complete the 20-statements test (e.g., respondents give 20 answers to "I am ____"), and others do. Asian Americans who do not list their ethnicity tend to have self-concepts similar to European Americans, and those who do list their ethnicity tend to have self-concepts similar to Koreans. Rhee, Uleman, and Lee (1996) observe that Asian Americans and European Americans differ in terms of general collectivism and collectivism with their families, as well as with respect to individualism not involving their relatives.

A few published studies have compared individualistic and collectivistic tendencies of members of two or more Asian American ethnic groups. Doherty et al. (1994), for example, report that Japanese Americans and Chinese Americans are similar with respect to idiocentric tendencies. Singelis and Sharkey (1995) also do not find any differences in either independent or interdependent self construals among Chinese Americans, Japanese Americans, Korean Amer-

TABLE 3.3 Individualistic and Collectivistic Tendencies by Ethnicity

	CA	JA	KA	FA	VA
Independent self construals	5.79	5.52	5.63	5.72	5.80
Interdependent self construals	5.31	5.07	5.07	5.35	5.27
Individualistic values	5.43	5.41	5.44	5.48	5.20
Collectivistic values	5.46	5.56	5.26	5.61	5.51

SOURCE: Survey of Asian American Communication.
NOTE: CA = Chinese American; JA = Japanese American; KA = Korean American; FA = Filipino American; VA = Vietnamese American. Scores range from 1 to 7.

icans, and Filipino Americans in Hawaii. Wink (1997) notes that Chinese American and Korean American ethnicity is associated positively with interdependent self construals and collective identities, and associated negatively with independent self construals and self-direction.

Unreported data from two studies can be used to examine ethnic differences in interdependent and independent self construals (Min-Sun Kim made this data available). Kim, Sharkey, and Singelis' (1994) data yields no differences among Asian American ethnic groups for interdependent self construals (Chinese Americans = 4.81; Filipino Americans = 4.95; Japanese Americans = 4.91; Korean Americans = 4.88) or independent self construals (Chinese Americans = 5.79; Filipino Americans = 6.06; Japanese Americans = 5.97; Korean Americans = 5.95) in Hawaii. Similarly, Kim and Kitani's (1998) data provide no differences among Asian American ethnic groups in Hawaii for interdependent self construals (Chinese Americans = 5.13; Filipino Americans = 4.95; Japanese Americans = 5.20; Korean Americans = 4.88) or independent self construals (Chinese Americans = 4.59; Filipino Americans = 4.91; Japanese Americans = 4.48; Korean Americans = 4.74).

The Survey of Asian American Communication contains measures of self construals and values that can be used to examine ethnic differences in individualistic and collectivistic tendencies. Table 3.3 presents the average scores for independent self construals, interdependent self construals, individualistic values, and collectivistic values for each of the five ethnic groups. There are no differences in any of the four measures across the five Asian American ethnic groups (also, there were no differences when only those who strongly identify with their ethnic groups were tested). Asian Americans individualistic and collectivistic tendencies also are not influenced by whether they are born in the

TABLE 3.4 Individualistic and Collectivistic Tendencies by Where Asian Americans Are Born and the Language Spoken at Home When They Were Children

	Where Born		Language Spoken	
	U.S.	*Not U.S.*	*English*	*Not English*
Independent self construals	5.66	5.77	5.81	5.64
Interdependent self construals	5.22	5.23	5.11	5.26
Individualistic values	5.40	5.45	5.47	5.36
Collectivistic values	5.53	5.49	5.51	5.49

SOURCE: Survey of Asian American Communication.
NOTE: Scores range from 1 to 7.

United States or another country or by which language was spoken in their homes when they were children (English/not English; see Table 3.4).

The findings for the Survey of Asian American Communication regarding similarities in individualistic and collectivistic tendencies are consistent with all of the studies comparing Asian American ethnic groups. The research to date, therefore, suggests that members of the various Asian American ethnic groups in the United States have similar individualistic and collectivistic tendencies. This is to be expected at one level since all the ethnic groups share a common Asian collectivistic heritage. Individual Asian Americans' individualistic and collectivistic tendencies, however, might be influenced by their ethnic and cultural identities, as well as by their generation in the United States. These factors are examined in the next chapter.

CONCLUSION

The experiences of members of Asian American ethnic groups vary as a function of their different immigration experiences in the United States. The specific immigration experiences that Asian American ethnic groups had are a function of when they came to the United States, how many came, and the response of European Americans to their immigration.

Asian Americans' experiences in the United States also are influenced by the ethnic institutional support that was available when they arrived. Asian Americans who arrived in the United States and lived in large ethnic enclaves, for example, had different experiences than those who arrived and lived among European Americans. In the absence of ethnic enclaves, ethnic churches, ethnic social organizations, and ethnic stores provide support for maintaining ethnic behaviors.

Asian Americans' experiences in the United States also are affected by whether they came alone or with their families. Those who came with their families had support structures that those who came alone did not have. Immigrant families initially were based on the family structure in the home country. As Asian Americans adapt to the United States, the family also adapts.

There is tremendous variation in the members of the different Asian American ethnic groups. Asian Americans, nevertheless, appear to have similar individualistic and collectivistic tendencies that influence their communication patterns.

Understanding Asian Americans' communication is not as simple as recognizing their cultural heritages and immigrant experiences. Asian Americans differ tremendously in the degrees to which they identify with their ethnic groups (i.e., ethnic identities) and with the mainstream U.S. culture (i.e., cultural identities). These issues are examined in the next chapter.

NOTES

1. See Yee, Huang, and Lew (1998) for a general discussion of Asian American families.
2. See Chan (1991) and Takaki (1989) for general histories of Asian Americans. See Ng (1998b) for a history of Asian American immigration.
3. I draw heavily on Kitano and Daniels (1995) in this section and the sections on ethnic group-specific immigration patterns. Where I use other sources, I cite them. If there is no citation, the material presented is drawn from Kitano and Daniels.
4. See Ng (1998c) for a discussion of Taiwanese in the United States.
5. See Tchen (1999) for a discussion of Chinese in New York City before Chinatown began; see Kwong (1987), Kinkead (1992), and Lim (1998) for portraits of Chinatowns.
6. For general discussions of Chinese American families see Hamilton (1996), Ng (1998a), and Yu (1995).
7. See Ishiikuntz (1997) for a discussion of intergenerational relationships across Asian American ethnic groups.
8. See Daniels (1972); Daniels, Taylor, and Kitano (1991); Hansen (1997); Hansen and Mitson (1974); and Tateishi (1984).
9. See Nagata (1993) and Takezawa (1995) for discussions of the redress movement.
10. See Miyamoto (1984) for a study of the Seattle Japantown.
11. See Hope and Jacobson (1995) for a general discussion.
12. See also Espiritu (1995) and Posadas (1999).
13. For general discussions see Cimmarusti (1996) and Heras and Revilla (1992).
14. See Hurh (1998) and Min (1998) for general discussions.

Chapter Four

Ethnic and Cultural Identities

Individuals can be born Chinese Americans, Filipino Americans, Japanese Americans, Korean Americans, or Vietnamese Americans and view their ethnicities as important parts of who they are. Alternatively, these individuals may not view their ethnicities as important parts of who they are or may view themselves as Asian Americans, not Chinese Americans, Filipino Americans, Japanese Americans, Korean Americans, or Vietnamese Americans. Asian Americans can be born outside the United States, move to the United States, and come to view themselves mainly as "Americans." Others may be born in the United States and never view themselves as "Americans." As these examples indicate, there can be tremendous variations in how Asian Americans view themselves with respect to their ethnicities and the mainstream U.S. culture.

Just because Asian Americans trace their heritages to specific Asian American ethnic groups does not mean they will think or act as members of those ethnic groups. The extent to which Asian Americans identify with their ethnic groups (i.e., the strength of their ethnic identities) influences the degree to which they think and act as members of their ethnic groups. The stronger Asian Americans' ethnic identities, the more they think and act based on their ethnicities. Asian Americans, however, do not just identify with their ethnic groups; they also identify to some extent with the mainstream U.S. culture (i.e., they

89

have cultural identities). The stronger Asian Americans' cultural identities, the more the U.S. culture influences how they think and behave.

The way Asian Americans think of themselves is not as simple as having identities based on being Chinese Americans, Filipino Americans, Japanese Americans, Korean Americans, or Vietnamese Americans and having identities based on the U.S. culture. Some Asian Americans come from mixed heritages (e.g., have Japanese Americans and European Americans as parents). Identity issues for mixed-heritage Asian Americans are more complex than for mono-heritage Asian Americans. Furthermore, Asian Americans might not just think of themselves as Chinese Americans, Filipino Americans, Japanese Americans, Korean Americans, or Vietnamese Americans; they may also think of themselves as Asian Americans (i.e., have *panethnic* identities). Asian Americans' ethnic identities might influence their behavior in some situations, their cultural identities might influence their behavior in other situations, and their panethnic identities might influence their behavior in still other situations.

I begin this chapter by looking at broad issues of ethnic and cultural identities. Following this, I overview issues of panethnicity. Next, I examine the models that have been proposed to explain Asian Americans' ethnic and cultural identities. I conclude with a discussion of how ethnic and cultural identities are related to issues of generation in the United States and ethnic language abilities.

ETHNICITY AND ETHNIC IDENTITY

Ethnicity and race are different. Ethnicity can be based on national origin, race, religion, or some combination of these (Gordon, 1964). Race is based on biological characteristics; ethnicity is based on cultural characteristics shared by people of a particular race, religion, or national origin. Wu and Foster (1982) point out that "ethnicity has to do with social and cultural distinctions among individuals, groups, and roles. It is not related directly to racial or physical differences" (p. 279). My focus here and throughout the remainder of the book is on ethnicity, not race, because ethnicity influences communication, not race. Race, however, cannot be ignored. European Americans often use Asian Americans' race to categorize them as Asian Americans (or Chinese Americans, Vietnamese Americans, etc.). When this happens, Asian Americans recognize that their identities cannot be separated from race. Omi and Winant (1994) refer to this as "racialized ethnicity."

I begin this section with a discussion of what ethnicity is. Following this, I examine Asian Americans' ethnic and cultural identities in general. Next, I outline issues of ethnic identities for mixed-heritage Asian Americans. I conclude this section by looking at collective self-esteem—the positive feelings associated with Asian Americans' ethnic and cultural identities.

Ethnicity

There are many ways to define ethnicity. Ethnicity, for example, can be viewed as involving members of groups using some aspect of the groups' cultural backgrounds to separate themselves from others (DeVos, 1975). It also can be viewed as "those individuals who identify themselves as belonging to the same ethnic category" (Giles & Johnson, 1981, p. 202). More generally, ethnicity can be viewed as the most general or inclusive identity individuals use to define themselves (Barth, 1969).

There are three primary ingredients used in defining ethnic groups:

> (1) The group is perceived by others in the society to be different in some combination of the following traits: language, religion, race, or ancestral homeland with its related culture; (2) the members also perceive themselves to be different; and (3) they participate in shared activities built around their (real or mythical) common origin and culture. (Yinger, 1994, pp. 3-4)

If any one of these three ingredients are present in an interaction, ethnicity is influencing what is happening.

Wu and Foster (1982) argue that ethnicity is based on "important" cultural distinctions, not "minor" ones. Distinctions in terms of language or national origin, for example, are important distinctions, and differences such as the way people dress or their hairstyles are minor differences. People grouped together because of language or national origin constitute ethnic groups, but people grouped together because of the way they dress or their hairstyles are not ethnic groups.

Recognizing their ethnicities helps Asian Americans define who they are. Ethnicity offers

> communality in language, a series of customs and symbols, a style, rituals, and appearance, and so forth, which can penetrate life in many ways. These trappings of ethnicity are particularly attractive when one is continually confronted by others who live differently. . . . If I see and experience myself

as a member of an ethnic category or group, and others—fellow members and outsiders—recognize me as such, "ways of being" become possible for me that set me apart from the outsiders. These ways of being contribute to the *content* of my self-perceptions. In this sense, I *become* my ethnic allegiance; I experience any attack on the symbols, emblems, or values (cultural elements) that define my ethnicity as an attack on myself. (Roosens, 1989, pp. 17-18)

Ethnicity, therefore, is important because it influences the way individuals view themselves and others.

Awareness of ethnicity develops at early ages. Preschool and early elementary school children are able to identify others who are members of their ethnic groups, but they cannot understand what ethnicity means (Gay, 1985). Consistency in children's perceptions of their ethnicities emerges around age eight (Aboud, 1984).

Ethnic and Cultural Identities

Ethnic and cultural identities are major social identities influencing Asian Americans' behavior (Gudykunst & Kim, 1997). Tajfel (1978) defines social identity as "that part of an individual's self-concept which derives from his [or her] knowledge of his [or her] membership in a social group (or groups) together with the value and emotional significance attached to that membership" (p. 63). Ethnic identities for Asian Americans, therefore, refer to their knowledge of memberships in particular Asian American ethnic groups (e.g., Chinese American, Japanese American) and the significance attached to those memberships. Ethnic identities do not refer to knowledge of memberships in the panethnic Asian American group as a whole. I use *panethnic identity* to refer to knowledge of membership in the Asian American group as a whole and the significance attached to that membership.

Cultural identities for Asian Americans refer to their knowledge of memberships in the mainstream culture of the United States and the significance attached to those memberships. (Note: If individuals live in another culture such as Canada, cultural identities refer to that culture; e.g., Chinese Canadians.) Sinclair, Sidanius, and Levin (1998) report that attachment to the U.S. culture and ethnic attachment are associated positively for European Americans and associated negatively for Asian Americans.

Social identities emerge from the tension between individuals' needs to be seen as similar to and fit in with other members of their social groups, and their needs to be seen as unique (Brewer, 1991). Individuals' needs to be seen as similar involve the general process of inclusion. Individuals' needs to be unique involve the general process of differentiation. These processes apply to ethnic and cultural identities as well. Most Asian Americans want to be members of their ethnic groups and, at the same time, be distinct from their ethnic groups (K. Smith, 1983).

Wu and Foster (1982) point out that ethnic identities are important because

> they help people set up expectations of how others are likely to act, and they carry with them statuses which define a person's culturally defined rights and obligations *vis-à-vis* others. In so doing, they play an important role in people's evaluations and explanations of others' behavior and in the way people plan their behavior to achieve their goals. (p. 280)

Asian Americans' ethnic identities provide guidelines for their behavior and frameworks for interpreting others' behavior.

Ethnic identities can be based on how Asian Americans identify themselves as well as how others (e.g., European Americans) identify them (Giles & Johnson, 1981). Asian Americans may claim memberships in ethnic groups by engaging in behavior associated with members of those ethnic groups, and others validate their claims (e.g., by treating them as members of the ethnic groups) (Wu & Foster, 1982). European Americans also can categorize Asian Americans as members of particular ethnic groups or as Asian American or Asian based on the European Americans' perceptions of Asian Americans' race, appearance, language (or dialect), or behavior.

Jen (1997) argues that how Asian Americans identify themselves involves identity politics. "In identity politics, to define oneself from without is to acknowledge 'the truth'; to define oneself otherwise is to deny the 'truth.' This sort of thinking represents a failure of self-knowledge. . . . A person is more than the sum of [his or] her social facts" (p. B-11). Tuan (1998) also points out that as racialized ethnics, Asian Americans

> maneuver between a maze of choices and constraints in constructing an identity for themselves. On the one hand, they feel constrained to identify in ethnic or racial terms because others continue to define, respond to, and treat them as separate from the American mainstream. . . . On the other

hand, there are signs of resistance and reappropriation as they struggle to work within imposed limitations and fashion an identity that resonates for them. (p. 151)

The identity that resonates for them may be associated with a specific ethnic group or a panethnic identity.

Ong (1996) argues that there are dual processes in which Asian Americans engage when negotiating identities: "being-made" and "self-making." Being-made refers to how Asian Americans' identities are influenced by the ethnic categories used in the United States. Self-making, in contrast, refers to how Asian Americans are active agents who speak and act for themselves in ways that are consistent or inconsistent with the ethnic categories used in the United States. Even though Asian Americans' identities are influenced by the ethnic categories used in the United States, they have room to "play" with their identi- ties. Play involves the maneuver room that is available because identities are inherently unstable (e.g., they can change from situation to situation) (Hall, 1991).

Sometimes there are differences in how individuals view themselves and how others see them (Wong, 1985). Many Asian Americans, for example, have been asked "Where do you come from?" by European Americans. Asian Americans may answer "San Francisco" or "New York." Most Asian Americans know that "the question, while often benign, is never completely innocent" (Lee, 1999, p. ix). To many European Americans, "San Francisco" or "New York" is not an acceptable answer and they ask the question again. Usually when this occurs, the European Americans are assuming that Asian Americans are not "American." Morrison (1992) points out that for many European Americans, being "American" is equated with being "white." Lee contends that when the question "Where do you come from?" is repeated, it implies "'you couldn't be from here.' It equates the Asian with the alien" (p. ix). In cases like this, Asian Americans view themselves as "Americans," and European Americans view them as "Asian."

Issues of how Asian Americans view themselves and how others view them also get manifested in other situations. At work, for example, some Asian Americans may not see themselves in ethnic terms and view themselves only as company employees. European American co-workers, in contrast, may always see them as Asian Americans or Japanese Americans or Filipino Americans. In this type of situation, the way others define Asian Americans and the ways

Asian Americans want to define themselves influence how Asian Americans view themselves in the situation.

Ethnicity tends to be an important part of Asian Americans' self-concepts (e.g., Johnson, 1976). Ethnic identities appear to be more important to how Asian Americans view themselves than how European Americans view themselves (e.g., Chin, 1983). This probably is the case for other non-European Americans in the United States as well. Individuals tend to activate ethnic identities when they are in the numeric minority.

Ethnic identities are more important to Asian Americans who are geographically or psychologically close to other Asian Americans than those who are not close with other Asian Americans (Hayano, 1981). Asian Americans' ethnic identities are influenced by their interpersonal relationships with other Asian Americans, as well as by where they live and the attitudes of the members of the mainstream culture (Yeh & Huang, 1996). Nagata (1993) reports that *Sansei* in California and the northwest have stronger ethnic preferences (e.g., feel more comfortable with other Japanese Americans than with European Americans) than those living in the Midwest or on the East Coast. She also observes that *Sansei* who were raised in neighborhoods of mostly Asian Americans have stronger ethnic preferences than those raised in mostly European American or equally European American and Asian Americans neighborhoods. *Sansei* who had a parent in the internment camps also have stronger ethnic preferences than those who did not.

Tuan (1998) suggests that ethnic identities may not be related highly to maintaining ethnic traditions. She reports that some Chinese Americans and Japanese Americans may claim strong identification with their ethnic groups even though they do not follow ethnic traditions.

Strength of Asian Americans' ethnic identities (e.g., how strongly they identify with their ethnic groups) is associated positively with individuals' self-esteem (e.g., how positively they feel about themselves as individuals) (Masuda, Matsumoto, & Meridith, 1970; also see Lay & Verkuyten, 1999). That is, the more Asian Americans identify with their ethnic groups, the greater their personal self-esteem (and collective self-esteem as well, see below). Positive ethnic identities, however, are not necessarily stable across time and situations (Sue & Morishima, 1982).

Identifying only with ethnic groups (as opposed to other social identities) can be dysfunctional (e.g., create mental health problems) (Palinkas, 1982). Pittinsky, Shih, and Ambady (1999) also argue that Asian American women's ethnic identities are sometimes adaptive (e.g., have positive consequences for them) and sometimes maladaptive. "The relative adaptiveness of an identity [e.g., ethnic or gender] to a particular social context influenced how individuals affectively oriented themselves toward that identity" (p. 513). Memories recalled for adaptive identities are more positive than memories recalled for maladaptive identities.

The importance of Asian Americans' ethnic identities is illustrated by the way Philip Gotanda, a Japanese American play writer, describes his experiences. Gotanda was raised in the United States but lived in Japan. Living in Japan helped him understand his ethnic identity:

> After I'd been living in Japan for about a year, I had an extraordinary experience. . . . I was walking down the streets and I looked over to my left and I saw a bank of televisions all lined up, and they were filled with a Japanese newscaster. I looked up at the billboard and there was a Japanese face, I looked at the magazines on display and they were filled with Asian faces; I looked ahead and I saw a sea of people coming toward me, all about my same height, with black hair, with skin that looked exactly like mine. . . . What I experienced for the first time was this extraordinary thing called anonymity—the sense of being able to be part of a group, of everything around me reinforcing what I was. I didn't have to second guess my obviousness, to be constantly aware that I was different. . . . in that instant in Tokyo something lifted from me, and I was able to move freely. . . . Of course, the longer I was in Japan the more I became aware of the fact that I wasn't strictly Japanese either, that I would never be Japanese Japanese —that I was Japanese-American. (Gotanda, 1991, pp. 9-10)

Gotanda's experiences clearly illustrate that ethnicity is something that many Asian Americans must address everyday of their lives in the United States.[1]

How Asian Americans experience their ethnicity and ethnic identities is influenced by where they are raised. Tuan (1998), for example, points out that racial identities appear to be more important than ethnic identities for Asian Americans raised in predominately European American communities. Asian Americans living in predominately European American communities in her study "all were made aware to varying degrees of being racially 'different' and were reminded in both inadvertent and meanspirited forms" (p. 104). Asian Americans raised in predominately ethnic communities (e.g., Chinatown) in Tuan's study experience a lot of freedom from thinking about themselves in racial or ethnic terms. They perceive themselves as "normal" within their ethnic communities (e.g., they do not stand out).

Data from the Survey of Asian American Communication indicate that whether or not Asian Americans were born in the United States influences the strength of their ethnic identities. Those not born in the United States have stronger ethnic identities than those born in the United States (born in United States = 4.13, not born in United States = 4.42, range = 1-7). Where Asian Americans were born, in contrast, does not influence the strength of their cultural identities (born in United States = 4.66, not born in United States = 4.49).

Strength of Asian Americans' ethnic identities also is influenced by their ethnicities. Table 4.1 displays the average scores for strength of ethnic and cultural identities for members of each ethnic group. Strength of cultural identities does not appear to be influenced by ethnicity. Vietnamese Americans ethnic identities, however, are stronger than those for members of other Asian American ethnic groups. Chinese Americans' and Korean Americans' ethnic identities are stronger than Japanese Americans' and Filipino Americans' ethnic identities. The strength of Vietnamese Americans' ethnic identities may be due to a large percentage of the respondents living in Little Saigon, and Vietnamese being the most recent immigrant group.

The data from the Survey of Asian American Communication are compatible with a study of Vietnamese Americans in southern California. Brody, Rimmer, and Trotter (1999) report that Vietnamese Americans view themselves as more Vietnamese than American. In response to the statement, "I think of myself as more Vietnamese than American," 49.1% strongly agree, 43.9% agree, 6% disagree, and 1% strongly disagree. An earlier study yields similar results. Baldwin (1984) notes that 86% of Vietnamese refugees see themselves as Vietnamese and 14% see themselves as Vietnamese *Americans*.

Ethnic Identities of Mixed-Heritage Asian Americans

Mixed-heritage Asian Americans generally have parents from different ethnic groups in the United States (e.g., African American/Japanese American, Chinese American/European American) (see Root, 1998, for a discussion of mixed-heritage Asian Americans). Mixed-heritage Asian Americans, however, also can include Asian Americans whose heritage was mixed before coming to the United States (e.g., Chinese Thais, Japanese Peruvians). "Amerasian" is the broadest term used to label mixed-heritage Asian Americans. This term origi-

TABLE 4.1 Strength of Ethnic and Cultural Identities by Ethnicity

	Chinese American	Filipino American	Japanese American	Korean American	Vietnamese American
Ethnic identities	4.42	4.19	4.01	4.52	4.81
Cultural identities	4.57	4.39	4.86	4.56	4.59

SOURCE: Survey of Asian American Communication.
NOTE: Scores range from 1 to 7.

nally was used for children of European American/Asian American couples, but today it is used broadly to apply to all mixed-heritage Asian Americans in the United States or other countries. I am focusing on mixed heritage rather than mixed race because it is ethnic heritage that influences behavior, not race.

Some mixed-heritage Asian Americans identify strongly with one heritage, some are torn between the two heritages, and some identify strongly with both heritages. Root (1992b) contends that "an individual can have simultaneous membership and multiple, fluid identities with different groups" (p. 6). She goes on to point out that

> a person of Black-Japanese heritage may look Filipino and may identify as both African American and Asian American. Similarly, a person of White-Asian background may . . . appear more similar to someone of European than Asian descent but may identify as a first-generation Japanese American. (p. 6)

These examples make it clear that identity issues are more complicated for mixed-heritage individuals in the United States than for mono-heritage individuals.[2]

Mixed-heritage Asian Americans who move to the United States also have multiple identities. Chinese Thais who migrate to the United States, for example, have multiple identities that they can use in different situations (Bao, 1999). To illustrate, Chinese Thais in the United States may define themselves as Thais when dealing with U.S. immigration officials or Thais in Thailand, Chinese Americans when dealing with European Americans or Chinese Americans, or as "Americans" if they assimilate into the mainstream U.S. culture or if it is to their advantage. Bao contends that ethnic and cultural identities also cannot be separated from gender because gender stereotypes influence the identities that Chinese Thais in the United States claim in different situations.

Some studies report no difference in the strength of ethnic identities for mono-heritage and mixed-heritage Asian Americans (e.g., Grove, 1991; Nakashima, 1988). Other studies do not find clear patterns when comparing mono-heritage and mixed-heritage individuals (e.g., Mass, 1992) or they find that mixed-heritage individuals have mixed-heritage ethnic identities (e.g., Stephan, 1992). Mixed-heritage Asian Americans can claim simultaneous identities (e.g., identities for both ethnic groups; Thornton, 1992), ethnic identities that are situation specific (e.g., Stephan, 1992), or their ethnic identities may change over their lifetimes (e.g., Root, 1990).

Many mixed-heritage Asian Americans are able to form integrated ethnic identities that are different from the ethnic groups to which they trace their heritages (e.g., Kich, 1992; Murphy-Shigematsu, 1987). There are problems that mixed-heritage Asian Americans face, but Stephan (1992) points out that "there are benefits of mixed-heritage status, including increased contact with members of one's heritage groups, enjoyment of the cultures of one's heritage, facility in languages spoken by one's heritage groups, and intergroup tolerance" (p. 62).

Collective Self-Esteem

Individuals try to achieve positive ethnic identities (Tajfel, 1978). Negative stereotypes and membership in what are sometimes perceived as "devalued" groups inhibit the development of positive ethnic identities (Spencer & Markstrom-Adams, 1990). There are individual differences in the degree to which Asian Americans have positive ethnic identities. Collective self-esteem is the degree to which individuals generally evaluate their ethnic groups positively (Luhtanen & Crocker, 1992). Asian Americans' level of collective self-esteem moderates the degree to which they try to protect or enhance their ethnic identities when they are threatened (Crocker & Luhtanen, 1990). When ethnic identities are threatened and individuals put down the members of outgroups threatening their ethnic identities, collective self-esteem increases (Branscombe & Wann, 1994).

There are four components to collective self-esteem (Luhtanen & Crocker, 1992). First, private collective self-esteem involves the degree to which Asian Americans evaluate their ethnic groups positively. Second, membership esteem involves the degree to which Asian Americans evaluate themselves as good members of their ethnic groups. Third, public collective self-esteem involves Asian Americans' perceptions about how others evaluate their ethnic groups.

Fourth, the importance of group memberships is the degree to which ethnic group memberships are central to how Asian Americans define themselves.

ASIAN AMERICAN PANETHNICITY

To fully understand Asian Americans' communication, issues relevant to specific Asian American ethnic groups must be addressed, and issues relevant to Asian Americans as a group must be addressed. The Asian American movement that began in the 1960s created new ways in which Asian Americans identify themselves (e.g., as Asian Americans instead of, or in addition to, as members of specific ethnic groups). In this section, I overview the Asian American movement and discuss issues of Asian American panethnicity.

Asian American Movement

The Asian American movement began in the 1960s at about the same time as the civil rights movement. Asian Americans working in the civil rights movement realized that they had more in common with blacks than with whites. "As individuals, they too had experienced prejudice and discrimination; as a group, they too had been victims of institutional racism and had been excluded from mainstream society" (Wei, 1993, p. 13). Asian Americans' political activism began spontaneously in different parts of the country at about the same time.

On the West Coast, the impetus for the Asian American movement came from two sources: community activists and student activists (Wei, 1993). Community activists in San Francisco, for example, focused on conditions in Chinatown (e.g., poor housing conditions). These activists tried to get the city government to address the conditions of the people living in Chinatown. To this end, the activists held an all-day "informational convocation" in August 1968. About the same time, student activists at the University of California, Berkeley and San Francisco State College (now University) were raising issues of non-European Americans not being included in the university curriculum. The students wanted to establish ethnic studies programs and have control over the hiring of faculty and what was taught. The "Third World" strikes were held on the two campuses between November 1968 and March 1969.

At about the same time that Asian American student organizations were started on the West Coast, they also were formed on the East Coast (Wei, 1993). To illustrate, Columbia University and Yale University both had Asian American student organizations in the middle of the 1960s. Community activism also occurred at this time. Two Japanese American women, for example, wanted to establish a Japanese American community and cultural organization to which their children could go (Wei, 1993). One of the women's sons, however, convinced them that only a pan-Asian organization would work. They started the community-based organization "Asian Americans for Action" in 1968.

Asian American student organizations began in the Midwest about the same time as those on the East and West Coasts. The most active group was at the University of Michigan in Ann Arbor (Wei, 1993). Two academic conferences on Asian Americans were held in the Midwest in the middle of the 1970s. The focus of these conferences and the student activism in the Midwest was Asian Americans' ethnic identities (e.g., who are they, Asians, Americans, or some combination).

The concern that united the Asian American activists across the country was the Vietnam War (Wei, 1993). Asian American activists saw the War as "unjust *and* racist" (p. 39). "For Asian Americans, the antiwar movement crystallized their understanding of racial discrimination against Asians in America and convinced them that an intra-Asian coalition was an effective way of opposing it" (p. 42). Individual Asian Americans' main concern, however, remained their ethnic identities. One reason for this is that in trying to fit into the mainstream U.S. culture, many Asian Americans had rejected their Asian heritages. Many European Americans, however, did not see them as "Americans"; rather, Asian Americans were (and are still) viewed as "aliens" by many European Americans.

In reconciling their identities, "Asian American activists rejected the concept of dual heritage that artificially divided their identity into abstract Asian and American halves. Instead, they acknowledged a distinct Asian American identity that had evolved over the years, based on the experiences of Asians in America" (Wei, 1993, p. 47). Defining this identity required refuting stereotypes of Asian Americans.[3] "Asian Americans for a Fair Media" was one of the first groups to emerge to fight media stereotypes of Asian Americans.

In addition to fighting stereotypes, Asian Americans needed a way to preserve the past. Community-based organizations emerged to preserve the past of individual Asian American ethnic groups. To illustrate, the New York Chinatown History Project emerged to document the history of New York's Chinatown. This project eventually led to a Chinese American museum in New York. The Japanese American National Museum was formed in Los Angeles to document the history of Japanese Americans in the United States. The museum was originally in an old Buddhist Temple, but a new museum building was opened in 1999. Similar to New York, the Filipino American Historical Society was founded in Seattle.

The Asian American movement was not one cohesive group. The activists differed in terms of ideological viewpoints and in the political strategies they preferred. Wei (1993), nevertheless, concludes that "they resolved their 'identity crisis' by directly challenging the distorted images that have diminished them as individuals and degraded them as a group, replacing them with more accurate ones based on historical knowledge about themselves, and creating a pan-Asian counterculture that reflects their values and experiences" (p. 70).

Panethnicity

Many European Americans have treated Asian Americans as a panethnic group (i.e., as one homogeneous group without recognizing differences among the various groups) since the first Asian immigrants arrived in the United States. Espiritu (1992) points out that "panethnicity—the generalization of solidarity among ethnic groups—is largely a product of categorization. An imposed category ignores subgroup boundaries, lumping diverse people in a single, expanded 'ethnic' framework. Individuals so categorized may have nothing in common except that which the category uses to distinguish them" (p. 6).

The term "Asian American" emerged from European Americans' categorizing Asian Americans as one group (Espiritu, 1992). Shibutani and Kwan (1965) point out that members of groups in the numerical minority often come together when members of the "dominate" group do not recognize differences among them. Asian Americans' coming together during the Asian American movement had positive consequences. "Although it originated in the minds of outsiders, today the panethnic concept is a political resource for insiders, a basis on which to mobilize diverse people and to force others to be more responsive to their grievances" (Espiritu, 1992, p. 7).

Espiritu (1992) points out that Asian American panethnicity emerged from political and social bonds, not cultural bonds. Even though Asian American panethnicity emerged from political processes, this does not mean that there is not a common culture. Once panethnic groups are established, interaction among members of the various groups can create a panethnic culture. Espiritu (1992) claims that "as persons of diverse backgrounds came together to discuss their problems and experiences, they began to develop common views of themselves and of one another and common interpretations of their experiences" (p. 12). She goes on to say that "the constructions of pan-Asian ethnicity involves the creation of a common Asian American heritage out of diverse histories. Part of the heritage being created hinges on what Asian Americans share: a history of exploitation, oppression, and discrimination" (p. 17).

Espiritu (1992) suggests that at least three things must occur for Asian American panethnicity to continue to survive. First, panethnic organizations must be developed. Panethnic organizations provide places where Asian Americans can interact and form social networks with other Asian Americans. The interactions that take place lay the foundation for a panethnic consciousness.

The second thing needed for the survival of Asian American panethnicity is panethnic entrepreneurs. Panethnic entrepreneurs are "individuals who have a vested interest in pan-Asian activities" (Espiritu, 1992, p. 166). Panethnic entrepreneurs provide resources for supporting Asian American panethnic activities. Asian American social workers in Los Angeles, for example, came together to form the Asian Pacific Planning Council to lobby for money.

The third thing necessary for an Asian American panethnic identity to survive is individual panethnicity. If individual Asian Americans do not view themselves as Asian Americans instead of, or in addition to, members of their specific ethnic groups, Asian American panethnicity cannot survive.

Panethnic Identities

Lee (1996) conducted an ethnographic study at a high school on the East Coast where 18% of the students are Asian Americans. Lee isolates three groups of students who had some form of Asian American panethnic identity: "Asian-identified," "Asian new wave-identified," and "Asian American-identified."

The Asian-identified students in Lee's (1996) study generally have dual identities. "Loosely speaking, students would stress their pan-Asian identities in interracial situations and would stress their specific ethnic group affiliation within Asian circles" (p. 111). The use of the dual identities supports the situational nature of identities discussed earlier. The Asian-identified students tend to associate mainly with other students of Asian heritage and view family obligations as important. They also accept that European Americans cannot recognize differences among them.

The new wave-identified students in Lee's (1996) study include Chinese, Vietnamese, and Cambodian students who are part of the last wave of refugees to come to the United States. Like the Asian-identified students, this group of students uses two ethnic identities. In contrast to Asian-identified students, new wave-identified students do not view family obligations as important. Rather, "New wave students complained that their parents were 'old fashioned' and did not understand them" (p. 113).

Asian American-identified students in Lee's (1996) study see themselves as a combination of Asian and American. One female student said:

> I have experiences that are similar to other Asians in America. That my culture is not all Asian and it's not all American. It's something entirely different. And it's not like some people say, that it's a mixture. It's like a whole different thing. When I say I'm Asian American I feel like I establish a root for myself here. My parents view themselves as Vietnamese because their roots are in Vietnam. Being Asian American is like a way to feel that I belong. (Lee, 1996, p. 116).

Since this student does not see herself as a visitor, her Asian American identity can empower her (Lee, 1996).

Asian-identified and new wave-identified students tend to accept the position of Asian Americans in the U.S. culture (Lee, 1996). Asian American-identified students, however, tend to question the status of the dominant group and are confrontational with respect to the prejudice and discrimination they experience. Asian American-identified students think that "all Asian Americans should work together to fight racism" (p. 115).

The students in Lee's (1996) study develop panethnic identities, but these identities do not eliminate friction among the members of the different Asian American ethnic groups. Lee reports political arguments (e.g., arguments about Vietnamese troops in Cambodia), stereotyping (e.g., "You Chinese are all the same"), and the use of ethnic slurs (e.g., "You, Vietcong scum") in conversations between Asian Americans from different ethnic groups (p. 114). These internal conflicts do not necessarily lead to a breakdown in the association of the Asian American students. Lee concludes that the formation of panethnic identities among the students she studied was a "response to racial conditions in the United States" (p. 123).

Strobel (1996) points out that in U.S. cities with large Filipino American populations, Filipino American high school students tend to be viewed as Asian Americans by others. In high schools with small Filipino American populations, Filipino American students tend to identify themselves as Asian Americans. College students, in contrast, tend to identify themselves mainly as Filipinos in America or Filipino Americans. College students also "identify as Asian

Americans in certain circumstances, but it is not their primary identification" (p. 35). Strobel argues that at times it is difficult to separate panethnic and ethnic identities, and that panethnic identities do not take away from Filipino Americans' ethnic identities.

Tuan (1998) reports that one of the factors that has contributed to the development of panethnic identities developing among Japanese Americans and Chinese Americans is that the distinct cultural patterns associated with the specific ethnic groups (e.g., ethnic language usage, ethnic traditions) are "watered down," the later the Asian Americans' generation in the United States.

> Asian ethnics are coming to embrace a racialized and panethnic identity. Especially as distinct cultural patterns continue to be watered down and replaced by a more generalized Asian American culture, individuals are less likely to focus on ethnic differences and, instead, recognize the similarities linking their experiences. While the impetus for this boundary expansion may not have originated from group members, the resulting identity has taken on a life and meaning of its own as those members have taken to constructing a culture base reflecting their common experiences. (pp. 166-167)

Tuan argues that the development of panethnic identities is related to interethnic marriage with other Asian Americans.

Espiritu (1992) points out that one way that interpersonal panethnicity emerges is through Asian American interethnic marriages. Shinagawa and Pang (1996) argue that there has been a shift in Asian Americans' interethnic marriage patterns in recent years. In 1980, the majority of Asian American interethnic marriages were with European Americans. In 1990, however, Asian American interethnic marriage with other Asian Americans approached or exceeded that with European Americans. Shinagawa and Pang contend that shared Asian American identities have contributed to interethnic marriages. Interethnic marriage also contributes to developing panethnic identities. Interethnic marriages among whites, for example, contributes to the development of European Americans' panethnic identities (Alba, 1990).

MODELS OF ETHNIC AND CULTURAL IDENTITIES

There are several models of Asian American ethnic and cultural identities (Sue, Mak, & Sue, 1998). The models of ethnic and cultural identities in current usage include (1) the components model of identity, which focuses on the affective, cognitive, and behavioral aspects of identity (e.g., Phinney, 1992); (2) typological models of identity, which suggest that ethnic and cultural identities interact to influence behavior (e.g., Kitano, 1989, 1993a; Sue & Sue, 1971); (3) the orthogonal model, which suggests that ethnic and cultural identities have independent influences on behavior (e.g., Oetting & Beauvais, 1990-1991); and (4) developmental models of identity, which suggest that Asian Americans go through stages in the development of their identities (Sue & Sue, 1990). In this section, I discuss examples of the four models and then compare their relative utility in predicting Asian Americans' individualistic and collectivistic tendencies.

Components Model

Phinney (1992) suggests that there are three components to Asian Americans' ethnic identities: affective, cognitive, and behavioral. The affective component involves Asian Americans' having a sense of belonging, commitment, and positive attitudes toward their ethnic groups. Phinney (1990) points out that "positive attitudes include pride in and pleasure, satisfaction, and contentment with one's own group" (p. 504). Having only negative attitudes such as dissatisfaction with members of their ethnic groups, in contrast, may lead Asian Americans to reject their ethnic groups. Asian Americans, however, have both positive and negative attitudes toward their ethnic groups at the same time, and the balance of positive and negative attitudes can change over time.

The cognitive component of ethnic identities focuses on Asian Americans' knowledge about their ethnic groups (Phinney, 1992). Included in the cognitive component is the extent to which Asian Americans understand and/or are interested in the traditions, history, and values of their ethnic groups.

The behavioral component of ethnic identities involves the degree to which Asian Americans engage in the activities associated with their ethnic groups and the extent to which they are competent in these activities (Phinney, 1992). This can include, but is not limited to, eating ethnic foods, engaging in ethnic behavioral patterns, and speaking the languages of the ethnic groups.

The three components of ethnic identities in Phinney's (1992) model combine to determine Asian Americans' ethnic identities. The more positive Asian Americans' attitudes toward their ethnic groups, the more knowledge they have, and the more ethnic behaviors they use, the stronger their ethnic identities. Phinney (1991) argues that Asian Americans with strong ethnic identities identify as "group members, evaluate their group positively, prefer or are comfortable with their group membership, are interested in, knowledgeable about, and committed to the group, and are involved in ethnic practices" (p. 194).

Uba (1994) takes a slightly different position regarding the components of ethnic identities. She argues that there are three components of Asian Americans' ethnic identities: being conscious of ethnicity, adopting ethnic identities, and activating ethnic identities. Consciousness of ethnicity is "a knowledge of the cultural characteristics of one's own ethnic group" (p. 95). This component includes knowledge of the ethnic groups' customs and knowledge about how members of the ethnic groups are expected to behave. Consciousness, however, does not include an ability to explain the knowledge Asian Americans have about their ethnic groups to others. There is some evidence that many Asian Americans do not have high levels of ethnic consciousness. Phinney (1989), for example, reports that Asian Americans are more likely than African Americans and Latino Americans to report that they would prefer to be European Americans.

Adopting an "ethnic identity entails the incorporation of ethnic behavior patterns, values, and beliefs into the personality and a feeling that a person has of being connected in some way to other members of the ethnic group" (Uba, 1994, p. 95). Adopting ethnic identities does not require that Asian Americans incorporate all aspects of their ethnicity into their behavior. Asian Americans may have negative attitudes toward some aspect of their ethnicities and not incorporate that part of their ethnicities into their ethnic identities. Asian American women, for example, who reject the expectation that they be subordinate to men can adopt ethnic identities that do not incorporate this aspect of their ethnicities (Uba, 1994).

Activating ethnic identities involves using them to guide behavior (Uba, 1994).[4] Uba points out that activating ethnic identities is not a conscious decision Asian Americans make. Whether Asian Americans activate their ethnic identities depends on the situation. Asian Americans differ with respect to the situations that lead to activating their ethnic identities. Some, for example, may only activate their ethnic identities at ethnic celebrations; others may activate their ethnic identities in most situations.

Typological Models

Typological models generally are early attempts to understand ethnic identities. All typological models involve isolating different "types" of Asian Americans who are similar within a type and different from members of other types.

Sue and Sue's (1971) model was developed to describe differences among Chinese Americans, but they believe that it applies to other Asian Americans as well. This typological model focuses on three types of Asian Americans: traditionals, marginals, and Asian Americans. In this model, the traditional Asian American types strongly identify with their ethnic groups, but not with the mainstream culture. In other words, traditionals have strong ethnic identities and weak cultural identities. The marginal Asian American types reject their ethnic groups and identify with the mainstream culture. Individuals who fit in this type may have tendencies to deny that there is prejudice against members of their ethnic groups. The Asian American types develop identities that incorporate both parts of the original ethnic group and the mainstream culture. Individuals who fit this type may develop a "bicultural" orientation.

Kitano's (1989, 1993a) typological model is based on the degree to which Asian Americans assimilate or identify with their ethnic groups.[5] Assimilation in this model is viewed as the same as developing strong cultural identities. Kitano isolated four types. Type A (high-assimilation/low-ethnic identities) includes Asian Americans who have assimilated to the U.S. culture and do not identify with their ethnic groups. Kitano points out that these individuals are largely Westerners with "Asian faces." Type B (high-assimilation/high-ethnic identities) includes Asian Americans who strongly identify with their ethnic groups and have assimilated into the U.S. culture. Kitano views these individuals as "bicultural." Type C (low-assimilation/high-ethnic identities) includes Asian Americans who maintain traditional ethnic values and behaviors. Kitano suggests that this type includes recent immigrants and people who live in Asian communities. Type D (low-assimilation/low-ethnic identities) includes Asian Americans who do not strongly identify with their ethnic groups and have not assimilated into the U.S. culture. Kitano argues that these individuals do not have a sense of belonging to either their ethnic groups or the U.S. culture and are marginal or are "dropouts."

Kitano's model is similar to Berry's model of acculturation (Berry, 1990; Berry, Kim, & Boski, 1988). Berry's model is designed to apply to "dominant" and "subordinate" groups in a culture and is based on "yes" or "no" answers to two questions: (1) "Is it considered to be of value to maintain cultural identity and characteristics?" (Note: "Cultural identities" as Berry uses the term is the same as "ethnic identities" as I use the term here), and (2) "Is it considered to be of value to maintain relationships with other groups?" (Berry et al., 1988, p. 66; Note: This question deals with cultural identities as I use the term here). By combining the answers to the two questions, four types of acculturation emerge. Integration involves "yes" answers to both questions (strong ethnic identities/strong cultural identities). Marginalization comes from "no" answers to both questions (weak ethnic identities/weak cultural identities). Assimilation involves a "no" answer to Question 1 and a "yes" answer to Question 2 (weak ethnic identities/strong cultural identities). Separation comes from a "yes" answer to Question 1 and a "no" answer to Question 2 (strong ethnic identities/weak cultural identities).

All typological models assume that ethnic and cultural identities are combined in some way to influence Asian Americans' behavior. The orthogonal model, in contrast, assumes that ethnic and cultural identities operate independently of one another to influence behavior.

Orthogonal Model

Oetting and Beauvais (1990-1991) argue that identification with ethnic groups is independent of identification with the mainstream culture. In this model, Asian Americans have ethnic identities that are independent of their cultural identities. Which identity influences behavior depends on the situations. Oetting and Beauvais argue that Asian Americans' well-being depends on positively identifying with either their ethnic groups or their culture.

Two recent studies of Asian Americans provide support for the orthogonal model of identity. Chung and Ting-Toomey (1999) isolate two Asian American identity factors: "ethnic pride" and "ethnic exclusivity." The ethnic pride factor contained items associated with ethnic identities as they are conceptualized here. The ethnic exclusivity factor contained items that are the inverse of cultural identity as it is conceptualized here. The two factors do not interact to influence Asian Americans' relational expectations. This study, therefore, supports the orthogonal model.

Yee-Jung and Ting-Toomey (1996) isolate two Asian American identity factors: ethnic identity salience and cultural identity salience. The two factors have independent influences on conflict styles. This study, therefore, supports the orthogonal model. Yee-Jung and Ting-Toomey's data for Asian Americans are part of Ting-Toomey et al.'s (2000) larger study of multiple ethnic groups (African Americans, Asian Americans, European Americans, and Latino Americans). The results for the larger study are compatible with the results for Asian Americans.[6]

The orthogonal model of identity is consistent with work in social psychology on identity. R. Turner (1987), for example, argues that in most situations there is one identity guiding individuals' behavior. This model also allows for

Asian Americans to change the degree to which they identify with their culture and ethnic groups over time (Sodowsky, Kwan, & Pannu, 1995).

Developmental Models

Development models focus on how Asian Americans' ethnic identities develop and change over time. There are several stage models of ethnic identity.[7] The models are somewhat similar. I focus on Sue and Sue's (1990) model here. Sue and Sue propose that Asian Americans go through five stages in developing their ethnic identities: conformity, dissonance, resistance and immersion, introspection, and integrative awareness. These five stages describe potential processes that individual Asian Americans might experience.

The first stage in Sue and Sue's (1990) racial/cultural identity development model is conformity. During this stage, Asian Americans value the dominant culture over their ethnic groups, and they may deprecate their ethnic groups and themselves. "This is due, in large part, to the constant barrage of mass media that portrays Asian Americans in an unflattering light (e.g., passive, sneaky, sly, inhibited)" (Sue et al., 1998, p. 301). Young Asian Americans appear to view themselves negatively in comparison with European Americans (e.g., Arkoff & Weaver, 1966; Chang, 1975). Asian Americans at this stage may put themselves and their ethnic groups down, but support from other members of their ethnic groups can mediate the degree to which negative attitudes influence them.

The second stage of Sue and Sue's (1990) model is dissonance. Dissonance implies an inconsistency in Asian Americans' beliefs or in their beliefs and actions. At this stage, Asian Americans begin to recognize positive qualities of their ethnic groups (e.g., they meet other members of their ethnic groups who they see positively) and/or in themselves. Recognizing positive qualities leads Asian Americans to begin to question why they put themselves and their ethnic groups down and accept the dominant culture without question. During this stage, Asian Americans become aware of the "minority" status of their ethnic groups and the prejudice that is expressed toward members of their ethnic groups.

Resistance and immersion is the third stage in Sue and Sue's (1990) model. Asian Americans begin to resist the dominant culture and immerse themselves in the practices of their ethnic groups. Some Asian Americans may begin to distrust members of the dominant culture and look for examples of members of the dominant culture being prejudiced toward members of their ethnic groups.

They also may feel guilty about rejecting their ethnicities in the earlier stages. Asian Americans at this stage seek out information about their ethnic groups and begin to engage in ethnic practices.

The fourth stage, introspection, in Sue and Sue's (1990) model begins when Asian Americans recognize that their negative attitudes and anger toward the dominant culture are not productive. During this stage, Asian Americans also may begin to question whether they should subordinate their personal identities to their ethnic groups. They may experience dissonance with respect to their allegiance to their ethnic groups and their need for autonomy as individuals. Also at this stage Asian Americans begin to question whether accepting part of the dominant culture means they are rejecting their ethnicities.

The final stage of Sue and Sue's (1990) model involves integrative awareness. When Asian Americans reach this stage, they have worked out the conflicts between accepting the dominant culture and accepting their ethnicities, and they begin to feel secure in their ethnic identities. They recognize that they do not have to completely accept the mainstream culture or their ethnicities; they can "pick and choose" the aspects of both that they accept.

Sue and Sue (1990) point out that several issues need to be kept in mind regarding their developmental model. First, not everyone goes through the five stages in the same way. Where Asian Americans live, for example, may influence how they go through the stages (e.g., do they live in areas surrounded by other Asian Americans or in predominately European American neighborhoods). Second, going through the stages may not be a linear process. Some Asian Americans may jump from Stage 1 to Stage 3 and not go through Stage 2. Third, it is not clear whether individuals can go backward in the stages. To illustrate, once Asian Americans reach Stage 5, can they go back to Stage 3?

Comparing Models of Ethnic and Cultural Identity

The different types of models of ethnic identities discussed in this section were developed for different reasons. The components models generally are designed to describe the different factors that contribute to how Asian Americans develop senses of themselves as members of ethnic groups. One of the components models has been used to develop a measure of ethnic identity (i.e., Phinney's [1992] "multiplegroup ethnic identity measure").

Two of the typological models discussed (Kitano, 1989; Sue & Sue, 1971) and virtually all stage models were developed originally as descriptive frameworks that counselors can use to understand and treat Asian American clients.

There is, therefore, no research testing the validity of these models. Berry's (1990) typological model was developed to describe the different patterns of acculturation that immigrants have when they move to new cultures. There is research examining the ability of Berry's model to predict immigrants' intergroup attitudes (e.g., attitudes toward assimilation and pluralism; see Berry, 1990). The orthogonal model was developed as an explanatory framework, but it also has been applied to Asian Americans' mental health like the other models.

Two of the models give equal weight to ethnic and cultural identities and are directly comparable: typological and orthogonal. The typological models assume that ethnic and cultural identities do *not* act independently of one another but, rather, that they combine to form identity types that influence behavior. The orthogonal model, in contrast, assumes that ethnic and cultural identities are independent of one another and they have separate influences on behavior. The assumptions on which these models are based are diametrically opposed. These two models make different theoretical predictions regarding Asian Americans' individualistic and collectivistic tendencies, their abilities in their ethnic languages, use of English, and relationships with other members of their ethnic groups. It is possible to test some of the predictions these models make using data from the Survey of Asian American Communication.

Individualistic and Collectivistic Tendencies.   As indicated in Chapter 2, individualism involves a tendency to place individuals over ingroups (e.g., Triandis, 1995). Collectivism, in contrast, involves a tendency to place ingroups over individuals. There are at least two ways that individuals' individualistic or collectivistic tendencies can be assessed: their values and their self construals.

Individualistic values are values that emphasize the importance of individuals (e.g., being independent, social recognition; Schwartz, 1992). Collectivistic values, in contrast, are values that emphasize the importance of their ingroups (e.g., harmony with others, honoring parents). Individuals hold both individualistic and collectivistic values (Schwartz, 1990). Individualistic values, however, predominate in the mainstream U.S. culture, and collectivistic values predominate in Asian cultures.

Markus and Kitayama (1991) contend that individuals have independent and interdependent self construals. Emphasizing independent self construals involves viewing individuals as unique and separate from others. This self construal predominates in the mainstream U.S. culture. The interdependent self construal involves viewing the self as connected to or intertwined with others. The interdependent self construal is used predominately in Asian cultures. All individuals have both independent and interdependent self construals, but one tends to predominate (e.g., Gudykunst et al., 1996).

Given the orthogonal model of identities, it would be expected that Asian Americans with strong ethnic identities hold collectivistic values and use an interdependent self construal more than Asian Americans who weakly identify with their ethnic groups. It also would be expected that Asian Americans who strongly identify with the U.S. culture hold individualistic values and use an independent self construal more than Asian Americans who weakly identify with the U.S. culture.

Given the typological model of identities, it would be expected that Asian Americans with strong ethnic identities/weak cultural identities (separation) and those with strong ethnic identities/strong cultural identities (integration) would be the most collectivistic. The two groups should be relatively equal because both involve strong ethnic identities. Asian Americans with weak ethnic identities/strong cultural identities (assimilation) and those with weak ethnic identities/weak cultural identities (marginal) would be the least collectivistic, and the two groups should be relatively equal because both involve weak ethnic identities. It also would be expected that Asian Americans with strong cultural identities/weak ethnic identities (assimilation) and those with strong cultural identities/strong ethnic identities (integration) would be the most individualistic, and the two groups would be relatively equal because both groups involve strong cultural identities. Asian Americans with weak cultural identities/strong ethnic identities (separation) and weak cultural identities/weak ethnic identities (marginal) would be the least individualistic, and the two groups should be relatively equal because both involve weak cultural identities.

Language Usage. There are at least two aspects of language usage that should be influenced by Asian Americans' identities: the extent to which they communicate in English with family and friends, and their abilities to speak the languages of their ethnic heritages (e.g., the extent to which Vietnamese Americans speak Vietnamese). To some extent, it would be expected that these two are associated negatively with each other. That is, the less Asian Americans can speak the languages of their ethnic heritages, the more they communicate in English with family and friends.

Given the orthogonal model of identities, it would be argued that ethnic identities have the major influence on language usage because ethnic identities are associated with things specifically ethnic and cultural identities focus on be-havior *vis-à-vis* the larger culture. Specifically, it would be expected that Asian Americans who strongly identify with their ethnic groups have greater ethnic language abilities and use English less than Asian Americans who weakly iden-tify with their ethnic groups.

Given the typological model of identities, it would be expected that Asian Americans with strong ethnic identities/weak cultural identities (separation) and those with strong ethnic identities/strong cultural identities (integration) would have the greatest abilities in the language of their heritage and use Eng-lish the least, and the two groups should be relatively equal because both groups involve strong ethnic identities. Asian Americans with weak ethnic identi-ties/strong cultural identities (assimilation) and those with weak ethnic identi-ties/weak cultural identities (marginal) would have the least abilities in the lan-guages of their heritages and use English the most, and the two groups should be relatively equal because both involve weak ethnic identities.

Shared Networks. The networks (e.g., links between individuals) Asian Amer-icans have with other members of their ethnic groups should also be related to their ethnic and cultural identities. The number of acquaintances, friends, and close friends Asian Americans have with other members of their ethnic groups should be influenced by ethnic and cultural identities.

Given the orthogonal model of identities, it would be expected that ethnic identities, not cultural identities, would predict shared networks. Specifically, it would be expected that Asian Americans who strongly identify with their eth-nic groups share more networks with other Asian Americans than Asian Ameri-cans who weakly identify with their ethnic groups.

Given the typological model of identities, it would be expected that Asian Americans with strong ethnic identities/weak cultural identities (separation) and those with strong ethnic identities/strong cultural identities (integration) would have the greatest shared networks, and the two groups would be rela-tively equal because both involve strong ethnic identities. Asian Americans with weak ethnic identities/strong cultural identities (assimilation) and those with weak ethnic identities/weak cultural identities (marginal) would have the fewest shared networks, and the two groups should be relatively equal because both involve weak ethnic identities.

Testing the Two Models. Data from the Survey of Asian American Communi-cation are presented in Tables 4.2 and 4.3.[8] The data indicate that the four types

TABLE 4.2 Individualistic and Collectivistic Tendencies and Language Usage by Ethnic/Cultural Identity Type

	Marginal *WCID/WEID*	*Separation* *SEID/WCID*	*Assimilation* *WEID/SCID*	*Integration* *SCID/SEID*
Independent self construals	5.48	5.66	5.94	5.79
Interdependent self construals	4.84	5.35	5.25	5.56
Individualistic values	5.28	5.35	5.56	5.52
Collectivistic values	5.21	5.57	5.55	5.74
Ethnic language abilities	3.63	4.61	3.03	4.50
Percentage English	78.86	81.08	84.96	66.32
Shared networks	28.35	48.82	21.45	48.83

SOURCE: Survey of Asian American Communication.
NOTE: SEID = strong ethnic identity; WEID = weak ethnic identity; WCID = weak cultural identity; SCID = strong cultural identity; WCID/WEID = marginalization; SEID/WCID = separation; WEID/SCID = assimilation; SCID/SEID = integration. The "type" labels are based on Berry's (1990) model. For all measures except percentage English and shared networks, 1 = low score, 7 = high score. Percentage English and shared networks range from zero (0) to 100.

in the typological model influence independent self construals, interdependent self construals, collectivistic values (but not individualistic values), ethnic language abilities (but not use of English), and shared networks. If we look at the average values for the variables in Table 4.2, we find that they are in an order that is generally compatible with the predictions made from the typological model. There are, however, many significant differences between the means for various types that would be expected to be the same, and no significant differences where they would be expected. To illustrate, earlier it was argued that Asian Americans with weak ethnic identities/strong cultural identities (assimilation) and those with weak ethnic identities/weak cultural identities (marginal) have the fewest shared networks, and the two groups should be relatively equal because both involve weak ethnic identities. The two groups with weak cultural identities, however, are statistically different with respect to shared networks.

The data from the Survey of Asian American Communication do not appear to support specific predictions from the typological model. The typological model appears to be a reasonable predictor of immigrants' attitudes (e.g., assimilation versus pluralistic attitudes) (e.g., Berry, 1990). It does not, however, appear to clearly predict individualistic and collectivistic tendencies or language usage. To date, none of the studies that have included strength of ethnic

TABLE 4.3 Individualistic and Collectivistic Tendencies and Language Usage by Strength of Ethnic and Cultural Identities

	Ethnic Identity		Cultural Identity	
	Weak	Strong	Weak	Strong
Independent self construals	5.70	5.72	5.57	5.89
Interdependent self construals	5.04	5.44	5.09	5.38
Individualistic values	5.42	5.42	5.31	5.54
Collectivistic values	5.38	5.65	5.39	5.63
Ethnic language abilities	3.34	4.57	4.10	3.66
Percentage English	81.26	84.40	83.92	77.24
Shared networks	27.23	45.83	39.48	31.96

SOURCE: Survey of Asian American Communication.
NOTE: For all measures except percentage English and shared networks, 1 = low score, 7 = high score. Percentage English and shared networks range from zero (0) to 100.

and cultural identities (e.g., Chung & Ting-Toomey, 1999; Ting-Toomey et al., 2000) have found statistical interactions that are consistent with the typological model.

The data to test the orthogonal model are presented in Table 4.3. Strength of ethnic and cultural identities do not interact to influence the seven variables. Strength of ethnic identities influences interdependent self construals (but not independent), collectivistic values (but not individualistic), ethnic language abilities (but not English usage), and shared networks. The means for all variables are consistent with the theoretical predictions based on the orthogonal model (e.g., Asian Americans with strong ethnic identities are more collectivistic, speak their ethnic languages more, and share more ethnic networks than those with weak ethnic identities).

Strength of cultural identities influences independent and interdependent self construals as well as individualistic and collectivistic values. The results for independent self construals and individualistic values are consistent with the theoretical predictions based on the orthogonal model (e.g., Asian Americans with strong cultural identities have more individualistic tendencies than those with weak cultural identities). The results for interdependent self construals and collectivistic values are inconsistent with expectations (e.g., the data indicate that Asian Americans with strong cultural identities are more collectivistic than those with weak cultural identities). One reason for this may be that Asian Americans who strongly identify with the U.S. culture have not totally assimilated into mainstream the U.S. culture (e.g., even though they have adapted U.S. values, they still retain ethnic values as well). This is to be expected to some degree since ethnicity is racialized for Asian Americans. Furthermore, approximately half of the sample in this study are first-generation immigrants, and they would not be expected to lose their collectivistic values when they acculturate to the U.S. culture.

The data from the Survey of Asian American Communication are generally consistent with the typological model, but there are numerous areas where the data are not consistent with the theoretical predictions. Similarly, the data for strength of cultural identities are not totally consistent with the orthogonal model, but they are compatible with the nature of the sample studied. The data for strength of ethnic identities, however, are totally consistent with the orthogonal model.

The orthogonal model assumes that individuals have separate ethnic and cultural identities that can be activated in different situations. The orthogonal model also is supported better than the typological model when Asian Americans' individualistic and collectivistic tendencies, language usage, and shared networks are analyzed. The orthogonal model, therefore, will be used when ethnic identities are used in other analyses of the Survey of Asian American Communication.

ETHNIC IDENTITY, GENERATION, AND LANGUAGE ABILITY

There are two issues closely related to ethnic identities: generation in the United States and language usage. Many researchers, for example, assume that generation can be used to predict ethnic identities. Other researchers argue that ethnic identities and ethnic language abilities are related closely. I begin with generation.

Generation and Ethnic Identities

Asian Americans develop different forms and strengths of ethnic and cultural identities depending on whether they were born in the United States or in the Asian cultures to which they trace their heritages (Uba, 1994). Uba, for example, contends that Asian Americans whose ancestors have been in the United States for several generations are more likely to identify with the U.S. culture than those whose ancestors have not been in the United States as long.

Hansen (1952) proposes the "third generation return" hypothesis. Essentially he argues that first-generation immigrants maintain the values of the culture to which they trace their heritages more than do second-generation immigrants. Third-generation immigrants, however, tend to be more like the first-generation immigrants than second-generation immigrants. There is some research to support this hypothesis for Asian Americans. Phinney (1990), for example, reports that first-generation Chinese Americans have stronger ethnic identities than second-generation Chinese Americans, but subsequent generations have stronger ethnic identities than second-generation Chinese Americans. Ting-Toomey's (1981) research also suggests that there is a resurgence in ethnic identity for third-generation Chinese Americans. Rosenthal and Feldman's (1992) research also supports Hansen's hypothesis for first- and second-generation Chinese Americans, but they did not look at the third generation. Lyman (1968) suggests that *Nisei* and *Sansei* want to "recover" their Japanese culture and integrate into the mainstream, but research specifically on ethnic identities among Japanese Americans does not support Hansen's hypothesis (e.g., Connor, 1977; Wooden, Leon, & Tashima, 1988; see below).

Kitano (1993b) contends that "perhaps the only Japanese group in America that was not confused about their ethnicity was the original immigrant group, the *Issei*. They were from Japan; they knew it and identified with the culture of their upbringing" (p. 161). *Nisei* (second generation) and *Sansei* (third generation) have different experiences with ethnicity than the *Issei*. Fugita and O'Brien (1991) point out that for *Nisei*

> the role of helping fellow ethnics, although not verbally articulated, is an intrinsic part of their identity. On the other hand, the *Sansei's* definition of ethnicity places more emphasis on sharing "common interactional styles" with fellow ethnics . . . and a commitment to finding out about one's cultural and political heritage. . . . The different bases of ethnicity reflect differences in the social, economic, and political experiences of the persons in the two generations. (p. 162)

Sansei tend to have greater assimilation into the U.S. culture than *Nisei,* and ethnicity for *Sansei* revolves around "fitting in."

Montero (1980) reports that *Nisei*'s age influences their behavior. The younger that *Nisei* are, for example, the more involved they are in non-Japanese American organizations and the more non-Japanese Americans they have as close friends. Montero also observes that *Sansei* are more likely than *Nisei* to have non-Japanese American close friends. Levine and Rhodes (1981) note that *Sansei* are encouraged by their parents to interact with European Americans more than *Nisei* are.

Kitano (1976, Table B, pp. 206-207) reports generational differences in Japanese Americans' attitudes. *Issei* (78%) agree with the statement "Once a Japanese, always a Japanese" more than *Nisei* (63%) and *Sansei* (47%). *Issei* (81%) also agree with the statement "I would prefer attending an all Japanese church" more than *Nisei* (44%) or *Sansei* (40%). *Issei* (69%) endorse the statement "I would prefer being treated by a Japanese doctor when sick" more than *Nisei* (50%) and *Sansei* (26%). Finally, *Issei* (89%) agree with the statement "One can never let himself [or herself] down without letting the family down at the same time" more than *Nisei* (79%) and *Sansei* (59%), but a majority of all three generations still endorse a familial orientation.

Padilla, Wagatsuma, and Lindholm (1985) report that first-generation Japanese immigrants (*Issei*) are controlled externally and experience more stress than second- (*Nisei*) or third-generation (*Sansei*) Japanese Americans. First- and second-generation Japanese Americans also experience lower levels of self-esteem than third-generation Japanese Americans. Generation also is related to acculturation to the U.S. culture; the later the generation, the greater the acculturation.

Japanese Americans in Fugita and O'Brien's (1991) study perceive an erosion of their ethnic attitudes and behaviors as a function of generation (e.g., *Sansei* are perceived as more "Americanized" than *Nisei;* families are less close; fewer Japanese traditions are followed). Interestingly, both *Nisei* and *Sansei* report negative reactions to the erosion of Japanese traditions.

Several studies find that *Nisei* have stronger ethnic identities than *Sansei* (e.g., Masuda et al., 1970; Meridith, 1967; Newton et al., 1988). Other studies do not find any differences in the strength of ethnic identities for *Nisei* and *Sansei* (e.g., Connor, 1977; Matsumoto, Meridith, & Masuda, 1970) or that ethnic identities remain stable after the second generation (e.g., Wooden et al., 1988). These findings are inconsistent with Hansen's (1952) hypothesis because third-generation Japanese American ethnic identities are not stronger than second-generation Japanese Americans. Uba (1994) suggests that "ambiguity about generation (Matsumoto et al., 1970) is [a] possible reason for the conflicting findings. For example, if an *Issei* and a *Nissei* married, in what generation are their children?" (p. 110).

Moore (1999) examines values of second-, third-, and fourth-generation Japanese Americans. She reports differences between the second and third generations, and between the second and fourth generations on eight values: power (second = $-.61$; third = $-.21$; fourth = $.02$), achievement (second = 2.00; third = 2.60; fourth = 2.75), hedonism (second = 1.22; third = 1.83; fourth = 2.18), stimulation (second = $.05$; third = 1.02; fourth = 1.16), self-direction (second = 1.68; third = 2.37; fourth = 2.23), benevolence (second = 2.28; third = 2.65; fourth = 2.65), tradition (second = 1.12; third = $.73$; fourth = $.62$), and security (second = 2.33; third = 1.92; fourth = 1.83). For power and hedonism, the differences between third and fourth generations also are significant. Generally, the findings suggest a tendency for Japanese Americans to become more individualistic and less collectivistic, the later the generation in the United States.

Takahashi (1997) argues that there are differences in the generations for Japanese immigrants who came to the United States prior to and after World War II.[9] He contends that there are large numbers of *Shin Nisei* (new *Nisei*) whose parents emigrated to the United States after World War II. *Shin Nisei* tend to have grown up in suburban communities among European Americans. "Except through family ties and networks, ethnicity is not always salient in their early lives" (p. 209). Raised under these circumstances, *Shin Nisei* may reject their ethnic identities in favor of conforming to the mainstream U.S. culture. *Shin Nisei* who speak Japanese and have strong ties to the Japanese culture, however, tend to be given higher status than their "Americanized" counterparts in the ethnic communities. Takahashi points out that this is the opposite trend to the pre-World War II immigrants. Prior to World War II, *Nisei* who were Americanized were accorded more status than their more ethnic counterparts in Japanese American communities.

There also appears to be generational differences among Korean Americans. Min (1996), for example, reports generational differences between Korean immigrants and Korean Americans born in the United States, particularly with respect to Korean-African American conflicts. "Whereas Korean merchants [immigrants] have taken the position closer to the White group than to the Black group in the larger biracial division in the United States, many younger-generation Koreans have emphasized the need for a Korean-Black alliance to fight against the 'White system' " (p. 222). Min points out that the victimization of Korean American merchants in the 1992 Los Angeles riots had a "positive" effect on the younger generations' ethnic identities (e.g., they identified more strongly after the riots than before). The positive effects of the riots on the younger generations' ethnic identities has increased the solidarity of the Korean American community in Los Angeles (Min, 1996).

Moon and Song (1998) report that Korean immigrant mothers and their adolescent daughters have similar values in some areas but different values in other areas. They are similar in terms of valuing learning Korean and Korean history/customs, as well as not giving up their Korean identities when adjusting to the United States, and both think this is possible. The mothers accept traditional sex roles more than do their daughters. The daughters think that moving out of the home before marriage and marrying across ethnic boundaries are more acceptable than do their mothers.

Park (1999) examines the ethnic identities of the 1.5 generation Korean Americans (i.e., foreign-born Koreans who immigrated to the United States before age 12). This generation tends to see themselves as neither Korean nor American. One typical male respondent said, "I'm not completely comfortable with Koreans or whites, and I do not have absolute mastery over the Korean or English languages. Therefore, I'm caught in the middle of the two cultures" (p. 151).

Second-generation Korean Americans do not tend to feel caught in the middle. Hong and Min (1999), for example, report that the vast majority of the second-generation respondents see themselves as Korean American (72.2%) rather than Korean (21.3%). The vast majority of the first-generation immigrants, in contrast, view themselves as Koreans (73%) as opposed to Korean Americans (26%). Over 50% of the second-generation Korean Americans had Korean American best friends and dating partners. Hong and Min conclude that "second generation Korean adolescents seem to maintain strong Korean ethnic identity mainly because of the cultural and historical homogeneity of the Korean group" (p. 171).

Data from the Survey of Asian American Communication indicate that there are not significant differences in strength of ethnic identities across the first four generations in the United States (first = 4.38; second = 4.42; third = 4.12; fourth = 4.21). There also are no differences in cultural identities across four generations (first = 4.51; second = 4.48; third = 4.98; fourth = 4.51).

Language and Ethnic Identities

The language individuals speak is a major way they mark boundaries between their ethnic groups and others' ethnic groups. This is true in informal conversations with strangers, acquaintances, and friends, as well as in formal communication situations (e.g., talking to supervisors at work). Wu and Foster (1982) point out that "language ability, which is often a fundamental part of the cultural dimension of ethnicity, tells us a great deal of what to expect from a person" (p. 128).

There are at least four reasons why language is an important aspect of ethnicity (Giles & Coupland, 1991). First, language is one of the major criteria for ethnic group membership. Some researchers argue that ethnic groups cannot survive without their ethnic languages (see Edwards, 1985). Some members of ethnic groups may consider ethnic linguistic abilities as necessary for "full and 'legitimate' membership" in their ethnic groups (Giles & Coupland, 1991, p. 96).

The second reason that language is important to ethnicity is that language often is used by outgroup members to categorize individuals as members of ethnic groups (Giles & Coupland, 1991). If Asian Americans speak their ethnic languages, others probably will make the inference that they identify with their ethnic groups. Use of ethnic languages, however, may not be as important as having it available. DeVos (1975) claims that "ethnicity is frequently related more to the symbol of a separate language than to its actual use by all members of a group" (p. 15).

The third reason that language is an important aspect of ethnicity is that language provides an emotional component to ethnic identities (e.g., members of ethnic groups feel more close to one another when speaking ethnic languages than when speaking English) (Giles & Coupland, 1991). If members of ethnic groups make the effort to learn the languages of their heritages, other members of their ethnic groups perceive them positively.

The fourth reason that language is an important aspect of ethnicity is that it facilitates ingroup cohesion (Giles & Coupland, 1991). Speaking ethnic languages, for example, clearly separates members of different Asian American ethnic groups from European Americans. Separating themselves from European Americans promotes feelings of solidarity within Asian American ethnic groups.

Table 4.4 presents U.S. Bureau of the Census data for Asian Americans aged 24 or under in 1990. There are minor variations across ethnic groups, but over 50% of each group (over 60-70% for most groups) of Asian Americans are either English monolinguals or fluent bilinguals.

A large percentage of Asian Americans live in a home where a language other than English is spoken. (Note: This does not necessarily mean that all individuals in the home speak a language other than English.) The percentages of

TABLE 4.4 Generation and Language Usage of Children, Adolescents, and Young Adult Asian Americans (in percentages)

	Chinese American	Filipino American	Japanese American	Korean American	Vietnamese American
Generation[a]					
Second or later	68.2	74.0	84.1	70.7	55.2
1.5	16.3	13.7	6.1	17.8	26.9
First	15.5	12.3	9.8	11.5	16.9
Language Usage					
English monolingual	21.8	57.9	64.5	36.5	9.5
Fluent bilingual	45.2	30.1	16.0	40.9	44.9
Limited bilingual	23.2	9.2	10.3	14.2	30.2
No English	9.8	2.8	9.2	8.4	15.4

SOURCE: U.S. Bureau of the Census (1993).
NOTE: Percentages are not weighted.
a. Second or later generation includes those born in the United States and foreign-born immigrating to the United States before age 5; 1.5 generation includes foreign-born immigrating to the United States between ages 5 and 12; first generation includes foreign-born immigrating to the United States at age 13 or over.

children and adolescents (aged 0-17) living in a home where a language other than English is spoken are 60% or above for all groups except Filipino Americans and Japanese Americans (i.e., Chinese Americans = 76.9%, Filipino Americans = 35.7%, Japanese Americans = 35.0%, Korean Americans = 59.8%, and Vietnamese Americans = 90.2%). The percentage of young adults (aged 18-24) living in a home where a language other than English is spoken is higher for most groups (i.e., Chinese Americans = 80.9%, Filipino Americans = 54.3%, Japanese Americans = 36.3%, Korean Americans = 93.7%, Vietnamese Americans = 91.1%) (U.S. Bureau of the Census, 1993).

When Asian Americans learn English influences their views of themselves with respect to their identities. Rhee et al. (1995) asked Asian Americans to take the 20-statements test (i.e., provide 20 answers to "I am _____"). They report that Asian Americans who learned English as a first language or learned English before the age of three are less likely to include their ethnicities as answers than are Asian Americans who learned English later.

Kuo (1974) observes that Chinese American families influence children's bilingual language acquisition. When the families' general orientation is to use Chinese (e.g., parents speak Chinese to children), children tend to be more proficient in Chinese than in English. Children's English proficiency is highest when their parents are naturalized citizens and serve more American food than Chinese food. Kuo concludes that families influence children's Chinese language abilities but do not take away from children's English abilities.

Hong and Min (1999) point out that under 10% of second-generation Korean Americans report being fluent in Korean. The vast majority rate their ethnic language abilities as good or fair. Almost 90% of their second-generation respondents, in contrast, report they are proficient in English. The respondents also tend to use English more than Korean when talking to Korean American friends and half Korean/half English when talking with their parents. Hong and Min conclude that second-generation Korean Americans prefer to use English in everyday communication.

Language usage in ethnic enclaves tends to fit a different pattern from the general population descriptions. Loo's (1998) study of the San Francisco Chinatown, for example, reveals that 63% are mainly monolingual in Chinese, 27% are Chinese-English bilinguals, and 10% are monolingual in English. He contends that these percentages are consistent with the figures for foreign-born Chinese American adults throughout the United States. Loo reports that current age and age at immigration are related to ability to speak English (e.g., the older the age, the less the English ability). These patterns probably generalize to other Asian American groups as well.

Ability to speak ethnic languages is related to generation in the United States among children. To illustrate, U.S. census data indicate that the percentage of fluent bilingual Asian American children decreases and the percentage of monolingual English speaking Asian American children increases from the first to the second generation in the United States (U.S. Bureau of the Census, 1993).

Zhou and Bankston (1998) argue that strength of ethnic identity is associated highly with the ability to read and write Vietnamese among Vietnamese American children growing up in the United States. They point out that "while there is a definite shift toward English, most Vietnamese children retain the language of their parents. Native language retention may be associated with continual contact with new arrivals, living with household members with limited English, and residence in Vietnamese communities" (p. 128).

The relationship between knowing a Philippine language and ethnic identity leads to arguments among members of the Filipino American community (Revilla, 1997). Some argue that "you need to know a Philippine language to have a strong identity" (p. 104). Revilla points out that Filipinos who are born in

TABLE 4.5 Language Usage by Ethnicity

	Chinese American	*Filipino American*	*Japanese American*	*Korean American*	*Vietnamese American*
Ethnic language abilities	3.79	4.15	3.00	4.74	4.94
Percentage of English	66.43	81.20	64.50	68.15	63.33
Shared ethnic networks	33.79	32.32	33.41	38.64	38.02

SOURCE: Survey of Asian American Communication.
NOTE: Ethnic language ability ranges from 1 (not at all fluent) to 7 (totally fluent). Percentage English and shared ethnic networks range from zero (0) to 100.

the United States who do not speak one of the languages used in the Philippines or who speak with an American accent "report being denigrated" by other Filipino Americans (p. 105). Revilla, however, goes on to argue that "despite the popular opinion that knowing a Filipino language is necessary to have a strong identity, research has indicated that this is not the case. It is possible for an individual to profess strong Filipino ethnic identity without knowing how to speak a Filipino language" (p. 105).

The Survey of Asian American Communication reveals differences across Asian American ethnic groups in terms of ethnic language abilities (which includes speaking, listening, reading, and writing) and percentage of conversations with family members and friends that take place in English (see Table 4.5). The relative order for ethnic language abilities (from highest to lowest) is Vietnamese Americans, Korean Americans, Filipino Americans, Chinese Americans, and Japanese Americans. Vietnamese American and Korean American scores are virtually the same, and each is different from the other three groups, which tend to differ among themselves.

A recent study of Vietnamese Americans in southern California yields results similar to the Survey of Asian American Communication. Brody et al. (1999) asked Vietnamese Americans "What languages do you speak?" Their responses are as follows: "only Vietnamese" (18%), "Vietnamese more than English" (46.5%), "both equally" (25.7%), "English more than Vietnamese" (9.4%), and "only English" (0.5%).

Filipino Americans have a greater percentage of conversations in English than Korean Americans, Chinese Americans, Japanese Americans, and Vietnamese Americans, and the percentages for the other four groups are virtually the same. Brody et al. (1999) report that 10.7% of adult Vietnamese Americans in southern California do not speak English at all, 40.2% speak English very little, 35.9% speak English moderately, and 13.7% speak English very well. There are no differences between males and females regarding ethnic language abilities (males = 3.81; females = 4.00), the percentage that use English is used to communicate with family and friends (males = 73.08; females = 82.56), or shared networks (males = 31.84; females = 35.39).

Where Asian Americans are born or the language spoken in their homes when they were children influence their language usage. The Survey of Asian American Communication indicates that Asian Americans born in the United States have less ethnic language ability and use English in conversations with family and friends more than Asian Americans not born in the United States (see Table 4.6). Similarly, Asian Americans who grew up in homes where English was the predominate language have less ethnic language ability and use English in conversations with family and friends more than those who grew up in homes where ethnic languages were spoken.

Relationships Among Identity, Generation, and Language

Data from the Survey of Asian American Communication allow me to examine the interrelationships among strength of ethnic and cultural identities, generation, individualistic tendencies, collectivistic tendencies, ethnic language abilities, use of English, and shared networks (see Table 4.7). Table 4.7 presents the correlations across the ethnic groups.[10]

There is a small negative association between generation and strength of ethnic identities and a small positive association between generation and strength of cultural identities. The results for ethnic identities are consistent with previous research on generation and ethnic identities (e.g., Masuda et al. 1970; Meridith, 1967; Newton et al., 1988). The results for ethnic identities, however, do not support Hansen's (1952) third-generation return hypothesis (i.e., members of the third generation exhibit values and behaviors similar to members of the first generation).

Kitano (1976) suggests that generation should be associated negatively with collectivistic tendencies and positively with individualistic tendencies for Japanese Americans. This argument should extend to other Asian American groups as well. This, however, is not the case in the Survey of Asian American Communication. Generation is not associated with individualistic or collectivistic tendencies. The results for the Survey of Asian American Communication are con-

TABLE 4.6 Language Usage by Where Asian Americans Are Born and the Language Spoken at Home When They Were Children

| | *Where Born* | | *Language Spoken* | |
	United States	*Not United States*	*English*	*Not English*
Ethnic language abilities	2.96	4.84	2.53	4.85
Percentage of English	87.25	66.29	92.95	64.14
Shared ethnic networks	29.18	37.10	25.52	36.62

SOURCE: Survey of Asian American Communication.
NOTE: Ethnic language abilities range from 1 to 7. Percentage English and shared network range from zero (0) to 100.

sistent with Rosenthal and Feldman's (1992) research, which does not reveal differences in individualism between first- and second-generation Chinese Americans.

Generation is associated negatively with ethnic language abilities. As expected, the higher the generation, the lower the ethnic language abilities. This association is consistent with previous studies of generation and ethnic language abilities (e.g., Zhou & Bankston, 1998). Strength of ethnic identities also is associated positively with ethnic language abilities. This is consistent with research suggesting that Asian Americans who identify with their ethnic groups also maintain ethnic language abilities (e.g., Zhou & Bankston, 1998). As would be expected, ethnic language abilities is associated positively with shared networks, interdependent self construals, and collectivistic values. Ethnic language abilities also is associated negatively with use of English with family members and friends. These results suggest that collectivistic orientations, sharing networks with other members of the ethnic groups, and not using English facilitate maintaining ethnic language abilities.

Strength of ethnic identities is associated positively with interdependent self construals and collectivistic values. This is consistent with Yeh and Huang's (1996) argument that Asian Americans' ethnic identities are associated with collectivism. Rosenthal and Feldman (1992) did not find a relationship between Chinese identities and collectivism, but they did not formally measure strength of Chinese ethnic identities. Strength of ethnic identities also is associated positively with shared networks. The results for shared networks are consistent with research on Japanese Americans in Hawaii that found an association between

TABLE 4.7 Associations Among Individualistic and Collectivistic Tendencies, Language Usage, and Generation

	1	2	3	4	5	6	7	8	9
1. Independent self construals									
2. Interdependent self construals	.45								
3. Individualistic values	.40	.16							
4. Collectivistic values	.24	.37	.49						
5. Ethnic language abilities	-.10	.13	-.03	.13					
6. Percentage English	.09	-.02	-.03	-.06	-.32				
7. Shared networks	-.03	.12	-.02	.15	.26	.27			
8. Strength of ethnic identities	.04	.22	.09	.23	.30	.11	.26		
9. Strength of cultural identities	.20	.17	.20	.16	-.14	.00	-.09	-.10	
10. Generation	-.05	-.06	.03	-.04	-.37	.09	-.05	-.12	.14

SOURCE: Survey of Asian American Communication.
NOTE: Correlations with a magnitude of +/−.10 or greater are significant at $p < .05$.

ingroup identification (i.e., strength of ethnic identities) and shared ethnic networks (Gudykunst, Sodetani, & Sonoda, 1987). Rosenthal and Feldman (1992) also report that having Chinese identities is associated with maintaining ethnic networks for Chinese Americans.

CONCLUSION

Issues of Asian Americans' ethnic and cultural identities are complicated. Asian Americans' identities are not as simple as Asian Americans' deciding the extent to which they identify with their ethnic groups and the mainstream U.S. culture. Since Asian Americans' identities are racialized, frequently they are classified as Asian Americans (or Chinese Americans, Filipino Americans, Japanese Americans, Korean Americans, or Vietnamese Americans) whether they want to be or not. Asian Americans can "play" with their ethnic and cultural identities, but they cannot ignore identity politics.

In addition to dealing with identities associated with their specific ethnic groups, Asian Americans have to address issues of panethnic identities. There are both positive (e.g., political power) and negative (e.g., differences among Asian American ethnic groups are ignored) consequences of panethnic identities. Again, identity politics cannot be ignored.

Several models of Asian Americans' ethnic and cultural identities have been proposed. None of the models fits all Asian Americans experiences with their ethnicities. The orthogonal model, which assumes that ethnic and cultural identities are independent of one another, however, appears to be consistent with predictions based on individualistic and collectivistic tendencies. This model also allows ethnic and cultural identities to be situation specific and to change over time.

NOTES

1. See Yamamoto (1999) for a discussion of Japanese American women's identities; see Min and Kim (1999) for narratives of Asian American professionals' ethnic identities; see Lee (1998) for a comparison of Asian Americans' ethnic identities in Philadelphia; see Belden (1997) for Chinese Americans' ethnic identities.

2. See Root (1992a) for studies of different aspects of mixed-heritage Asian American identities; see Thornton (1996) for a discussion from a race perspective; see Lott (1998) for a discussion of legal issues.

3. For discussions of stereotypes in popular media, see Lee (1999), Marchetti (1993), and Xing (1998).

4. Uba uses the term "adhibition" instead of *activating*.

5. Kim and Kim (1998) adapted Kitano's model specifically to Korean Americans; Kitano (1993a) is specific to Japanese Americans.

6. There are interaction effects in Ting-Toomey et al.'s (2000) study, but the results are not consistent with the typological models.

7. Example models include Atkinson, Morton, and Sue's (1989) minority identity development model; Ibrahim, Ohnishi, and Sandhu's (1997) model specific to South Asian Americans; Kich's (1992) model of identity development for mixed-heritage Asian Americans; Phinney's (1993) three-stage model of identity formation; and Sue and Sue's (1990) racial/cultural identity development model. See Ying and Lee (1999) for a discussion of adolescent identity development; see Tse (1999) for a recent "test" of the model.

8. For these analyses, the continuous measures of ethnic and cultural identities were dichotomized using median splits.

9. See Portes (1994) for a general discussion of the "new" second generation.

10. No major differences were observed between these correlations and those controlling for the individual ethnic groups.

Chapter Five

Asian American
Communication Patterns

$\mathcal{J}$n the previous two chapters, I examined Asian American ethnic groups and Asian Americans' ethnic and cultural identities—the major factors that influence Asian Americans' communication. The focus of this chapter is on Asian American communication patterns. There is, however, very little research that directly compares communication patterns across Asian American ethnic groups. Throughout the chapter, I summarize the research that has been conducted, and I also present data from the Survey of Asian American Communication where applicable.

I divide this chapter into two sections. In the first section, I examine expectations for communication. The expectations that Asian Americans have for how they are supposed to communicate influence how they actually communicate. In the second section, I review studies of Asian Americans' communication styles. Communication styles are communication tendencies that are used consistently over time and across situations.

COMMUNICATION EXPECTATIONS

Expectations involve individuals' anticipations and predictions about how others will communicate with them. Expectations are derived in large part from the social norms and communication rules that individuals learn as part of their socialization into their cultures, ethnic groups, and families. Individuals generally are not highly aware of their expectations for communication. Asian Americans' expectations, nevertheless, influence their communication whether they are aware of their expectations or not.

I begin this section with the nature of expectations. Next, I discuss relational expectations and emotional reactions to violating expectations. Following this, I look at expectations for the ways that communication messages are structured. I conclude this section with stereotyped-based expectations.

Nature of Expectations

"People who interact develop expectations about each others' behavior, not only in the sense that they are able to predict the regularities, but also in the sense that they develop preferences about how others *should* behave under certain circumstances" (Jackson, 1964, p. 225). Individuals' cultures and ethnicities provide guidelines for appropriate behavior and the expectations they use in judging others' communication competency. To illustrate, Burgoon and Hale (1988) point out that in the mainstream U.S. culture

> one expects normal speakers to be reasonably fluent and coherent in their discourse, to refrain from erratic movements or emotional outbursts, and to adhere to politeness norms. Generally, normative behaviors are positively valued. If one keeps a polite distance and shows an appropriate level of interest in one's conversational partner, for instance, such behavior should be favorably received. (p. 61)

The rules for what is a polite distance and what constitutes an emotional outburst vary across cultures and ethnic groups within the U.S. culture.

At the outset, it can be argued that European Americans and Asian Americans have different expectations for communication because of their different cultural heritages (e.g., European Americans tend to be individualistic, Asian Americans tend to be collectivistic). There is, however, no basis to speculate on differences in expectations among Asian American ethnic groups.

Relational Expectations

Burgoon and Walther (1990) argue that expectancies involve individuals' thoughts about "anticipated behavior that may be generalized or person specific" (p. 235). Relational expectations may be prescriptive or predictive. "Prescriptive expectations are one's beliefs about what behaviors should be performed or avoided, while predictive expectations are one's beliefs about what behaviors are likely to occur" (Kelley & Burgoon, 1991, p. 41).

Predictive relational expectations can be used to examine communication differences across Asian American ethnic groups. Kelley and Burgoon (1991) isolate seven dimensions of predictive relational expectations: intimacy (e.g., "Desire to move our conversations to deep levels"), dominance ("Try to control the interaction"), receptivity ("Not care what I think"), informality ("Keep our discussions informal"), arousal/noncomposure ("Be frustrated with me"), distance ("Create a sense of distance between him- or herself and me"), and equality/trust ("Want me to trust him or her").

Relational Expectations for Dating Relationships. Chung and Ting-Toomey (1999) examine the influence of ethnic and cultural identities on Asian Americans' intraethnic and interethnic dating expectations. The intraethnic dating partners are members of the same ethnic groups as the respondents, and the interethnic dating partners are European Americans.

Chung and Ting-Toomey (1999) report that strength of "ethnic pride" (ethnic identity) does not influence relational expectations for dating partners. There is, however, an interaction between "ethnic exclusivity" (the inverse of cultural identity) and the ethnicity of the dating partner for six of the seven dimensions of relational expectations (only informality is not affected). Generally, the results suggest that Asian Americans who are strong in ethnic exclusivity tend to have negative expectations for interethnic dates with European Americans (e.g., expect them to be dominant, distant, and to involve arousal, low intimacy, low receptivity, and low trust).

Relational Expectations Across Ethnic Groups. The Survey of Asian American Communication contained measures for five of the relational expectation dimensions: receptivity, intimacy, control, arousal, and trust/equality. Respondents were asked to indicate what their expectations are for the five dimensions when they communicate with members of their ethnic groups.

Table 5.1 presents the average scores for the five relational expectations by Asian American ethnic groups. There are no significant differences in expectations for communication across the five ethnic groups. There also are no differences in expectations based on where Asian Americans were born (i.e., United States/not United States) or the language spoken in their homes when they were children (i.e., English/not English). These results are probably due to members of the five ethnic groups in the Survey of Asian American Communication sharing similar levels of individualism and collectivism (see Chapter 3).

Table 5.2 presents the average scores for the five dimensions of expectations by strength of ethnic and cultural identities. Strength of cultural identities does not influence relational expectations. Strength of ethnic identities influences intimacy and trust/equality. Asian Americans who strongly identify with their ethnic groups expect their interactions with members of their ethnic groups to be more intimate and trusting than Asian Americans who do not strongly identify with their ethnic groups.

The influence of strength of ethnic identities on intimacy and trust appears to be due to Asian Americans' who strongly identify with their ethnic groups being more collectivistic than those who do not identify strongly with their ethnic groups. Intimacy and trust are associated with emphasizing interdependent self construals (being collectivistic) and shared networks with other Asian Americans. Expectations for receptivity, control, and arousal, in contrast, are associated with emphasizing independent self construals (being individualistic).

Violations of Expectations: Shame and Guilt

When individuals violate expectations, they respond emotionally. The two most common emotions experienced are shame and guilt. "Guilt accompanies moral transgressions, acts that violate ethical standards" (Liem, 1997, p. 369). Shame, in contrast, "is provoked by exposure of the self to an audience, real or symbolic, in whose eye the actor [or actress] experiences his or her total being as profoundly flawed" (p. 369). Liem contends that "guilt motivates a desire to compensate or seek absolution, whereas shame triggers the wish to flee or hide" (p. 369).

Liem (1997) reports that guilt for European Americans emerges when they do something they know is wrong (e.g., cheating to win a contest) and no one knows about it. Guilt (rather than shame) is triggered because there is no public recognition of their wrongdoing. European Americans experience shame as be-

TABLE 5.1 Relational Expectations by Ethnicity

	Chinese American	Filipino American	Japanese American	Korean American	Vietnamese American
Receptivity	4.63	4.75	4.67	4.42	4.65
Intimacy	5.18	4.97	4.75	4.71	4.93
Control	3.73	3.29	3.22	3.66	3.49
Arousal	2.89	2.72	2.66	3.16	2.42
Trust/Equality	5.41	5.28	5.15	4.94	5.37

SOURCE: Survey of Asian American Communication.
NOTE: Scores range from 1 to 7.

TABLE 5.2 Relational Expectations by Strength of Ethnic and Cultural Identities

	Ethnic Identity		Cultural Identity	
	Weak	Strong	Weak	Strong
Receptivity	4.69	4.58	4.58	4.71
Intimacy	4.62	5.10	4.69	5.02
Control	3.28	3.64	3.36	3.56
Arousal	2.83	2.70	2.78	2.76
Trust/Equality	4.97	5.45	5.02	5.40

SOURCE: Survey of Asian American Communication.
NOTE: Scores range from 1 to 7.

ing "embarrassed" or "feeling ashamed." Shame emerges when what European Americans do wrong becomes public knowledge, especially when others are physically present. The shame European Americans experience is not shared by others. In other words, it is based on the independent self construal.

Guilt emerges for Asian Americans from moral transgressions in hierarchical relationships. Asian Americans experience guilt when they perceive that they have not done their "duty" (Liem, 1997). Shame for Asian Americans emerges when their wrongdoing becomes public. The feelings of shame, however, are not limited to the individuals engaging in the wrongdoing; it is shared by other ingroup members (e.g., the family). Shame, therefore, is based on the interdependent self construal for Asian Americans. To illustrate, if Asian Americans are arrested, they feel shame, and the members of their families also feel shame. If Asian Americans are highly acculturated to the mainstream U.S.

culture, however, they may not think that ingroup members share their shame, even when the ingroup feels shame because of the acculturated individuals' behavior (Liem, 1997).

Closely related to shame is embarrassment. Embarrassment is an emotional response to being evaluated by others. It involves threats to individuals' public identities. Singelis and Sharkey (1995) examine susceptibility to embarrassment among Asian Americans and European Americans in Hawaii. They report that independent self construals are related negatively to susceptibility to embarrassment, and interdependent self construals are related positively to susceptibility to embarrassment. These relationships hold for European Americans, Japanese Americans, Chinese Americans, and Filipino Americans, but not for Korean Americans (but a very small sample of Korean Americans was used). The reason that susceptibility to embarrassment is related positively to interdependent self construals and negatively to independent self construals is that when individuals define themselves as interdependent with others, they are highly concerned about what others think of them.

Singelis and Sharkey (1995) also note that when self construals are taken into consideration, there are ethnic differences in susceptibility to embarrassment. Specifically, European Americans are less susceptible to embarrassment than Chinese Americans, Filipino Americans, Japanese Americans, and Korean Americans, but there are no differences among the Asian American ethnic groups. If self construals are not taken into consideration, however, there are no ethnic differences in susceptibility to embarrassment. Singelis and Sharkey conclude that self construals are better predictors of susceptibility to embarrassment than ethnicity.

Conversational Constraints

Individuals have expectations for how communication messages should be structured. Kim, Sharkey, and Singelis (1994) refer to these expectations as "interactive constraints." They isolate three major constraints that operate across cultures: "concern for clarity," "concern for avoiding hurting the hearer's feelings," and "concern for avoiding negative evaluations by the hearer." Concern for clarity is "the likelihood that an utterance will make one's intention clear and explicit" (p. 119). Concern for hearers' feelings involves the likelihood that messages will allow listeners to maintain their self-images. Concern for avoiding negative evaluations is the likelihood that "an utterance does not cause dislike, devaluation, or rejection by the hearer" (p. 120).

Kim et al. (1994) report that emphasizing independent self construals is related positively to concern for clarity. This is consistent with individualists' emphasizing low-context communication. Emphasizing interdependent self construals is related positively with concern for others' feelings and with concern for avoiding negative evaluations. These findings are consistent with collectivists' focus on high-context communication.

Kim et al.'s (1994) study includes European Americans and Asian Americans in Hawaii, but they do not report ethnic differences. Unreported data from this study (Min-Sun Kim made the data available) indicate that there are no differences between European Americans and Asian Americans for the three interactive constraints. Furthermore, there are no differences among the Chinese Americans, Japanese Americans, Filipino Americans, and Korean Americans in this study. These findings suggest that it is individuals' individualistic or collectivistic tendencies (e.g., their self construals), not their ethnicity, that influences their concerns regarding interactive constraints.

Unreported data from Kim and Sharkey's (1995) study (made available by Min-Sun Kim) of a multinational corporation also yields no significant differences among Asian Americans in Hawaii regarding interactive constraints. Kim and Sharkey, however, do find that European Americans are less concerned with avoiding negative evaluations than are Asian Americans.

Politeness Rules

Another area where there are differences in Asian Americans' and European Americans' expectations for communication involves rules for politeness. Politeness rules allow individuals to minimize the frictions between themselves and others with whom they are communicating. Hill et al. (1986) argue that politeness is "one of the constraints on human interaction, whose purpose is to consider others' feelings, establishing levels of mutual comfort, and promote rapport" (p. 349).

Rules for politeness are culturally based. Ogawa and Gudykunst (1999) isolate differences in politeness rules in Japan and the United States that are generally consistent with individualism and collectivism. Ogawa and Gudykunst's U.S. sample contains sufficient Asian Americans to compare their responses with European Americans.

Table 5.3 contains the 18 (of 105 rules) politeness rules from Ogawa and Gudykunst's (1999) study on which there are differences between Asian Americans and European Americans. The rules that Asian Americans endorse more than European Americans involve maintaining smooth interactions, maintaining harmony, recognizing own and others' social standing, protecting self-images (face), being formal, and being reserved. The rules that Asian Americans endorse more than European Americans tend to be associated with a collectivistic orientation. The rules that European Americans endorse more than Asian Americans involve not talking only about oneself, not giving others orders, asking others how they have been, and listening to others.

Expectations for Silence

Individuals have expectations for when it is appropriate to talk and be silent in conversations. It might be expected that Asian Americans use silence more than European Americans. Hasegawa and Gudykunst (1998) examine attitudes toward silence in Japan and the United States. The results generally are compatible with expectations based on individualism-collectivism.

Hasegawa and Gudykunst's (1998) U.S. sample contains sufficient Asian Americans to compare their responses with European Americans. Asian Americans have a more negative view of silence when communicating with strangers than do European Americans. Given that strangers' behavior can be unpredictable and Asian Americans tend to prefer smooth interpersonal relationships, it would be expected that Asian Americans would be uncomfortable with silence when communicating with strangers. Both Asian Americans and European Americans use silence strategically (e.g., to get others to do things) more when communicating with strangers than with close friends.

Stereotypes

Lippman (1922) refers to stereotypes as "pictures in our heads." He points out that stereotypes have both cognitive and affective components:

[Stereotyping] is not merely a way of substituting order for the great blooming, buzzing confusion of reality. It is not merely a shortcut. It is all these things and more. It is a guarantee of our self-respect; it is the projection upon the world of our own sense of value, our own position and our own rights. The stereotypes are, therefore, highly charged with feelings that are attached to them. (pp. 63-64)

TABLE 5.3 Politeness Rules for Asian Americans and European Americans

	European Americans	Asian Americans
Do not touch others.	3.37	4.23
Make the conversation smooth.	4.52	5.25
Emphasize my social standing.	2.58	3.50
Do not talk only about myself.	5.59	4.82
Tell others I want to meet them again.	3.80	4.61
Lie to preserve harmony with others.	2.93	4.07
Protect my self-image.	3.96	5.16
Formally greet others.	4.35	5.05
Do not give others orders.	5.18	4.59
Ask questions about others' status.	2.99	3.84
Sum up the conversation before it ends.	3.16	3.93
Protect my reputation.	4.20	4.86
Ask others how they have been.	5.85	5.25
Listen when others speak.	6.30	5.86
Behave formally.	3.89	5.09
Try to read the other person's mind.	2.67	3.48
Emphasize others' social standing.	2.59	3.64
Be reserved.	3.42	4.23

SOURCE: Unreported data from Ogawa and Gudykunst (1999).
NOTE: Only rules with significant differences are presented. Scores range from 1 (not required to be polite) to 7 (always required to be polite).

Stereotypes, therefore, are cognitive representations of groups that influence individuals' feelings toward members of the groups being stereotyped.

Stereotypes Create Expectations. Stereotypes create expectations regarding how members of individuals' ingroups and members of outgroups will behave. Unconsciously, individuals assume that their expectations are correct, and individuals behave as though they are. Hamilton, Sherman, and Ruvolo (1992) point out that stereotypes operate as a source of expectancies about what a group as a whole is like (e.g., Hispanics), as well as about what attributes that individual group members are likely to possess (e.g., Juan Garcia). Their influence can be pervasive, affecting the perceiver's attention to, encoding of, inferences about, and judgments based on that information. And the resulting interpretations, inferences, and judgments typically are made so as to be consistent with preexisting beliefs that guided them. (p. 142)

Individuals, therefore, unconsciously try to confirm their expectations when they communicate with others.

Individuals' stereotypes constrain others' communication and lead to stereotype-confirming communication. Stated differently, stereotypes can create self-fulfilling prophecies. Individuals tend to see behavior that confirms their expectations, even when it is absent. Individuals ignore disconfirming evidence when they are not highly conscious of their communication. Hamilton et al. (1992) point out that

perceivers can influence a person with whom they interact by constraining the person's behavior. However, perceivers typically do not recognize this influence or take it into consideration when interpreting the target's behavior. Although a target person's behavior may be affected by perceiver-induced constraints, it is often interpreted by the perceiver as a manifestation of the target's personality. (p. 149)

Snyder and Haugen (1995) suggest that individuals' tendencies to engage in confirming behaviors depends on their goals in the interaction. If individuals' goals are to adjust to others and have smooth interactions, they tend to engage in stereotype-confirming behaviors. If their goals are to gather information about others, in contrast, they do not necessarily engage in stereotype-confirming behaviors.

Asian, Asian American, and European American Stereotypes. There are only a few studies of stereotypes of Asian Americans. European Americans, however, often apply their stereotypes of Asians to Asian Americans. Chinese and Japanese are included in a series of studies that examined national stereotypes of undergraduate students. In these studies, students are provided with 85 adjectives that might apply to different groups, and the students are asked to check the adjectives that applied to each group.

The first study (Katz & Braly, 1933) indicates that "Americans" (read whites in the United States) are industrious (48% checked this trait), intelligent (47%), and materialistic (33%). Japanese are viewed as intelligent (45%), industrious (43%), and progressive (24%). Chinese are seen as superstitious (74%), sly (29%), and conservative (29%). A follow-up study (Gilbert, 1951) reveals essentially the same traits associated with each group.

The third study (Karlins, Coffman, & Walters, 1969) reveals that "Americans" (read as whites in the United States) are materialistic (67%), ambitious (42%), pleasure loving (28%), and industrious (23%). Chinese are seen as loyal to family ties (50%), tradition loving (32%), industrious (23%), and quiet (23%). Japanese are viewed as industrious (57%), ambitious (33%), efficient (27%), and loyal to family ties (23%). The view of whites remains relatively stable over the 34 years between the first and third study. The view of Japanese Americans also is relatively stable, but efficient and loyal to family ties replace progressive. The stereotype with the greatest change is that of Chinese. It changes from one that was highly negative in 1933 to one relatively positive in 1969.

Maykovich (1971) examines European Americans' and Japanese Americans' stereotypes of Japanese Americans in California. *Nisei* view Japanese Americans as industrious (62%), reserved (52%), loyal to family (50%), neat (50%), conservative (48%), ambitious (38%), and courteous (32%). Japanese American college students (*Sansei* or *Yonsei*) see Japanese Americans as quiet (60%), conservative (54%), loyal to family (40%), reserved (38%), and tradition loving (30%). Japanese American elementary school students view Japanese Americans as quiet, shy, not speaking in class (68%); intelligent, smart, getting good grades (82%); and traditional, loyal to family (56%).

European American adults in Maykovich's (1971) study see Japanese Americans as loyal to family (77%), ambitious (50%), courteous (50%), industrious (50%), efficient (42%), and tradition loving (31%). European American college students view Japanese Americans as loyal to family (67%), ambitious (51%), intelligent (38%), industrious (35%), and courteous (27%). European American elementary school students see Japanese Americans as quiet, shy, not speaking in class (78%); intelligent, smart, getting good grades (65%); and traditional, loyal to family (36%).

There is a high degree of correspondence in the Japanese Americans' and the European Americans' stereotypes of Japanese Americans in Maykovich's (1971) study. One reason for this may be that the study was conducted in Sacramento, a city with a relatively large Japanese American population. The larger the Japanese American population, the more likely European Americans have contact with Japanese Americans. The greater the contact, the more correspondence would be expected between Japanese Americans' stereotypes of Japanese Americans and European Americans' stereotypes of Japanese Americans.

Ogawa (1971) suggests that the stereotypes of Japanese Americans as "being 'highly Americanized' or 'just like whites' have remained fairly consistent" over the years (p. 28). He also points out that Japanese Americans are viewed as "exceptionally law-abiding" and "strongly family-oriented" in popular magazines (p. 32).

Yum and Wang (1983) examine the favorableness of the stereotypes that members of the various ethnic groups in Hawaii have for one another. Generally, members of each ethnic group tend to have the most favorable stereotypes of their own groups with one exception. The exception is that European Americans tend to have slightly more positive views of Japanese Americans than of their own group. European Americans' ratings (scores range from 1-6) are European Americans = 4.65; Japanese Americans = 4.73; Korean Americans = 4.40; Filipino Americans = 4.26. The corresponding scores for Japanese Americans are Japanese Americans = 5.16; European Americans = 4.69; Korean Americans = 4.64; Filipino Americans = 4.57. The Korean Americans' scores are Korean Americans = 4.73; European Americans = 4.88; Japanese Americans = 4.71; Filipino Americans = 3.65. The Filipino Americans' scores are Filipino Americans = 5.67; European Americans = 5.11; Japanese Americans = 4.93; Korean Americans = 4.49. The favorableness of the stereotypes is influenced by having friends among the other group. Stereotype favorableness is higher for individuals who have at least one friend among the other groups than for individuals who do not have a friend among the other groups.

Dion, Pak, and Dion (1990) argue that Asian Americans' collectivistic orientations influence the attributes they use to stereotype others. They contend that collectivists tend to use group-related attributes to stereotype others more than individualists, who focus on person-related attributes. Dion et al. report that Chinese Canadians who are highly involved in the Chinese community (an indicator of collectivism) use physical attractiveness to stereotype other members of their ethnic groups less than those who are not highly involved in the community.

Ogawa (1971) contends that there is some consistency between stereotypes of Japanese Americans and their actual behavior. He argues that Japanese Americans' behavior may be due to self-fulfilling prophecies; that is, European

Americans have stereotypes of Japanese Americans, and Japanese Americans behave in ways that fulfill these stereotypes.

Such a prophecy fulfillment is evident in social settings today, especially on the classroom level. Anglo students and teachers stereotype their fellow Japanese-Americans as "intelligent," "industrious," "courteous," and "quiet." Consequently, the Japanese students, wishing to be accepted by their peers, behave in a manner compatible to these stereotypes. They become conditioned to behave, think, and live according to a value system based upon a prophecy made for them by the dominant Anglos. (p. 65)

This analysis may also apply to other Asian American ethnic groups as well. It is impossible to determine the accuracy of Ogawa's analysis. It does, however, provide a plausible explanation for why there is some consistency in European Americans' stereotypes of Japanese Americans and Japanese Americans' behavior.

Social Distance. Another way to look at individuals' expectations for members of ethnic groups is to look at the social distances they expect between themselves and members of various groups. Social distance is the tendency to approach or withdraw from members of different groups (Bogardus, 1968). Social distance is assessed using a scale that indicates how close respondents want members of other groups to be to them: 1 = admit to close kinship by marriages; 2 = admit to my club as personal chums; 3 = admit to my street as neighbors; 4 = admit to employment in my occupation; 5 = admit to citizenship in my country; 6 = admit as visitors only to my country; and 7 = would exclude from my country.

Bogardus (1968) summarizes European Americans social distance scores for various groups over 40 years. Chinese, Japanese, Koreans, Filipinos, and Japanese Americans were included in the studies. In 1926, the scores are European Americans = 1.10; Chinese = 3.36; Filipinos = 3.00; Japanese = 2.80; and Koreans = 3.60 (Japanese Americans were not included in 1926). In 1946, the scores are European Americans = 1.04; Japanese Americans = 2.90; Chinese = 2.50; Japanese = 3.61; Filipinos = 2.76; and Koreans = 3.05. In 1956, the scores are European Americans = 1.08; Japanese Americans = 2.34; Chinese = 2.68; Filipinos = 2.46; Japanese = 2.70; and Koreans = 2.83. In 1966 the scores are European Americans = 1.09; Japanese Americans = 2.14; Chinese = 2.34; Japa-

nese = 2.41; Filipinos = 2.31; and Koreans = 2.51. The scores are relatively stable over the 40-year period, but note the drop in the scores for Japanese in 1946
as a result of World War II.

Kinloch (1973) examines social distance among ethnic groups in Hawaii;
the tendencies of members of each group to reject the members of the other
groups. European Americans tend to accept members of other ethnic groups
(percentage rejecting each group is in parentheses): Chinese Americans
(9.5%), Japanese Americans (9.5%), Korean Americans (12.5%), and Filipino
Americans (14.9%). Chinese Americans tend to accept all groups except Filipino Americans: Japanese Americans (9%), Korean Americans (16%), and Filipino Americans (30.2%). Japanese Americans also tend to accept members of
each group except Filipino Americans: Chinese Americans (7.8%), Korean
Americans (12.7%), and Filipino Americans (25.2%). Korean Americans also
tend to accept Filipino Americans the least: Chinese Americans (9.2%), Japanese Americans (4.9%), and Filipino Americans (21.7%). Filipino Americans
accept Korean Americans the least: Chinese Americans (7.9%), Japanese
Americans (8.8%), and Korean Americans (14.8%).

Stereotypes of Asian American Ethnic Groups.   To the best of my knowledge,
there are no published studies comparing the specific stereotypes of more than
two Asian American ethnic groups. I included a section on stereotypes on the
Survey of Asian American Communication regarding stereotypes to fill this
void. Twenty-two adjectives were included on the survey. Rather than just
checking adjectives, respondents were asked to indicate the degree to which
each adjective applied to their ethnic groups.

Table 5.4 presents the average scores for members of Asian American ethnic
groups' stereotypes of their own ethnic groups. There are significant differences on 12 of 22 traits: ambitious, compassionate, friendly, aggressive, industrious, deceitful, cooperative, warm, quiet, pleasure loving, emotional, and
talkative.

1. *Ambitious:* Filipino Americans and Korean Americans perceive themselves to be the most ambitious, Chinese Americans and Vietnamese
   Americans perceive themselves the least ambitious, and Japanese Americans are in the middle.

2. *Compassionate:* Vietnamese Americans perceive themselves to be the
   most compassionate, Filipino Americans perceive themselves the least

TABLE 5.4 Stereotypes of Own Ethnic Group by Ethnicity

	Chinese American	Filipino American	Japanese American	Korean American	Vietnamese American
Intelligent	5.99	5.90	6.13	6.00	5.79
Ambitious	5.40	6.03	5.76	5.92	5.38
Compassionate	4.78	5.39	4.78	4.87	5.21
Conservative	5.56	5.16	5.83	5.26	5.34
Friendly	5.29	5.76	5.04	5.21	5.19
Aggressive	4.06	4.34	3.74	5.11	4.11
Materialistic	4.69	5.18	4.72	4.76	4.53
Industrious	4.99	5.28	5.78	5.26	4.57
Deceitful	3.38	3.99	2.89	3.76	3.17
Arrogant	3.44	3.66	3.24	4.16	3.49
Cooperative	4.79	5.54	5.32	4.63	5.11
Warm	4.82	5.48	4.82	4.34	5.34
Conventional	4.75	4.76	5.09	4.97	4.66
Quiet	4.74	4.42	5.37	4.18	4.49
Pleasure loving	4.58	5.55	4.94	5.16	4.94
Honest	5.17	5.21	5.44	5.05	5.38
Sincere	5.14	5.24	5.41	4.76	5.28
Progressive	5.06	5.24	5.44	5.32	5.04
Tradition loving	5.88	5.93	5.46	5.68	5.64
Competitive	5.25	5.50	5.44	5.58	5.21
Emotional	4.25	5.65	4.63	4.47	5.06
Talkative	4.07	5.38	4.06	4.82	4.43

SOURCE: Survey of Asian American Communication.
NOTE: Scores range from 1 (not characteristic of my ethnic group) to 7 (very characteristic of my ethnic group).

compassionate, and Chinese Americans, Japanese Americans, and Korean Americans fall in the middle.

3. *Friendly:* Filipino Americans perceive themselves to be the most friendly, Japanese Americans perceive themselves to be the least friendly, and Chinese Americans, Korean Americans, and Vietnamese Americans fall in the middle.

4. *Aggressive:* Korean Americans perceive themselves to be the most aggressive, Japanese Americans perceive themselves to be the least aggressive, and Chinese Americans, Filipino Americans, and Vietnamese Americans fall in the middle.

5. *Industrious:* Japanese Americans perceive themselves to be the most industrious, Vietnamese Americans perceive themselves to be the least industrious, Chinese Americans, Filipino Americans, and Korean Americans fall in the middle.

6. *Deceitful:* Filipino Americans and Korean Americans perceive themselves to be the most deceitful, Japanese Americans perceive themselves to be the least deceitful, and Chinese Americans and Vietnamese Americans fall in the middle.

7. *Cooperative:* Filipino Americans perceive themselves to be the most cooperative, Chinese Americans and Vietnamese Americans perceive themselves to be the least cooperative, and Japanese Americans and Vietnamese Americans fall in the middle.

8. *Warm:* Filipino Americans and Vietnamese Americans perceive themselves to be the warmest, Korean Americans perceive themselves to be the least warm, and Japanese Americans and Chinese Americans fall in the middle.

9. *Quiet:* Japanese Americans perceive themselves to be the quietest, Korean Americans perceive themselves to be the least quiet, and Chinese Americans, Filipino Americans, and Vietnamese Americans fall in the middle.

10. *Pleasure loving:* Filipino Americans perceive themselves to be the most pleasure loving, Chinese Americans perceive themselves to be the least pleasure loving, and Japanese Americans, Korean Americans, and Filipino Americans fall in the middle.

11. *Emotional:* Filipino Americans perceive themselves to be the most emotional, Vietnamese Americans perceive themselves to be the second most emotional, Chinese Americans perceive themselves to be the least emotional, Japanese Americans and Korean Americans fall between the Vietnamese Americans and Chinese Americans.

12. *Talkative:* Filipino Americans perceive themselves to be the most talkative, Chinese Americans and Japanese Americans perceive themselves to be the least talkative, and Korean Americans and Vietnamese Americans fall in the middle.

The Asian Americans in the Survey of Asian American Communication do not differ on the other 10 traits.

Generally, Filipino Americans perceive that they are more ambitious, compassionate, friendly, cooperative, warm, pleasure loving, emotional, and talkative than members of the other Asian American ethnic groups. Japanese Americans perceive that they are more industrious, cooperative, and quiet than members of the other Asian American ethnic groups. Korean Americans perceive that they are more aggressive than members of the Asian American ethnic groups. Vietnamese Americans perceive that they are more compassionate and warm than members of the other Asian American ethnic groups. The traits on which Filipino Americans perceive themselves to be the highest tend to be traits not associated with Confucian philosophy, which is important among Chinese Americans, Japanese Americans, Korean Americans, and Vietnamese Americans.

Strength of cultural and ethnic identities also influences Asian Americans' stereotypes of their own ethnic groups (see Table 5.5). Asian Americans who strongly identify with the U.S. culture perceive their ethnic groups to be more intelligent, more ambitious, more conservative, and more honest than those who do not strongly identify with the U.S. culture. Asian Americans who strongly identify with their ethnic groups perceive their ethnic groups to be more compassionate, more friendly, more aggressive, more honest, and more sincere than those who do not strongly identify with their ethnic groups.

COMMUNICATION STYLES

Norton (1978) defines communication style as "the way one verbally and paraverbally interacts to signal how literal meaning should be taken, interpreted, filtered, or understood" (p. 99). Norton (1983) suggests that "style is a message about content" (p. 19). Communication style tells others how to interpret the content of messages that individuals transmit. Style involves individuals' recurring patterns of communication. In other words, style involves patterns of communication that individuals use across situations. Norton isolates numerous communication styles that predominate in the mainstream U.S. culture (e.g., dominant, dramatic, animated, aggressive, attentive, contentious, relaxed, friendly, open).

TABLE 5.5 Stereotypes of Own Group by Strength of Ethnic and Cultural
Identities

	Ethnic Identity		Cultural Identity	
	Weak	*Strong*	*Weak*	*Strong*
Intelligent	5.92	5.95	5.81	6.08
Ambitious	5.72	5.60	5.52	5.82
Compassionate	4.80	5.18	5.01	4.93
Conservative	5.35	5.42	5.22	5.57
Friendly	5.17	5.46	5.30	5.29
Aggressive	4.08	4.43	4.29	4.16
Materialistic	4.91	4.81	4.81	4.93
Industrious	5.24	5.07	5.12	5.22
Deceitful	3.56	3.39	3.64	3.29
Arrogant	3.74	3.44	3.64	3.56
Cooperative	4.92	5.20	4.99	5.12
Warm	4.94	5.14	5.01	5.03
Conventional	4.71	4.90	4.84	4.73
Quiet	4.72	4.68	4.65	4.73
Pleasure loving	5.00	5.06	5.01	5.04
Honest	5.04	5.36	5.00	5.38
Sincere	5.01	5.34	5.06	5.29
Progressive	5.19	5.33	5.16	5.39
Tradition loving	5.66	5.82	5.65	5.83
Cooperative	5.47	5.45	5.45	5.50
Emotional	4.71	4.83	4.69	4.83
Talkative	4.43	4.68	4.48	4.62

SOURCE: Survey of Asian American Communication.
NOTE: Scores range from 1 (not characteristic of my ethnic group) to 7 (very characteristic of my ethnic group).

In this section, I review various Asian American communication styles,
including low- and high-context communication, face negotiation styles, conflict styles, and persuasive styles. I begin with low- and high-context communication.

Low- and High-Context Communication

As indicated in Chapter 2, Hall (1976) isolates two broad communication styles that differentiate the predominate styles of communication used in the mainstream U.S. culture and Asian collectivistic cultures: low-context and high-context communication. Low-context communication occurs when the vast majority of the information needed to interpret messages is in the explicit message (e.g., what is said). Low-context communication tends to be direct, explicit, and precise. High-context communication occurs when the vast majority of the information needed to interpret messages is in the situation or internalized in the individuals interpreting messages (e.g., Japanese know that when they ask other Japanese a direct question that requires a "yes" or "no" and the others are silent, the silence means "no"). High-context communication tends to be indirect, and sometimes it is ambiguous. It requires that listeners figure out what is meant by using their knowledge of the situation or cultural information they have internalized.

In this section, I examine several different aspects of Asian Americans' communication that involve high-context messages. I begin with Japanese American communication styles. Following this, I discuss Chinese Americans' beliefs about talk. Next, I look at emotional communication and conversational patterns. In the final section, I present data for low-context and high-context communication across the five ethnic groups studied in the Survey of Asian American Communication.

Japanese American Communication Style. All descriptions of Japanese American communication style are consistent with Hall's (1976) description of high-context communication (e.g., Johnson & Johnson, 1975; Johnson, Marsella, & Johnson, 1974; Kitano, 1993a; Lyman, 1971, 1988; Miyamoto, 1986, 1988) (Note: These writers do not use the label "high-context communication," but their descriptions are consistent with Hall.) Johnson and Johnson (1975), for example, argue that several aspects of Japanese communication styles are reflected in Japanese American communication styles: (1) paying attention to the social status of the individuals with whom they are communicating, (2) not being highly assertive, (3) vagueness in communication that derives from the Japanese language, (4) consciously being indirect, (5) a tendency to be silent during verbal interaction, and (6) an emphasis on interpreting others' nonverbal communication.

Kitano (1993a) argues that at least two aspects of Japanese communication styles are reflected in Japanese Americans' behavior, including *Sansei* (third generation) and *Yonsei* (fourth generation): use of indirect communication and low levels of verbal participation, especially in groups. To illustrate, he points out that Japanese American parents tend to correct their children when they do something wrong by saying something indirect like "A good child does it this way" rather than directly scolding them. Japanese Americans' communication depends "in part on explicit communications, to be sure, but it also depends much more than in the [European] American case on sensing and inferring each others' attitudes and feelings" (Miyamoto, 1988, p. 111).

Kitano (1976) suggests that Japanese Americans socialize children so as to minimize their verbal interaction.

> The most distinctive characteristic of Japanese [American] family interaction was, and still remains, the absence of prolonged verbal exchanges. Although some of the common strategies to gain support through manipulation or cajoling were present, very few problems were resolved through open discussion between parents and children. Instead arguments were one-sided, and most *Nisei* can remember the phrase "*da- mot-to-le*" (keep quiet) that concluded them. Verbalization, talking out of mutual discussion, were actively discouraged. (p. 72)

Japanese Americans often use the same patterns as in the family in other social situations. Kitano (1993a) points out that he sees these patterns in *Sansei* and *Yonsei* students in his classes. Similarly, Johnson and Marsella (1978) contend that *Sansei* in Hawaii may hold traditional Japanese attitudes and use a Japanese style of communication, even when they do not speak Japanese.

Johnson and Johnson (1975) believe that Japanese *enryo* ("reticence," "reserve") influences Japanese Americans' behavior, and it may be one of the reasons there are low levels of verbal interaction among Japanese Americans. They point out that *enryo* involves "a cluster of behaviors which are related to the communication of humility, deference, [and] reticence" (p. 456). Kitano (1976, 1993a) also believes that *enryo* continues to affect Japanese Americans' behavior today. Kitano (1976) suggests that *enryo*

> has both a positive and a negative effect on Japanese (American) social interaction. For example, take observations of Japanese in situations as diverse as their hesitancy to speak out at meetings; their refusal of any invitation, especially the first time; their refusal of second helpings; their accep-

tance of a less desired object when given a free choice; their lack of verbal participation, especially in an integrated group; their refusal to ask questions; and their hesitancy in asking for a raise in salary—these may all be based on *enryo*. (p. 125)

Enryo is related to Japanese Americans' desire not to stand out from the group and their desire not to assert themselves as separate individuals. Johnson and Johnson point out that *Sansei* may not know the term, but they are familiar with the behaviors associated with *enryo*.

Kitano (1993a) suggests that the Japanese values and behavior that survive and are still used by Japanese Americans today are those that they have found to be functional. "Those that have been retained serve a useful purpose, those that have had less value tend to be discarded or modified" (p. 143).

Several writers contend that Japanese values and behavior influence Japanese Americans' behavior more than is obvious. Miyamoto (1986), for example, suggests that *Nisei* may appear "American" at work when interacting with European American co-workers, but they may maintain Japanese behavior with family and friends. Similarly, Tamura (1994) contends that Japanese Americans may be direct, aggressive, and individualistic in public interacting with European Americans and be traditional, group-oriented, and indirect with family and friends. Nishi (1995) argues that what appears to be assimilation to the mainstream U.S. culture over one or two generations may only be superficial acculturation to food preferences, dress, language usage, and communication patterns. Deep-seated values, emotional responses to life crises, and the ways Japanese Americans give emotional support may still be similar to the Japanese model.

Chinese Americans' Beliefs About Talk. Wiemann, Chen, and Giles (1986) contend that individuals have beliefs about talk and silence, and these beliefs influence the communication strategies individuals use. They suggest that in informal situations, individuals' tendencies with respect to whether they should talk or be silent, how much they should talk, and when they should talk are functions of their beliefs about talk, their personalities (e.g., extroverts talk more than introverts), and situational factors (e.g., some situations specify who should talk). To illustrate, European Americans tend to believe that when there are pauses in conversations (i.e., silences), they should fill them (i.e., talk).

Wiemann et al. (1986; see Giles, Coupland, & Wiemann, 1992, for a summary of the study) isolate four dimensions of beliefs about talk. The first dimension is affiliation/assertiveness (e.g., "I take responsibility for breaking the ice by talking when I meet someone"). The second dimension involves using talk as a way to control others or situations (e.g., "I engage in small talk to avoid intimate topics"). The third dimension focuses on the extent to which individuals engage in small talk (e.g., "I enjoy small talk"). The fourth dimension is tolerance of silence (e.g., "I think that people generally talk more than they should").

Wiemann et al. (1986) report that European Americans believe that talk should be used to create affiliation more than Chinese or Chinese Americans. European Americans also engage in more small talk than Chinese Americans, but the difference is not significant. European Americans see talk as a source of control more than Chinese, with Chinese Americans falling in between the other two groups. Finally, Chinese have a greater tolerance for silence than either European Americans or Chinese Americans. The European American tendency to use talk to create affiliations and control others is consistent with low-context communication. In low-context communication, verbal interaction is the way that individuals get to know others and get what they want.

One shortcoming of Wiemann et al.'s (1986) study is that they do not take the Chinese Americans' ethnic identities or individualistic and collectivistic tendencies into consideration. It may be that the Chinese Americans in this study do not identify strongly with their ethnic group or are not collectivistic. If this is the case, it would explain why there are not differences between the European Americans and Chinese Americans on three of the four dimensions.

Asian Americans' Emotional Communication. Members of Asian cultures tend to moderate the expression of emotions (e.g., hide their emotions) more than European Americans (e.g., Friesen, 1972). Kao, Nagata, and Peterson (1997) argue that this difference extends to European Americans and Asian Americans. They report that Asian Americans are more emotionally restrained in their families than European Americans.

Several researchers examine whether Chinese Americans follow the Asian tendency. Tsai, Levenson, and Carstensen (1992), for example, find no physiological (e.g., heart rate) difference between European Americans and Chinese Americans in response to films arousing sadness and amusement. Similarly, Lee and Levenson (1992) observe no physiological difference between European Americans' and Chinese Americans' responses to sudden loud noises.

Tsai and Levenson (1997) examine European American and Chinese American romantic couples' emotional responses when they discuss conflicts. They report no physiological differences between the two groups when they discuss conflicts. The Chinese Americans, however, have fewer periods of positive affect than European Americans when conflicts are discussed. Tsai and Levenson also note that the more acculturated Chinese Americans are to mainstream U.S. culture, the less moderated and the less controlled their emotional responses are.

Samter et al. (1997) compare European Americans and Asian Americans use of emotional support in same-sex friendships. Emotional support helps individuals cope with the stress and disappointments of everyday life. Samter et al. report that European Americans and Asian Americans view comforting skills as equally important. European Americans and Asian Americans also perceive emotion-focused goals (e.g., help people who are upset to talk about what they are feeling) as equally important. European American men and Asian American men view problem-focused goals (e.g., help them solve their problem) as equally important, but Asian American women see problem-focused goals as more important than do European American women.

Samter et al. (1997) also note that European American men and Asian American men perceive highly person-centered messages (e.g., messages that focus on the other person's feelings) to be equally sensitive. European American women, in contrast, view highly person-centered messages as more sensitive and effective than do Asian American women. Asian American women, on the other hand, see comforting messages low in person centeredness (e.g., telling others how they should feel) as more sensitive than European American women.

Samter et al.'s (1997) results are hard to explain. They suggest that the results may be due to the Asian Americans' collectivism, but this explanation does not fully account for the results since the only differences to emerge were between European American women and Asian American women. Unfortunately, Samter et al. did not assess the Asian Americans' individualistic or collectivistic tendencies or their ethnic identities. It might be that the Asian American women in the study are more collectivistic or have stronger ethnic identities than the Asian American men in the study.

Doherty et al. (1994) examine ethnic influences on love and attachment in Hawaii. They report no differences among Chinese Americans, European Americans, and Japanese Americans in terms of their likelihood of being in love, their passionate (e.g., romantic) love, or companionate (e.g., friendship) love. There also are no differences in terms of the attachment styles (i.e., feeling secure, anxious, avoidant) among the three groups. Doherty et al. also note that idiocentrism (individualistic tendency) is not related to attachment styles. The results of this study might be due to Japanese Americans and Chinese Americans in the study not strongly identifying with their ethnic groups. Ethnic identity, however, was not assessed.

Conversational Time Patterns. Ethnicity influences the rhythms individuals use in their conversations. The rhythms involve the sequences of vocalizations and pauses used in conversations. The rhythms individuals establish provide information about the individuals communicating and their relationship to one another (Welkowitz et al., 1984a, 1984b).

Feldstein et al. (1981) examine the conversational patterns of English-speaking Canadians and bilingual Chinese Canadians. They report that Chinese Canadians use longer periods of silence, regardless of whether they are speaking Chinese or English, than English speakers. Chinese Canadians use shorter periods of vocalization than English speakers, and their vocalizations are shorter when they speak English than when they speak Chinese.

Welkowitz et al. (1984b) look at conversational time patterns of European American and Japanese American children (eight years old) in Hawaii. They find that the Japanese American children take shorter turns (e.g., talk less at one time) than the European American children in same-ethnicity dyads. Welkowitz et al. argue that these results may be due to Japanese Americans being more introverted than European Americans. Meridith (1966) notes that Japanese Americans are more introverted than European Americans.

Welkowitz et al. (1984b) also report that Japanese American boys take fewer turns to speak but have longer turn duration and longer pauses than Japanese American girls. These results are inconsistent with traditional Japanese American sex roles, and they may suggest that Japanese American sex roles do not emerge by age eight. European American girls use fewer turns but take longer turns and have longer pauses than Japanese American girls in same-ethnicity dyads. When the Japanese American girls speak with Japanese American boys or European Americans, they speak less than with Japanese American girls. Welkowitz et al. argue that these differences may be due to the Japanese American girls being more "feminine" than European American girls. Meridith (1969) finds that Japanese American females score higher in femininity than European American females.

Welkowitz et al. (1984a) look at conversational time patterns in Japanese American children and adults. They report that the adults use more turns, have longer turns, and have longer pauses than the children. Male adults also take more turns and have shorter pauses than the female adults in same-sex dyads.

Welkowitz et al. suggest that "Japanese-American males become more active verbally with age than females" (p. 135). Since the male adults are different from the boys in only one area, they suggest that the adult gender differences may be due to female submissiveness rather than male dominance.

Asian Americans' Communication Styles. The Survey of Asian American Communication contained measures of 15 communication styles (10 styles from Norton, 1983, and 5 styles from Gudykunst, Matsumoto et al., 1996). As indicated earlier, communication styles are general tendencies that individuals use over time and across situations. The following are brief definitions of each style:

1. *Being dramatic* involves picturesque speech, the tendency to exaggerate, and to tell jokes (Norton).
2. *Being contentious* involves demanding that others be precise and show proof of what they are saying (Norton).
3. *Being animated* involves using facial expressions and using gestures (Norton).
4. *Being relaxed* involves being calm and not being nervous (Norton).
5. *Being attentive* involves being able to repeat what others say and being empathic (Norton).
6. *Being open* involves revealing personal things about the self and expressing feelings (Norton).
7. *Being friendly* involves encouraging others and being tactful (Norton).
8. *Being precise* involves being accurate and precise (Norton).
9. *Being expressive nonverbally* involves others' being able to "read" individuals' nonverbal expressions and showing emotions when they communicate (Norton).
10. *Communicator image* involves individuals' viewing themselves as good communicators (Norton).
11. *Being indirect* involves being ambiguous and individuals' making others guess what they mean (Gudykunst, Matsumoto et al.).
12. *Making inferences* involves understanding what others mean when they are indirect or unclear (Gudykunst, Matsumoto et al.).
13. *Being sensitive* involves maintaining harmony with others and not offending others (Gudykunst, Matsumoto et al.).

TABLE 5.6 Communication Styles by Ethnicity

	Chinese American	Filipino American	Japanese American	Korean American	Vietnamese American
Using feelings to guide behavior	4.37	4.58	4.35	4.36	4.64
Using silence	3.75	3.54	3.48	3.93	3.76
Being dramatic	3.96	4.21	3.68	4.15	3.97
Being contentious	4.17	4.02	3.95	4.08	4.25
Being animated	4.39	4.54	4.24	4.38	4.52
Being relaxed	3.85	4.11	3.96	4.21	4.02
Being attentive	4.73	4.82	4.80	4.76	5.00
Being open	4.25	4.19	3.89	4.19	4.32
Being friendly	4.87	4.90	5.06	4.67	4.91
Being precise	4.61	4.66	4.65	4.73	4.70
Being nonverbally expressive	4.52	4.44	4.19	4.25	4.54
Inferring meaning	4.63	4.62	4.81	4.65	4.70
Being indirect	3.66	3.58	3.63	3.70	3.83
Being sensitive	5.03	5.06	5.31	4.84	5.30
Communicator image	4.56	4.84	4.52	4.62	4.72

SOURCE: Survey of Asian American Communication.
NOTE: Scores range from 1 to 7.

14. *Using feelings to guide behavior* involves orienting to people through their emotions and basing their behavior on their feelings (Gudykunst, Matsumoto et al.).
15. *Using silence* involves being comfortable with silence in conversations (Gudykunst, Matsumoto et al.).

Generally, Norton's 10 styles involve low-context communication and Gudykunst, Matsumoto et al.'s 5 styles involve high-context communication, except using feelings to guide behavior.

Table 5.6 presents the average scores for the 15 communication styles by ethnic group. There are no significant differences among the ethnic groups for

TABLE 5.7 Communication Styles by Strength of Ethnic and Cultural Identities

	Ethnic Identity		Cultural Identity	
	Weak	*Strong*	*Weak*	*Strong*
Using feelings to guide behavior	4.28	4.62	4.24	4.68
Using silence	3.70	3.66	3.71	3.62
Being dramatic	3.87	4.10	3.87	4.12
Being contentious	3.98	4.27	4.14	4.09
Being animated	4.26	4.58	4.35	4.50
Being relaxed	3.95	4.07	3.99	4.03
Being attentive	4.70	4.91	4.54	5.10
Being open	4.10	4.23	4.10	4.25
Being friendly	4.78	4.97	4.72	5.05
Being precise	4.45	4.86	4.55	4.76
Being nonverbally expressive	4.30	4.54	4.41	4.41
Inferring meanings	4.52	4.87	4.47	4.94
Being indirect	3.47	3.77	3.64	3.58
Being sensitive	4.95	5.19	4.89	5.27
Communicator image	4.51	4.82	4.47	4.87

SOURCE: Survey of Asian American Communication.
NOTE: Scores range from 1 to 7.

any of the communication styles. Similarly, there are no differences in communication styles based on where Asian Americans were born (i.e., United States/not United States) or the language spoken in the home when they were children (i.e., English/not English). One possible reason for these results is that there are no differences in the degree of individualism or collectivism across the five ethnic groups studied.

Table 5.7 presents the average scores for the 15 communication styles by strength of ethnic and cultural identities. Asian Americans who strongly identify with their ethnic groups view themselves as more precise, inferring meanings more, and having more positive communicator images than those who do not identify strongly with their ethnic groups. Strongly identifying with their ethnic groups leads to Asian Americans' having positive images of themselves as communicators. Also, strongly identifying with their ethnic groups makes it possible for Asian Americans to infer meanings of the other members of their ethnic group when they are indirect.

Strength of cultural identities influences using feelings to guide behavior, being dramatic, being attentive, inferring meanings, and being sensitive. Each of these styles is used more by Asian Americans who identify strongly with the U.S. culture than by Asian Americans who do not identify strongly with the U.S. culture. Using feelings to guide behavior, being dramatic, and being attentive are aspects of low-context communication that would be expected of individuals who identify with the U.S. culture. Being sensitive and inferring meanings, in contrast, would tend to be associated with high-context communication. It appears that Asian Americans who identify with the U.S. culture still see it as important to understand (e.g., infer meanings) and be sensitive toward other members of their ethnic groups.

Emphasizing independent self construals is associated positively with using feelings to guide behavior, being dramatic, being contentious, being animated, being attentive, being open, and being precise. All these styles involve low-context communication and would be expected to be used by individualists. Emphasizing interdependent self construals is associated positively with being sensitive and making inferences. These styles involve high-context communication and would be expected to be used by collectivists.

Strength of cultural identities is associated positively with using feelings to guide behavior, being dramatic, being attentive, and being precise. Strength of ethnic identities is associated positively with being indirect, being sensitive, and making inferences. Only silence is associated positively with ethnic language ability, and only being animated is associated positively with percentage of English used to communicate with family and friends.

Unreported analyses from Gudykunst, Matsumoto et al.'s (1996) study can be used to examine differences in communication styles between Asian Americans and European Americans. There are no differences on four of eight communication styles: ability to infer meanings, sensitivity, using feelings to guide behavior, and positive attitudes toward silence. European Americans are more dramatic, more open, and more precise than Asian Americans. Asian Americans are more indirect than European Americans. Emphasizing independent self construals is related positively to ability to infer meanings, using feelings to guide behavior, being open, and being precise. Emphasizing interdependent self construals is associated positively with being indirect, being sensitive, and positive attitudes toward silence.

Face Negotiation

Face involves individuals' projected images of themselves in social situations (Ting-Toomey, 1988). The way face is used in the United States suggests that it is something that individuals claim for themselves without implications for their ingroups. The concept of face, however, originated in China, and the Chinese conceptualization involves ingroups (e.g., Hu, 1944). Ho (1976), for example, conceptualizes face as

> the respectability and/or deference which a person can claim for himself [or herself] from others, by virtue of the relative position he [or she] occupies in his [or her] social network and the degree to which he [or she] is judged to have functioned adequately in that position and acceptability in his [or her] general conduct. (p. 883)

Ho's definition is consistent with Hu's original discussion of Chinese face.

Ho (1976) also suggests that face is "never a purely individual thing. It does not make sense to speak of the face of an individual as something lodged within his [or her] person; it is meaningful only when his [or her] face is considered in relation to that of others in the social network" (p. 882). Morisaki and Gudykunst (1994) extend Ho's position and argue that face in individualistic cultures like the mainstream culture in the United States is based on independent self construal, and face in Asian collectivistic cultures is based on interdependent self construal.

The initial conceptualizations of face do not link it to politeness (e.g., Ho, 1976; Hu, 1944). Brown and Levinson's (1978) politeness theory, however, links face to politeness. They isolate three factors that influence how polite individuals are expected to be: (1) the relational distance between individuals, (2) the relative power individuals have, and (3) how face-threatening their behavior is. Perceptions of these three factors vary across cultures and across ethnic groups in the United States.

Implications of Cross-Cultural Studies. There are several differences in how face is managed by European Americans and Asians that should apply to differences between European Americans and Asian Americans. The Asian tendencies should apply to Asian Americans who identify strongly with their ethnic groups and who are collectivistic.

Following Brown and Levinson (1978), Holtgraves and Yang (1992) argue that the relational distance between individuals (e.g., status differences) influences how polite they are required to be when managing their own and others' face. The greater the relational distance, the more politeness is required (politeness protects others' face). Holtgraves and Yang contend that European Americans pay less attention to the relational distance between themselves and others than do Koreans. Given the same relational distances, European Americans are less polite than Koreans. Based on Holtgraves and Yang's work, it could be argued that Asian Americans pay more attention to relational distances than do European Americans. Furthermore, if relational distances are the same, it can be argued that Asian Americans are more polite than European Americans.

Cocroft and Ting-Toomey (1994) report that European Americans use antisocial and self-presentation strategies to manage face more than Japanese. Japanese, in contrast, use indirect face maintenance strategies more than European Americans. Given Cocroft and Ting-Toomey's research, it can be argued that European Americans will use more self-oriented, direct strategies to manage face than Asian Americans. Asian Americans, in contrast, would be expected to use more indirect, other-oriented strategies to manage face than European Americans.

Cupach and Imahori (1993) contend that European Americans are more likely than Japanese to use humor and aggression to manage face issues in social predicaments. Japanese, in comparison, are more likely than European Americans to apologize. Imahori and Cupach (1994) observe that European Americans use humor as a way to maintain face in embarrassing situations more than Japanese; Japanese use remediation (e.g., the correction of behavior) as a way to manage face more than European Americans. These results suggest that European Americans are more likely to use humor in threatening or embarrassing situations than Asian Americans. Asian Americans, in contrast, are more likely to apologize or try to correct their behavior to manage face in embarrassing situations than European Americans.

Yeh and Huang (1996) argue that Asian Americans have high face concerns. They suggest that "face includes the positive image, interpretations, or social attributes that one claims for oneself or perceives others to have accorded one. If one does not fulfill expectations of the self, then one loses face" (p. 651). Shon and Ja (1982) point out that Asian Americans with high face concerns are likely to try to conform to interpersonal expectations that others have for them. When Asian Americans have high face concerns, they tend to use shame to control their own behavior and others' behavior (Shon & Ja, 1982; Yeh & Huang, 1996). Fear of loss of face for Chinese immigrants is related to their ethnic identities; the stronger individuals' identities, the greater their face concerns (Kwan & Sodowsky, 1997).

Self-Effacement. European Americans tend to engage in self-enhancement more than Asians, and Asians tend to be more self-effacing than European Americans (Kitayama et al., 1997; Yik, Bond, & Paulhus 1998). Akimoto and Sanbonmatsu (1999) suggest that these tendencies may be due to the role of self-effacing in maintaining ingroup harmony. "Modesty may allow one to avoid offense and thereby maintain a sense of social or collective harmony. For example, if one behaves modestly by playing down one's performance, no one can be threatened or offended" (p. 160).

Japanese Americans engage in self-effacing behavior (Akimoto & Sanbonmatsu, 1999). European Americans tend to perceive individuals who engage in self-effacing behaviors as less competent than individuals who do not. Japanese Americans' self-effacing behavior, however, may not reflect negative self-evaluations. Rather, when Japanese Americans describe their behavior modestly, they may be behaving in ways that they perceive are appropriate.

Akimoto and Sanbonmatsu (1999) gave Japanese Americans and European Americans a test and then interviewed them about their performance, with the interviews being audio-recorded. Both groups were given the same feedback on their performance. In the interviews, Japanese Americans make fewer favorable statements about their performance than European Americans (when they were told they performed equally well). When asked to provide written statements about their performance, Japanese Americans also make less favorable comments about themselves than European Americans. Furthermore, Japanese Americans engage in more self-effacing behaviors in public than in private.

Observers who could not tell the interviewees' ethnicity rated the audiotapes of the interviews with European Americans and Japanese Americans about their performances. The observers rate Japanese Americans as having performed less well than European Americans (Akimoto & Sanbonmatsu, 1999). Japanese Americans also are perceived as less competent and less likely to be offered a job than European Americans.

Akimoto and Sanbonmatsu (1999) suggest two possible explanations for their findings. First, the Japanese Americans in the study are following the Japanese self-effacing communication rules. Second, Japanese Americans self-efface in public to gain acceptance. Self-effacing may be a strategy that Japanese Americans use to avoid being disliked. Unfortunately, Akimoto and

Sanbonmatsu did not assess Japanese Americans' individualistic or collectivistic tendencies, or their ethnic identities. Having this information would help to understand why the Japanese Americans responded the way they did in this study.

Conflict Styles

Conflict involves anything from minor disagreements between individuals to wars between nations. Conflict is inevitable in any ongoing relationship; it is going to happen whether individuals want it to or not. Roloff (1987) isolates several sources of conflict. First, conflicts occur when individuals misinterpret one another's behavior. Second, conflicts arise from perceptions of incompatibility, such as perceiving that personality or group characteristics are not compatible. Third, conflicts arise when individuals disagree on the causes of their own or others' behavior.

Implications of Cross-Cultural Studies. Olsen (1978) argues that conflicts arise from either instrumental or expressive sources. Expressive conflicts arise from a desire to release tension, usually generated from hostile feelings. Instrumental conflicts, in contrast, stem from a difference in goals or practices. Ting-Toomey (1985) suggests that members of individualistic cultures "are more likely to perceive conflict as instrumental rather than expressive in nature," and members of collectivistic cultures "are more likely to perceive conflict as expressive rather than instrumental in nature" (p. 78). It might, therefore, be argued that Asian Americans perceive conflict in more expressive terms than European Americans, and European Americans perceive conflict in more instrumental terms than Asian Americans.

Members of individualistic cultures often separate the issue on which they have conflicts from the people with whom they have conflicts (Ting-Toomey, 1985). Members of collectivistic cultures, in contrast, generally do not distinguish conflicts from the people with whom they have conflicts. It is plausible that Asian Americans also do not separate the issues on which they have conflicts from the individuals with whom they have conflict, whereas European Americans do.

Ting-Toomey (1985) argues that in individualistic cultures conflicts are likely to occur when individuals' expectations of appropriate behavior are violated. Conflicts in collectivistic cultures, in contrast, are likely to occur when groups' normative expectations for behavior are violated. Asian Americans, therefore, should perceive conflicts to occur when their ingroups standards are violated.

Ting-Toomey (1985) suggests that members of individualistic cultures are likely "to possess a confrontational, direct attitude toward conflicts," and members of collectivistic cultures are likely "to possess a non-confrontational, indirect attitude toward conflicts" (p. 9). Most writers (e.g., Kitano, 1993a) suggest that Asian Americans prefer nonconfrontational approaches to conflict.

Ting-Toomey (1994) believes that members of individualistic cultures take a short-term view of managing conflict, and members of collectivistic cultures tend to take a long-term view of managing conflict. Collectivists' long-term orientation toward conflict is a function of lifelong commitments to their ingroups. Given the importance of families to Asian Americans, it would be expected that Asian Americans have a more long-term attitude toward conflict than do European Americans.

Ting-Toomey (1994) also contends that members of collectivistic cultures prefer to avoid face-to-face meetings and use mediators to manage conflicts more than do members of individualistic cultures. The mediators used in Asian cultures tend to have relationships with both parties having conflicts (e.g., if two employees have a conflict, their supervisor would mediate). The use of mediators allows conflicts to be managed without direct confrontation. If confrontation can be avoided, harmony in relationships can be maintained. It would be expected that Asian Americans would prefer ingroup mediators more than would European Americans.

Members of individualistic and collectivistic cultures also use different styles to manage conflict. Conflict styles refer to individuals' typical mode of managing conflict in different situations (Ting-Toomey, 1988). Ting-Toomey (1988) argues that members of individualistic cultures prefer direct styles of dealing with conflict, such as integrating or compromising. Members of collectivistic cultures, on the other hand, prefer indirect styles of dealing with conflict that allow all parties to preserve face. They tend to use obliging and avoiding styles of conflict resolution or avoid the conflict all together.

Asian American Conflict Styles. Ting-Toomey et al. (2000) examine conflict styles used by Asian Americans, African Americans, European Americans, and Latino Americans. The only style on which Asian Americans differ from the other groups is use of the avoiding style. Ting-Toomey et al. report that Asian Americans and Latinos use avoiding more than African Americans, and that

Asian Americans use avoiding more than European Americans. These results are consistent with Asian Americans' using a collectivistic style of managing conflict.

Kim and Kitani (1998) examine the conflict styles that European Americans and Asian Americans use in romantic relationships in Hawaii. They report that European Americans use the dominating style more than Asian Americans. Asian Americans, in contrast, use the integrating, obliging, avoiding, and compromising styles more than European Americans.

Kim and Kitani (1998) also look at how self construals influence the use of conflict styles. They note that emphasizing independent self construals is related to the use of a dominating conflict style. Emphasizing interdependent self construals, in contrast, is related to the use of integrating, obliging, avoiding, and compromising styles.

Kim and Kitani (1998) argue that the integrating, obliging, avoiding, and compromising styles cluster together as "non-force" styles. Kim and Kitani's results are consistent with Kim and Hunter's (1995) study, which indicates that using integrating, obliging, avoiding, and compromising conflict styles is related to other-face concerns (as opposed to self-face concerns).

Anxiety/Uncertainty Management

Anytime individuals communicate, anxiety and uncertainty are factors that influence the effectiveness of their communication. Uncertainty arises from individuals' inabilities to predict or explain others' behavior, attitudes, or feelings (Berger & Calabrese, 1975). Individuals need to be able to predict, for example, which of several alternative behaviors others will choose to employ.

When two individuals meet, the situational communication rules provide guidelines for predicting others' behavior. When the situation does not reduce uncertainty sufficiently to make individuals feel comfortable, they try to reduce uncertainty by gathering information about those with whom they are communicating.

Anxiety refers to individuals' feelings of being uneasy, tense, worried, or apprehensive about what might happen when they are communicating with others (Stephan & Stephan, 1985). If anxiety is too high, individuals do not feel comfortable communicating with others. Anxiety and uncertainty are related negatively to effective communication (Gudykunst, 1995). Effective communication involves minimizing misunderstandings.

Gudykunst and Nishida (in press) examine anxiety, uncertainty, and effectiveness of communication in Japan and the United States. The U.S. data from this study contains sufficient Asian Americans to compare their responses with European Americans. There are no differences between Asian Americans and European Americans with respect to anxiety. Asian Americans have greater uncertainty communicating with strangers than do European Americans. European Americans, in contrast, have greater uncertainty communicating with close friends than do Asian Americans. Overall, European Americans perceive their communication to be more effective than Asian Americans. For both Asian Americans and European Americans, there is greater anxiety and uncertainty and less effectiveness communicating with strangers than communicating with close friends.

The Survey of Asian American Communication contains measures of anxiety, uncertainty, and perceived effectiveness of communication. Table 5.8 presents the average scores for anxiety, uncertainty, and perceived effectiveness of communication when Asian Americans communicate with members of their ethnic groups by ethnicity. There are no differences in these three variables based on ethnicity. Also, there are no differences based on where Asian Americans were born (United States/not United States) or the language spoken in their homes when they were children (English/not English).

Table 5.9 presents the average scores for anxiety, uncertainty, and perceived effectiveness of communication when Asian Americans communicate with members of their ethnic groups by strength of cultural and ethnic identities. Strength of ethnic identities does not influence any of the variables. Strength of cultural identities, however, influences anxiety and perceived effectiveness. Asian Americans who strongly identify with the U.S. culture experience less anxiety and perceive their communication to be more effective than those who do not strongly identify with the U.S. culture.

Persuasive Strategies

Some writers (e.g., Miller & Steinberg, 1975) argue that one of the primary functions of communication is social influence (e.g., individuals communicate to get others to do what they want them to do). Persuasive strategies are the general types of messages that individuals use to persuade or influence others.

Members of collectivistic cultures take the context into consideration and select persuasive strategies that are socially appropriate and appropriate to the

TABLE 5.8   Anxiety, Uncertainty, and Effectiveness by Ethnicity

	Chinese Americans	Filipino Americans	Japanese Americans	Korean Americans	Vietnamese Americans
Anxiety	3.32	3.29	3.30	3.44	3.18
Uncertainty	3.22	3.32	3.18	3.34	3.43
Effectiveness	5.10	5.17	5.26	4.82	5.07

SOURCE: Survey of Asian American Communication.
NOTE: Scores range from 1 to 7.

context. Members of individualistic cultures, in contrast, focus on the individuals they are trying to persuade and use persuasive strategies that may be perceived as socially inappropriate (Gudykunst & Ting-Toomey, 1988).

Burgoon et al. (1982) report that in comparison to European Americans, Asian Americans prefer to use the strategies of "promise" (e.g., "If you comply, I will reward you."), "positive expertise" (e.g., "If you comply, you will be rewarded by the nature of things."), "pregiving" (e.g., rewarding the person before request), "liking" (e.g., person is friendly to get the other in good frame of mind), "positive altercasting" (e.g., "A person with 'good' qualities would comply."), "negative altercasting" (e.g., "Only a person with 'bad' qualities would not comply."), "positive self-feeling" (e.g., "You will feel better about yourself if you comply."), and "positive self-esteem" (e.g., "People you value will think better of you if you comply."). All of these strategies tend to involve high degrees of social acceptability, as opposed to strategies that involve psychological force (e.g., "People you value will think worse of you if you do not comply") or punishing activities (e.g., punishing someone and making stopping the punishment contingent on compliance).

Miller, Reynolds, and Cambra (1982) examine persuasive strategy selection among European Americans, Japanese Americans, and Chinese Americans. European Americans use aversive stimuli more than Chinese Americans and Japanese Americans. European Americans also use threats more than Japanese Americans. Japanese Americans use altruism less than Chinese Americans.

Miller et al. (1987) argue that the intensity of language used influences the persuasive process. They look at language intensity in European Americans', Chinese Americans', and Japanese Americans' persuasive messages in Hawaii. Miller et al. report that ethnicity and gender combine to influence individuals'

TABLE 5.9 Anxiety, Uncertainty, and Effectiveness by Strength of Ethnic and Cultural Identities

| | *Ethnic Identity* | | *Cultural Identity* | |
	Weak	*Strong*	*Weak*	*Strong*
Anxiety	3.39	3.25	3.42	3.21
Uncertainty	3.24	3.28	3.33	3.18
Effectiveness	5.07	5.15	4.94	5.26

SOURCE: Survey of Asian American Communication.
NOTE: Scores range from 1 to 7.

language intensity. Specifically, Chinese American men and Japanese American men use more intense language than Chinese American women and Japanese American women. There is, however, no difference in language intensity between European American men and women. The results of the study are consistent with the relative roles of men and women in the three ethnic groups.

CONCLUSION

The research reviewed in this chapter indicates that there are differences in communication between Asian Americans and European Americans. Many of these differences are compatible with individualistic and collectivistic tendencies of European Americans and Asian Americans, respectively.

The research reviewed in this chapter also suggests that with the exception of ingroup stereotypes, there are not systematic differences in communication among Chinese Americans, Japanese Americans, Filipino Americans, Korean Americans, and Vietnamese Americans. The similarities in communication across these five ethnic groups appear to be due to shared collectivistic cultural heritages (see below). This is not to say that there are no differences in communication across Asian American ethnic groups. Only that the areas examined so far do not reveal differences. Future research that examines communication linked to dimensions of cultural variability on which Asian Americans differ may reveal consistent differences (e.g., Asian cultures differ in terms of power distance, and therefore, there may be differences in communication in relationships of unequal power).

Strength of ethnic and cultural identities appears to predict clear patterns of communication. Strength of ethnic identities is related to communication associated with Asian Americans' cultural heritages (e.g., high-context communication). Strength of cultural identities, in contrast, is associated with direct, low-context communication associated with the mainstream U.S. culture.

Asian Americans' independent and interdependent self construals influence their communication and appear to be better predictors of communication expectations and styles than ethnicity. The results for self construals for Asian Americans are consistent with research that has been conducted in Asian cultures. To illustrate, Gudykunst, Matsumoto et al. (1996) report that self construals are better predictors of communication styles than cultural differences. One reason for this is that cultural individualism-collectivism should only predict behavior that is based on cultural norms and rules (see Chapter 2). Communication styles are not based on norms or rules; they are based on individuals' preferences.

The communication patterns examined in this chapter focus on communication patterns between individuals. The role of communication in the acculturation of Asian immigrants to the United States is examined in the next chapter.

Chapter Six

Communication and Acculturation

$\mathcal{I}$n the previous chapters, I have discussed how Asian Americans' generation in the United States influences their communication. In these discussions, generation was treated like any other factor influencing Asian Americans' communication. Generation in the United States, however, is not like other factors I have discussed (e.g., ethnic identities). First-generation (i.e., individuals who come to the United States at age 13 or later) and 1.5-generation (individuals who come to the United States before age 13) experiences in the United States are different from other generations of Asian Americans' experiences. First-generation and 1.5-generation Asian Americans are born in Asian cultures and move to the United States. Second and subsequent generations of Asian Americans, in contrast, are born and raised in the United States.

The number of Asian immigrants has been increasing since the 1965 Immigration Act. Kitano and Daniels (1995) point out that "by the beginning of the 1990s, Asian Americans were constituting some 42 percent of all legal immigration to the United States and there was every indication that its incidence would continue to be high" (p. 19). Understanding Asian Americans' adaptation to the United States, therefore, remains an important issue.

Being born in one culture and moving to another culture requires some degree of acculturation to the new cultural environment. Asian immigrants' acculturation to the U.S. culture is influenced by their communication with members of the mainstream U.S. culture and by their communication with members of their ethnic communities. Communication is central to Asian immigrants' acculturation.

I divide this chapter into three sections. In the first section, I overview the general process of adaptation that occurs when Asian immigrants move to the United States. In the second section, I examine Asian immigrants' communication acculturation to the United States. In the final section, I discuss Asian Americans' interethnic dating and marriage. This material is included here because Asian Americans' interethnic marriage with European Americans is one indicator of immigrants' assimilation to the U.S. culture.

THE ACCULTURATION PROCESS

Asian immigrants' acculturation to the United States is an ongoing process. Asian immigrants' acculturation is influenced by adaptation processes that are occurring (e.g., learning about the U.S. culture), as well as by the U.S. view of how immigrant groups should integrate into the U.S. society (e.g., should immigrant groups assimilate into the U.S. culture?). I begin the discussion of the acculturation process with the individual adaptation process.

The Adaptation Process

When children grow up in Asian countries, they are socialized into the cultural practices and traditions of those countries by their parents, by the schools they attend, by their interactions with their peers, and by the mass media to which they are exposed. This process of enculturation teaches children what they need to know to be perceived as competent members of the Asian cultures in which they are raised, including competencies in verbal and nonverbal communication. Through the enculturation process, Asians develop cultural and ethnic identities associated with the cultures in which they are raised. In many, but not all, Asian cultures, ethnic and cultural identities are similar or the same because the cultures tend to be highly homogeneous.

When individuals born and raised in Asian cultures move to the United States and interact with members of the mainstream U.S. culture, several processes occur. They begin to learn new values and behaviors that help them function in the U.S. culture. This process of learning new values and behavior leads to some degree of acculturation into the U.S. culture. Kim (1978a) defines acculturation as "the process of cognitive, attitudinal, and behavioral adaptation to the new cultural system" (p. 199).

As Asian immigrants acculturate to the U.S. culture, they may forget or unlearn some of the values and/or behavior of their original cultures. This process is referred to as deculturation. As Asian immigrants deculturate with respect to their cultures of birth and acculturate to the U.S. culture, they begin to develop U.S. cultural identities. Asian immigrants' cultural identities associated with their cultures of birth are their ethnic identities in the United States.

The changes that Asian immigrants go through as they adapt to the U.S. culture generally do not involve changes in the basic values that they learned when they were socialized in their cultures of birth (e.g., the importance of the family ingroup). Basic values are hard to change. Rather, the changes that take place generally involve more superficial values and aspects of behavior (e.g., language spoken, meeting role expectations). Asian immigrants, for example, can fulfill role expectations in the U.S. culture (e.g., expectations for performing their jobs at work) without changing the basic values they learned when they were socialized in their native Asian cultures. Some Asian immigrants, however, may also change their basic values. How individual immigrants respond depends on their experiences in the United States and their adaptive readiness (discussed below).

Assimilation Versus Pluralism

All societies have explicit or implicit policies about how members of immigrant groups are expected to act with respect to the host societies. Some societies expect members of immigrant groups to assimilate (e.g., fully integrate) into the host societies. Other societies allow members of immigrant groups to continue to maintain their ethnicities (e.g., pluralism). The United States does not have an official policy, but until recently, assimilation was the implicit policy and what European Americans' expect of immigrants.

Assimilation refers to the process of giving up one culture and taking on the characteristics of another. In the case of Asian immigrants, this means giving up their Asian cultural heritages and becoming "Americans." Park (1950), for example, argues that the "cycle of contact, competition, accommodation, and eventual assimilation [among ethnic groups] is apparently progressive and unreversible" (p. 13). The predominate metaphor used for the assimilation view of interethnic relations is the "melting pot." In this metaphor, immigrants who come to the United States are expected to give up their old cultural ways and think and act like "Americans." In this way, they "melt" into the U.S. culture.

Gordon (1964) suggests that there are seven subprocesses of assimilation to the U.S. culture: (1) cultural or behavioral assimilation (e.g., changing cultural patterns to those of the United States; Gordon calls this type of assimilation "acculturation"), (2) structural assimilation (e.g., entering U.S. institutions), (3) marital assimilation (e.g., large-scale interethnic marriage), (4) identification assimilation (e.g., development of U.S. cultural identities), (5) attitude receptional assimilation (e.g., the "absence of prejudice"), (6) behavior receptional assimilation (e.g., the "absence of discrimination"), and (7) civic assimilation (e.g., the "absence of value and power conflict") (p. 71). Gordon agues that "not only is the assimilation process mainly a matter of degree, but, obviously, each of the stages or subprocesses distinguished above may take place in varying degrees" (p. 71).

Glazer (1993) points out that "in almost all of the discussion of Americanization until about World War II, the discussion had only Europeans in mind" (p. 126). In other words, it was assumed that immigrants from Europe would assimilate into the U.S. culture. Park (1930) argues that "in a vast and cosmopolitan society such as in America, the chief obstacle to assimilation seems to be not cultural differences but physical traits" (e.g., race) (p. 282).

The assimilation view of interethnic relations often leads to the use of race as a metaphor for "Americanness," where being "American" is viewed as being "white" (Morrison, 1992, p. 42). This metaphor only works, however, when the population of the United States is predominately white. It will not work when European Americans become a numerical minority sometime in the 21st century. The changes in the ethnic composition of the United States are redefining what it means to be an "American." "The deeper significance of American's becoming a majority nonwhite society is what it means to the national psyche, to individuals' sense of themselves and their nation—their idea of what it is to be an American" (Henry, 1990, p. 30).

The assimilation view of relations between ethnic groups was first challenged in the 1960s during the civil rights movement. Scholars studying ethnicity began to argue that total assimilation was not possible for non-white ethnic groups and that the "melting pot" actually never existed in the United States (e.g., Glazer & Moynihan, 1975; Novak, 1971; also see Alba & Nee, 1997). A pluralistic view of ethnicity began to emerge. In the pluralistic view, ethnicity "is an internal attitude which predisposes, but does not make compulsory, the display of ethnic identification in interaction. When it facilitates self-interest, ethnic identity will be made self-evident; it is left latent when it would hinder" (Hraba & Hoiberg, 1983, p. 385).

When members of ethnic groups decide to exert their ethnicities in the pluralistic view depends on the particular circumstances in which they find themselves (Glazer & Moynihan, 1975). The metaphor often used to explain the pluralistic model is a "tossed salad" where the parts of the salad (e.g., ethnic groups) exist in harmony side by side and, at the same time, combine to form something larger than any of the parts alone (e.g., the U.S. society).

Some writers contend that pluralism leads to problems with respect to relations between ethnic groups. Schlesinger (1991), for example, argues that

> instead of a transformative nation with an identity all of its own, America increasingly sees itself as preservative of old identities. Instead of a nation composed of individuals making their own free choices, America increasingly sees itself as composed of groups more or less indelible in their ethnic character. (p. 2)

Schlesinger goes on to suggest that these processes lead to ethnic polarization.

Assimilation is a one-way process. In the assimilation view of interethnic relations, Asian immigrants are expected to change to adapt to the U.S. culture (i.e., give up their old cultural ways and adopt U.S. cultural ways). The U.S. culture does not change; it absorbs the immigrants who are now "Americans." Some models of acculturation, in contrast, suggest that the adaptation of immigrants to the U.S. culture is a two-way process (e.g., Teske & Nelson, 1974). That is, immigrants adapt to the U.S. culture, and the U.S. culture adapts or changes in some way in response to the presence of the immigrants' ethnic groups. It can be argued that the larger the number of immigrants, the more the U.S. culture must adapt to the immigrants' ethnic groups.

The U.S. society has adapted, at least to some degree, to Asian immigrant groups. Wei (1993), for example, claims that the Asian American movement contributes to pluralism in the United States.

> Without necessarily intending to do so, the Asian American Movement has validated ethnic pluralism. Instead of increasing social fragmentation and Tribalism, as some people feared might happen, it has enlarged the defini-

tion of who can be an American by serving as an effective means for Asian Americans to assert, on their own terms, their right to belong to the society and to be treated as respected and responsible members of it. (pp. 274-275)

Without the Asian American movement, Asian Americans might not be accepted in the United States to the degree that they are.

Both assimilation and pluralism involve group-level relations between ethnic groups. That is, both focus on how members of ethnic groups arriving in the United States are expected or allowed to interact with the larger society and how members of the groups are treated. If the assimilation model predominates, at the individual level, immigrants are expected to give up their ethnic identities and develop strong cultural identities. If the pluralism model dominates, at the individual level, immigrants are allowed, but not necessarily expected, to maintain their ethnic identities. At the same time, they are allowed, but not necessarily expected to develop U.S. cultural identities. There is no inconsistency in having strong cultural identities and strong ethnic identities (Alba, 1990; Takezawa, 1995). Pluralism, therefore, allows individual immigrants to make choices about how they define themselves.

As indicated earlier, there are no official policies regarding assimilation or pluralism in the United States. The United States differs from countries like Canada where government policies dictate the co-existence of the Anglophone and Francophone cultures. Many European Americans in the United States still expect immigrants to assimilate into the U.S. culture. These same European Americans, however, also may racialize Asian Americans' ethnicity and treat Asian Americans as "aliens."

COMMUNICATION ACCULTURATION

Kim's (1977a, 1979a, 1988, in press) theory of communication acculturation provides a framework for examining the role of communication in Asian Americans' acculturation to the United States. Kim argues that immigrants' acculturation is influenced by their personal communication (e.g., their cognitive abilities, their affective orientations, and behavioral skills), their social communication (e.g., use of ethnic interpersonal and mass media communication channels, use of U.S. interpersonal and mass media communication channels), their adaptive predispositions (e.g., cultural/racial background, open-mindedness), and the host environmental conditions (e.g., hosts' attitudes toward immigrants).

Kim's theory is a general theory of communication acculturation (e.g., it applies to immigrants' acculturation in any culture). In this section, I use it as a framework for explaining Asian immigrants' acculturation to the U.S. culture. I begin with personal communication.

Personal Communication

Personal communication includes those factors that help Asian immigrants develop the competencies necessary to communicate effectively and appropriately in the United States (e.g., with European Americans). There are three major areas where competencies are necessary: cognitive abilities, affective orientations, and behavioral skills.

Cognitive Abilities. Cognitive abilities involve those abilities that help Asian immigrants understand the U.S. society and understand European Americans. Kim (1988) suggests that "during the initial phases of adaptation, strangers' [Asian immigrants'] perceptions of the new environment [the United States] tend to be overly simplistic, inaccurate, and unrealistic" (p. 94). Asian immigrants tend to use broad categories and stereotypes to understand the United States when they first arrive. Asian immigrants need to develop cognitive complexity with respect to the ways that they perceive the U.S. culture and "Americans" in order to acculturate.

As Asian immigrants live in the United States, they begin to learn about the U.S. culture, and they begin to see similarities and differences among "Americans." Recognizing similarities and differences leads to the development of cognitively complex perceptions of individuals in the United States, and this allows immigrants to develop the abilities to take the perspective of "Americans."

Kim (1978a) reports that Korean immigrants in Chicago are able to point out differences between Korean friendships and European American friendships more easily than they are able to point out similarities. She also observes that Korean immigrants perceptual complexity becomes more complex during their first three years in the United States, then levels off for the next five years. After about nine years in the United States, Korean immigrants develop additional perceptual complexity regarding the United States.

Asian immigrants' cognitive complexity influences how they view European Americans and their stay in the United States. Kim (1978a), for example, reports that the more cognitively complex Korean immigrants are, the more positive their attitudes are toward European Americans and the more satisfied they are with living in the United States. Kim (1977a, 1978a) also observes that perceptual complexity is associated positively with communicating with European Americans and the use of U.S. mass media. Yum (1982) notes that cognitive complexity is related positively to Korean immigrants' abilities to acquire information that helps them acculturate to Hawaii and to the diversity of their communication networks (e.g., the extent to which they included European Americans).

Another cognitive factor that influences Asian immigrants' acculturation is locus of control. Locus of control involves the extent to which individuals perceive that rewards come from within themselves or from external sources (Rotter, 1966). Yum (1988a) reports that European Americans have the highest internal locus of control, followed by Korean Americans and Japanese Americans, and that Filipino Americans have the least internal locus of control among the four groups in Hawaii. She also observes that having an internal locus of control is associated positively with communicating with European Americans for Korean Americans and Filipino Americans in Hawaii.

Affective Orientation. Asian immigrants not only need to develop cognitive complexity about the U.S. culture, they also need the emotional drive to want to adapt to the U.S. culture (Kim, 1988). The most critical affective orientation that influences Asian immigrants' adaptation to the United States is their adaptive or acculturation motivation. "The more intense their adaptive motivation, the more they are likely to show enthusiasm and dedication in their efforts to become functional in the host [U.S.] society" (Kim, 1988, pp. 99-100).

Kim (1977a) notes that acculturation motivation increases the longer Korean immigrants are in Chicago. She also observes that acculturation motivation is associated positively with participation in U.S. communication channels. To illustrate, the greater Korean immigrants' acculturation motivation, the more they engage in interpersonal communication with European Americans, the more they use U.S. mass media (Kim, 1977a), and the more they participate in U.S. social organizations (Kim, 1977b). Kim (1979b) also reports that acculturation motivation is associated positively with English competence among Indochinese refugees.

Behavioral Skills. In addition to cognitive abilities and affective orientations, Asian immigrants need behavioral skills to interact in the United States. Kim

(1988) points out that "through trial and error, strangers [Asian immigrants] are able to expand their behavioral capability to integrate sequences of verbal and non-verbal activities in a relatively smooth and automatic manner" (p. 103). Asian immigrants, for example, often learn to speak English by rehearsing what they want to say before they interact with European Americans. The more they practice speaking English, the more smooth and automatic their abilities become.

The major behavioral skill that facilitates Asian immigrants' adaptation to the United States is their English proficiency. Kim (1977a) reports that Korean immigrants' English proficiency is influenced by their age at immigration, their length of stay in the United States, and their education. The older Korean immigrants are when they immigrate to the United States, the less their English proficiency (Kim, 1977a). The more education Korean immigrants have in Korea before immigration, the greater their English competency (Kim, 1977a). The longer Korean immigrants stay in the United States, the greater their abilities to use English (Kim, 1977a; Yum, 1982). The more positive Indochinese refugees' self-images, the greater their English competency (Kim, 1989). Yum (1982) also observes that cognitive complexity and internal locus of control (as opposed to external locus of control) are associated positively with English fluency.

English competency influences many aspects of Asian immigrants' acculturation. English competency is associated positively with interpersonal communication with European Americans and use of U.S. mass media among Koreans (Kim, 1977a) and participating in U.S. organizations (Kim, 1977b). English proficiency is related positively with having European American acquaintances, casual friends, and intimate friends among Koreans (Kim, 1977b) and Indochinese refugees (Kim, 1979b). English competency is associated negatively with alienation from the U.S. society among Indochinese refugees (Kim, 1979b, 1990; Nicassio, 1985). English fluency also is associated positively with immigrants' abilities to gather the information they need to acculturate and having European Americans in their communication networks (Yum, 1982).

Social Communication

Kim (1988) argues that immigrants' culture learning comes through their social communication in the host culture. Social communication includes

Asian immigrants' interpersonal communication with European Americans and their use of U.S. mass media (e.g., newspapers, radio, television). In order to understand Asian immigrants' acculturation, their social communication with European Americans must be examined in light of their social communication within their ethnic communities. I begin with interpersonal communication.

Interpersonal Communication. Kim (1988) points out that "all migrants are removed from most, if not all, of the long-standing friends, family, relatives and co-workers with whom they participated in interpersonal communication activities" when they move to a new culture (pp. 105-106). Obviously, the extent to which this occurs for Asian migrants depends on the conditions of their move to the United States (e.g., some migrants move to the United States alone, some move to be with family members, some move with their families). Once Asians arrive in the United States, "They are faced with the task of constructing a new set of relationships that is critical to meeting their personal and social needs" (p. 106).

In the United States, Asian immigrants can form relationships with other members of their ethnic groups, European Americans, or members of other ethnic groups. My focus in this section is Asian Americans' communication with members of their own ethnic groups or with European Americans. Most Asian immigrants form relationships both with members of their ethnic groups and with European Americans. In fact, communication with members of Asian Americans' own ethnic communities is associated positively with communication with European Americans (Kim, 1978a, 1979b; Inglis & Gudykunst, 1982).

The length of Asian immigrants' stay in the United States influences their communication with members of their ethnic communities and their communication with European Americans. The number of ethnic and European American acquaintances both increase with Koreans' length of stay in the United States (Kim, 1978a). This does not mean, however, that length of stay increases the overall amount of ethnic communication. The longer the length of stay, the less the communication with members of the ethnic communities and the greater the communication with European Americans (Kim, 1978b).

How Asian immigrants view themselves influences their interactions with European Americans. Indochinese refugees' self-images, for example, are associated positively with having European American acquaintances (Kim, 1989). Informal and formal communication with members of the mainstream

U.S. culture helps Asian immigrants ease their loneliness and find solutions for handling their problems (Kim, in press). At the same time, interpersonal contacts in the mainstream culture allows Asian immigrants to learn U.S. cultural values. Overall, involvement in the U.S. culture is associated positively with personal and interpersonal adjustment to the United States (Nguyen, Messe, & Stollak, 1999).

Asian immigrants' interpersonal communication with European Americans is associated positively with their use of U.S. mass media (Kim, 1978a; Inglis & Gudykunst, 1982). Interpersonal communication with members of the mainstream culture and use of U.S. media helps immigrants understand the U.S. culture (Lindgren & Yu, 1975). Asian immigrants interpersonal communication with European Americans also is related positively with their attitudes toward European Americans and with their satisfaction with living in the United States (Kim, 1978a).

Asian immigrants' ethnic communication also influences their acculturation. Ethnic communication is associated positively with satisfaction with living in the United States, especially in the short term (but the association is much higher between communication with European Americans and satisfaction; Kim, 1978a). Involvement in the ethnic community is associated negatively with personal adjustment (i.e., distress; Nyuyen et al., 1999). Emphasizing ethnic communication appears to have a negative influence on overall acculturation, especially in the later stages of acculturation (J. Kim, 1980). Emphasizing ethnic communication inhibits developing competence in U.S. communication patterns and participating in U.S. social processes which, in turn, hinders long-term acculturation (Yang, 1988). The influence of ethnic communication on acculturation is particularly problematic when the coethnics are poorly acculturated (Hsu, Grant, & Huang, 1993).

Ethnic communication helps immigrants initially adjust to living in the United States and provides social support during the initial phases of acculturation. Involvement in the ethnic community is associated positively with having good family relationships (Nguyen et al., 1999). Ethnic communication decreases as immigrants become involved in U.S. social processes and learn English (Kim, Lee, & Jeong, 1982; Kim, 1989, 1990). Over the long term, ethnic interpersonal communication, especially the use of ethnic languages, facilitates immigrants' maintaining their ethnic identities. Maintaining ethnic identities, in turn, might take away from long-term acculturation, but this does not have to be the case. Recall from the discussion of ethnic and cultural identities in Chapter 4 that ethnic and cultural identities are independent of each other. Asian immigrants can maintain strong ethnic identities *and,* at the same time, develop strong U.S. cultural identities. Interacting with other members of their ethnic communities appears to be important for Asian Americans to be comfortable with their place in the U.S. society (e.g., Gehrie, 1976; Osajima, 1989).

There are differences in social communication across Asian American ethnic groups. Kim (1978b) reports that a greater percentage of Korean Americans (66.0%) have acquaintances with members of their own ethnic group than do Japanese Americans (35.3%). A greater percentage of Japanese Americans (46.6%), in contrast, have European American acquaintances than do Korean Americans (23.4%). A greater percentage of Japanese Americans have casual friends among their own group (49.8%) and with European Americans (78.6%) than do Korean Americans (own group = 38.8%; European Americans = 16.2%). About the same percentage of Japanese Americans (41.9%) and Korean Americans (43.0%) have intimate friends from their own ethnic group, but a greater percentage of Japanese Americans (73.6%) have intimate friendships with European Americans than Korean Americans (18.4%).

Brody, Rimmer, and Trotter (1999) look at interaction patterns of Vietnamese Americans in southern California. When asked "With whom do you socialize," 11.8% of the respondents indicate only with Vietnamese Americans, 37.4% indicate more Vietnamese Americans than non-Vietnamese Americans, 43.0% indicate both equally, and 7.7% indicate more non-Vietnamese Americans than Vietnamese Americans.

Kim (1978b) reports that *Issei* and *Sansei* have similar patterns of interpersonal communication; members of both generations have more relationships with European Americans than with Japanese Americans. The *Nisei,* in contrast, have as many relationships with Japanese Americans as with European Americans. Kim suggests that this may be due to the *Nisei*'s being the primary organizers of activities in the Japanese American community in Chicago. Kim also reports that *Issei* have more intimate friendships with non-European Americans than do *Nisei* or *Sansei.*

Overall, Kim (1978b) notes that Japanese Americans are more active in interpersonal communication with European Americans than are Korean Americans. For both groups, however, the number of communication relationships outside their own ethnic group decreases as the relationships become more intimate (e.g., there is less communication with European American intimate friends than with European American acquaintances).

Yum (1983) reports that European Americans have the largest communication networks in Hawaii followed by Filipino Americans, Japanese Americans, and Korean Americans (the only two groups not significantly different are European Americans and Filipino Americans). Yum also looks at whether social networks can predict acquiring information needed to acculturate for Korean Americans and Filipino Americans (the two immigrant groups in her study). She observes that the size of communication networks, frequency of interaction with European Americans, and the ethnic diversity of communication networks predict acquiring information needed to acculturate for Korean immigrants. These same factors, however, do not predict Filipino Americans' acquisition of information. This may be because Filipino Americans have more of the information needed to acculturate than Korean Americans.

Mass Communication. Depending on where they live, Asian immigrants can use either U.S. mass media (e.g., newspapers, radio, television), ethnic media, or both. Ethnic media tend to be available in areas where there are large ethnic communities. Use of ethnic media decreases and use of U.S. media increases with length of stay in the United States (Kim, 1978a). The use of ethnic media is related inversely to the use of U.S. media (Kim, 1978a).

Kim (1988) argues that the use of host mass media (e.g., Asian immigrants' use of U.S. media) allows immigrants to "learn about the broader ranges of the host cultural elements—its aspirations, tradition, history, myths, art, work, play and humor, as well as specific current issues and events" (p. 115). The use of U.S. media, therefore, provides Asian immigrants with information about European Americans and the U.S. culture that is not readily available from their interpersonal interactions with European Americans. U.S. newspapers and television also play an important role in immigrants' political socialization (Chaffee, Nass, & Yang, 1990).

Nagata (1969) observes that there are differences in U.S. media use among *Issei, Nisei,* and *Sansei.* The later the generation in the United States, the more U.S. media are used. Chang (1972) notes differences based on ethnic identity for Korean immigrants.

The use of U.S. media influences Asian immigrants' acculturation. The use of U.S. media, for example, is associated positively with attitudes toward European Americans (Inglis & Gudykunst, 1982; Kim, 1978a). Korean immigrants' use of U.S. media also is associated positively with their level of satisfaction with living in the United States (Inglis & Gudykunst, 1982; Kim, 1978a). Use of host mass media also is associated negatively with alienation toward the U.S. society among Indochinese refugees (Kim, 1990).

The length of time in the United States and English proficiency are associated negatively with reading ethnic newspapers (Kim, in press). The amount of interpersonal communication with European Americans is related negatively with use of ethnic media (Kim, 1978a). Overall, ethnic media use is less influential on maintaining ethnicity than is ethnic interpersonal communication (Lam, 1980).

Adaptation Predisposition

Kim (1988) isolates three factors that contribute to immigrants' adaptation predispositions: cultural/racial backgrounds, personality attributes, and orientation toward change. One factor that influences Asian immigrants predisposition to adapt to the United States has to do with the cultural differences between their native cultures and the United States (see Chapter 2). The more similar the native and host cultures are, the easier it is for immigrants to adjust to the host culture. Asian immigrants' race also influences how European Americans respond to them (see below).

Kim (1988) suggests that immigrants' personalities influence their acculturation in host cultures. Immigrants who are able to adapt most easily to new cultural environments tend to be those who are "open" and "resilient." Openness involves personality attributes such as open-mindedness and tolerance for ambiguity. Resilience includes attributes such as internal locus of control, persistence, self-confidence, and resourcefulness.

The extent to which immigrants are prepared for change also influences their acculturation. Kim (1988) suggests that one thing that prepares immigrants for change is formal education. Education expands individuals' cognitive abilities. Formal education is associated positively with Korean immigrants' acculturation potential, the availability of U.S. media, and Korean immigrants' interaction potential (Kim, 1977a). Formal education also is related positively to having European American acquaintances, casual friends, intimate friends, and participating in U.S. organizations (Kim, 1977b).

The circumstances of Asian immigrants' move to the United States also influence preparedness for change. If immigrants are able to plan ahead for their move to the United States, for example, their transition will be much easier than if they are forced to leave their homeland (e.g., refugees).

Host Environment Conditions

Host environmental conditions involve conditions in the U.S. society that influence Asian immigrants' adaptation to the U.S. culture. Numerous factors influence the host environmental conditions. In this section, I address four factors: interaction potential, institutional completeness of Asian Americans' ethnic communities, European Americans' attitudes toward immigrants, and the modes with which immigrants are incorporated in the U.S. culture.

Interaction Potential. Interaction potential involves the hosts' receptivity toward immigrants and the degree of opportunities that Asian immigrants have to interact with European Americans (Kim, 1977a). Immigrants tend to move to areas where they have some access to an ethnic support system (e.g., family, friends, ethnic organizations, ethnic churches; see institutional completeness in next section) (Chan & Lam, 1987; Hurh & Kim, 1990). This provides immigrants with a sense of security (Kim, in press). Living among coethnics, however, limits the potential that Asian immigrants have for interacting with European Americans. Living among members of the mainstream culture provides interaction potential to socialize with European Americans.

Interaction potential increases with length of stay in the United States (Kim, 1977a). Interaction potential also is associated positively with communicating with European Americans (Kim, 1977a), as well as having European American acquaintances, casual friends, and intimate friends (Kim, 1977b).

Institutional Completeness of Ethnic Communities. Breton (1964) argues that the number and strength of ethnic institutions (e.g., churches, fraternal organizations) influences immigrants' experiences. Breton refers to this as "institutional completeness." The greater the institutional completeness of ethnic communities, the more support the communities provide for immigrants in host cultures. Breton reports that immigrants living in communities with high levels of institutional completeness tend to form high proportions of their personal relations in the new culture within their ethnic groups.

Breton (1964) observes that different types of institutions have different influences on immigrants. Religious institutions have the greatest effect on immigrants, followed by ethnic publications; welfare organizations have the least influence. The presence of ethnic churches in a community, for example, leads to high levels of intraethnic relations, even among immigrants who are not members of the churches.

Kim's (1977a, 1977b, 1978a) research on the communication acculturation of Korean immigrants was conducted in Chicago. Chicago has a strong Korean ethnic community (about 25,000 Koreans when she conducted the research). It includes Korean churches, informal social groups, formal civic associations, numerous restaurants, numerous ethnic stores, Korean newspapers published in Korean, and Korean radio/television broadcasts. Many Koreans in Chicago also live in a centralized area.

Inglis and Gudykunst (1982) compared Kim's findings with data from Koreans in Hartford, Connecticut, a community with much less institutional completeness (only about 1,000 Koreans at the time the study was conducted). The Koreans were dispersed throughout the greater Hartford area at the time of the study. At the time of the study, there were two Korean churches, three Korean stores, and two Korean restaurants in Hartford. There were no Korean media available in Hartford.

There are several differences in the communication patterns in Kim's Chicago study and Inglis and Gudykunst's Hartford study. The Koreans in Hartford, for example, have lower levels of intraethnic communication with acquaintances than do the Koreans in Chicago. The levels of intraethnic communication with intimate friends is relatively similar in the two cities. The Chicago community provides more interaction potential for intraethnic communication than the Hartford community because of its size and institutional completeness. There also are several similarities in communication patterns in Chicago and Hartford. In both cities, Koreans who are active in intraethnic communication are active in interethnic communication with European Americans. One reason these two may be associated is that the immigrants may have used both Korean style communication and U.S. style communication in their intraethnic relationships. Broom and Kitsuse (1955) point out that "the ethnic community is a relatively safe place in which acculturated forms may be tried out, and interaction with the dominant group may be rehearsed" (p. 45). It may also be that when Koreans communicate within their ethnic networks they gather information from other Koreans that they can use to communicate with European Americans.

Overall, there are many similarities between the communication patterns of Koreans in Chicago and Hartford. The Hartford community is much less institutionally complete than the Chicago community, but the Hartford community does have some formal ethnic institutions. Breton (1964) suggests that it is not simply the numbers of ethnic institutions that is critical; rather it is the presence or absence of formal institutions. The presence of any formal institutions (particularly churches) provides the structure for ethnic communication to be supported.

European Americans' Attitudes Toward Immigrants. European Americans' attitudes toward immigrants affects immigrants' adaptation in the United States. Generally, European Americans believe that the level of immigration to the

United States should be lower than it has been in recent years. A nationwide Roper Center Poll conducted in 1990 (reported by Simon, 1993), for example, asked Americans whether the number of immigrants allowed into the United States should be more/increase (9%), should be the same/present level (29%), or should be fewer/decrease (48%) (14% indicated no opinion/don't know). This poll clearly suggests a preference that immigration not increase or should decrease in the future.

Perceptions of specific ethnic groups in the United States influence the acculturation experiences of members of those ethnic groups. A nationwide Gallup Poll conducted in 1982 (reported by Simon, 1993) examined perceptions of four Asian immigrant groups. Respondents were asked their perceptions of the immigrant groups in light of the groups' contribution to the U.S. society. Generally, perceptions of Japanese immigrants and Chinese immigrants are most positive: Japanese—good (47%), bad (18%); Chinese—good (44%), bad (19%). (Note: "Mixed feelings" and "don't know" responses are not reported.) Perceptions of Korean immigrants and Vietnamese immigrants are less positive and about the same: Koreans—good (24%), bad (30%); Vietnamese—good (20%), bad (38%). These results suggest that Japanese immigrants and Chinese immigrants generally have a more positive reception in the United States than Korean immigrants or Vietnamese immigrants. The perceptions of specific groups, however, might vary tremendously in different locations in the United States.

Most voters in the United States tend to think that Asian Americans do not experience discrimination (McQueen, 1991; see Cummings & Lambert, 1997, for African American anti-Asian sentiment). Similarly, only a small percentage of Asian Americans in California believe that "most people are prejudiced" (5%). Most Asian Americans in California think that "some people are prejudiced" (52%; 42% think "most people are not prejudiced") (Cain & Kiewiet, 1986). When the same Asian Americans are asked if they have experienced discrimination, 30% indicate they have experienced social discrimination and 15% have experienced economic discrimination. A poll of legal immigrants indicates that 90% feel welcome in the United States and 61% say they have never experienced discrimination as immigrants (*USA Today,* July 5, 1995, p. A1).

O'Brien and Fugita (1983) report that only a small percentage of *Nisei* (31.3%) and *Sansei* (12.8%) have experienced a "considerable amount" or a "great deal" of discrimination. A majority of *Nisei* (54.9%) and *Sansei* (54.8%) think there is job discrimination against Japanese Americans. The vast majority of *Nisei* (76.0%) and *Sansei* (74.3%) think that Japanese Americans "currently experience social discrimination."

The U.S. Commission on Civil Rights (1986, 1992) documents anti-Asian prejudice and discrimination. To illustrate, the Commission cites the distribution of flyers calling for boycotting Asian Americans' businesses and realtors who sell houses to Asian Americans in Brooklyn, New York, and Hayward, California. The Commission also reports incidents of vandalism, arson, and individuals throwing rocks/eggs at Asian Americans' homes. Based on recent figures, Asian Americans are the third most frequent victims of hate crimes.

Modes of Incorporating Immigrants. Portes and Rumbaut (1990) suggest that how the U.S. society responds to various immigrant groups is a function of three processes: government policies, societal reception, and ethnic communities. Government policies can be receptive, indifferent, or hostile. Policies are receptive when immigrants are allowed legal entry and given relocation assistance; policies are indifferent when legal entry is allowed, but there is no assistance; policies are hostile when there is active opposition to a group's entry. Societal reception can be either "prejudiced" or "non-prejudiced" (actually there is always some degree of prejudice). Portes and Rumbaut contend that the response to non-European American immigrants tends to be prejudiced (e.g., it is based on racial differences). Ethnic communities can be either weak (e.g., small numbers in the ethnic group, little occupational diversity such as only manual laborers) or strong (e.g., large numbers in the ethnic group, high occupational diversity; strong ethnic communities tend to have some degree of institutional completeness).

Portes and Rumbaut (1990) argue that immigrants' reception in the United States is based on a combination of the three processes. To illustrate, Vietnamese immigration involved receptive government policies (i.e., immigration was legal and most received relocation assistance). The societal response was "prejudiced." Baldwin (1984), for example, reports that 54% of the European Americans in Orange County, California, thought Vietnamese would take jobs away from European Americans, and 44% thought they were a source of potential violence. Initially, the Vietnamese ethnic community was weak (i.e., recall that initially Vietnamese were spread out throughout the United States so that the immigrants would not have a large influence on any specific community). As the Vietnamese moved around after their initial placement, however, the ethnic communities became strong (i.e., they moved to locations where there were large Vietnamese populations such as Little Saigon).

Portes and Rumbaut (1990) suggest that Koreans' immigration experience was different from the Vietnamese experience. The government policies toward Koreans was indifferent (i.e., their immigration was/is legal, but they received no relocation assistance). Like the Vietnamese, the Koreans experience a preju-diced societal reception. Koreans tend to immigrate to cities with existing eth-nic communities (e.g., Los Angeles, Chicago, New York) so their ethnic com-munities tend to be strong on arrival.

INTERETHNIC DATING AND MARRIAGE

A discussion of interethnic dating and interethnic marriage may seem out of place in a chapter on communication and acculturation. It is, nevertheless, an appropriate topic for this chapter. Recall Gordon's (1964) discussion of the seven subprocesses involved in assimilation. One of the seven sub-processes is marital assimilation. The extent to which Asian Americans marry European Americans is one indicator of their assimilation into the U.S. culture. To place the discussion of interethnic marriage in context, I begin with interethnic dating.

Interethnic Dating

There are relatively few studies of Asian Americans' interethnic dating. Some general patterns, however, appear to emerge from the studies that have been conducted.

Spickard (1989) suggests that generation in the United States is one of the major factors that influence Asian Americans' interethnic dating. He claims that Asian Americans' interethnic dating with European Americans is preva-lent among third-generation Asian Americans who do not live in ethnic en-claves and those who live outside the western part of the United States (e.g., away from large groups of Asian Americans). Nagata (1993) observes that Cal-ifornia *Sansei* are more likely to have dated another Japanese American than *Sansei* living in other parts of the country. She suggests this is because of the higher concentration of Japanese Americans in California than in other parts of the country. Johnson and Ogasawara (1984) also point out that Asian Ameri-cans from higher socioeconomic groups are more likely to date out of their eth-nic groups than those from lower socioeconomic groups.

Liu, Campbell, and Condie (1995) contend that Asian Americans prefer to date European Americans over members of other ethnic groups (e.g., of those not from their own group). Similarly, Revilla (1989) reports that only 31% of Filipino Americans prefer to date/marry members of their own group, and a vast majority of those who prefer non-Filipino Americans, prefer European

Americans. One reason for preferring European Americans may be who Asian Americans perceive to be attractive. Fujino (1992), for example, reports that both European Americans and Asian Americans rate European Americans as more attractive than Asian Americans.

Kitano et al. (1984) point out that Asian American women date outside their ethnic groups more than Asian American males. Two recent studies (Shinagawa & Pang, 1996; Tuan, 1998) suggest that the rate is leveling off for young Asian Americans. There are a couple of possible explanations for women dating outside their ethnic groups more than men.

One reason Asian American women may date out of their ethnic groups more than Asian American men has to do with gender stereotypes. Weiss (1970), for example, claims that European American men have positive stereotypes of Chinese American women (e.g., "sexy," "quiet," "subservient"). Chinese American women in turn have negative stereotypes of Chinese American men (e.g., "weak," "traditional," "old-fashioned") and positive stereotypes of European American men (e.g., "suave," "cool," "sophisticated," "sexy"). When asked why they dated Chinese American men, Chinese American women say things like "parental coercion," "respect for tradition," and "race conscious-ness." When asked about dating European American men, Chinese American women say things like they are "more fun on dates" and "more considerate" than Chinese American men, and they have "easygoing personalities." The combination of stereotypes and preconceptions facilitates Chinese American women dating European American men.

The influence of stereotyping on interethnic dating also may involve Asian American women not fitting Asian American men's stereotypes. One Japanese American woman who is married to a European American says:

[European Americans] were the only guys I was attracted to, felt more com-fortable with. I always would feel that Japanese guys [pause] I just wasn't what they were looking for, and they weren't what I was looking for either because I didn't fit into that conforming mold. I never kept up with all the things that were important to Japanese girls so I don't think I was desirable to them [Japanese guys], that I was ever on the list. And all the guys liked the same girls. There'd really be like a list of who was not desirable. I'm too outspoken and too intimidating. (Tuan, 1998, p. 121)

This woman's preference may be a function of both her stereotypes of Japanese American men and Japanese American men's stereotypes of Japanese American women.

Another potential explanation for Asian American women engaging in interethnic dating more than Asian American men involves issues of racism. Fujino (1992) suggests that Asian American men are expected to initiate dates. Since they are expected to initiate dates, Asian American men who perceive that they are subject to racism may not tend to initiate dates with European American women. Asian American women, in contrast, can determine whether European American men who approach them are highly racist and choose not to date those who are. Fujino argues that Asian American women's dating patterns, therefore, are not as influenced by racism as Asian American men's dating patterns.

Fujino (1997) examines interethnic dating among Chinese Americans, European Americans, and Japanese Americans at the University of California, Los Angeles. Overall, she finds that Japanese Americans date out of their ethnic group more than Chinese Americans, who date out of their group more than European Americans. A large percentage of all three groups, however, had at least one interethnic date: Japanese American men (86.5%), Japanese American women (85.7%), Chinese American men (75.3%), Chinese American women (69.2%), European American men (62.5%), and European American women (52.6%). The pattern is a little different when the overall percentage of dates *not* from their own ethnic groups is examined: Japanese Americans (64%), Chinese Americans (54%), European Americans (22%).

Fujino (1997) reports that Asian American women prefer to date and marry members of their own ethnic groups, followed by European Americans, and then other Asian Americans. Asian American men also prefer to date and marry members of their own groups, followed by other Asian Americans, then European Americans. Fujino also observes that Asian Americans who date European Americans had more European Americans in their high schools and neighborhoods than those who do not date European Americans. Asian American women who date European Americans have more liberal attitudes toward women's roles and place higher value on dating partners' attractiveness than those who do not date European Americans.

Fujino (1997) also notes that Asian American women who date European Americans come from families who have lived in the United States longer than those who do not date European Americans. Only 41% of the first-generation Asian American women had "significant" dating relationships with European Americans, while 65% of the second-generation Asian American women had "significant" dating relationships with European Americans, and 77% of the third-generation Asian American women had "significant" dating relationships with European Americans.

Interethnic Marriage

Interracial marriages have always been legal in some states, but 38 states had antimiscegenation laws at one time. To illustrate, California passed a law prohibiting marriages between people of European descent with "Negroes," "Mulattos," "Indians," "Mongolians," and people of "mixed-blood" in 1880. The law was amended in 1934 to include "Malays." The California law was found unconstitutional in 1948. Like California, 21 other state laws were overturned or repealed, but it was not until 1967 that the last 16 state laws were declared unconstitutional (U.S. Supreme Court, *Loving v. Virginia*).

Even though interethnic marriage is legal, there is still opposition to it in the United States. Fang, Sidanius, and Pratto (1998), for example, report that European Americans score 2.97 (5 = very much opposed) regarding interethnic marriages with Asian Americans. Asian Americans score 2.69 with respect to interethnic marriages to European Americans.

Since the 1940s, there have been numerous studies of the rates of Asian American interethnic marriage (e.g., Johnson & Ogasawara, 1984; Kikumura & Kitano, 1973; Kitano & Chai, 1982; Kitano, Fujino, & Sato, 1998; Kitano & Yeung, 1982; Kitano et al., 1984; Lee & Yamanaka, 1990; Shinagawa & Pang, 1988; Spickard, 1989; Sung, 1990). Generally, these studies suggest that Asian American women marry outside their ethnic group more than Asian American men. These studies also indicate that Japanese Americans tend to marry outside their ethnic group more than other Asian American ethnic groups. Shinagawa (1996) reports that 31.2% of Asian American husbands and 40.4% of Asian American wives had spouses from other ethnic groups in 1990. Japanese Americans (51.9%) and Filipino Americans (40.2%) account for the highest percentages of interethnic marriage.

Lee and Yamanaka (1990) examine interethnic marriage rates for Asian American men and women throughout the United States in 1980, and whether they married European Americans or members of other ethnic groups. (Note: The data are percentages of interethnic marriages.)

	Overall Rates of Interethnic Marriages		Marriages With European Americans	
	Females	Males	Females	Males
Chinese Americans	16.8	14.4	12.2	8.3
Filipino Americans	35.5	22.2	27.5	15.1
Japanese Americans	41.6	21.3	33.9	13.7
Korean Americans	44.5	7.5	36.1	4.4
Vietnamese Americans	28.9	5.5	24.9	4.2

These data clearly support the tendency for women to marry out of their ethnic groups more than men and for Asian Americans to marry European Americans more than members of other groups.

Asian Americans' interethnic marriage rates vary depending on the part of the country in which they live. Nagata (1993), for example, reports that *Sansei* in California have the lowest interethnic marriage rate (36%) and *Sansei* in the Midwest have the highest (72%), with those in the Northwest (46%) and on the East Coast (53%) in the middle. She suggests that this is due to the concentration of Japanese Americans in California. *Sansei* in California can meet more potential Japanese American spouses than those in other areas. Nagata also notes that religion influences interethnic marriages, with Christians (57%) marrying outside their ethnic group more than Buddhists (28%).

Kitano et al. (1998) examine interethnic marriages in Los Angeles and in Hawaii. The interethnic marriage rates in Los Angeles in 1989 are higher than in the country as a whole for most groups: Chinese Americans (33.9%), Filipino Americans (40.8%), Japanese Americans (51.9%), Korean Americans (11.0%), and Vietnamese Americans (26.5%) (Kitano et al., 1998, Table 7.5, p. 239). (Note: Gender breakdowns are not possible because the rates for gender were miscalculated in Table 7.5.) The Korean American interethnic marriage rate in 1989 is lower than it had been in earlier years in Los Angeles (e.g., in 1977 it was 34.1%).

Kitano et al. (1998, Table 7.6, p. 248) report that the interethnic marriage rates in Hawaii during the period 1980-1989 are even higher than those in Los Angeles:

	Men	Women
Chinese Americans	63.7%	66.9%
Filipino Americans	44.6%	54.3%
Japanese Americans	41.6%	47.6%
Korean Americans	47.3%	76.4%
Vietnamese Americans	30.7%	62.8%

Kitano et al. note that the interethnic marriage rate in Hawaii generally has increased since 1912 (see Fu & Heaton, 1997). (Note: Since European Americans are not in the numerical majority in Hawaii, marriage with them is not a good indicator of assimilation.)

Kitano et al. (1998) isolate the best predictors of Asian Americans' interethnic marriage using data from Los Angeles. They report that generation is the best predictor of interethnic marriage across Asian American ethnic groups. The later the generation in the United States, the greater the interethnic marriage rate. Second-generation Asian Americans are three times more likely to marry outside their ethnic groups than first-generation Asian Americans. Third-generation Asian Americans are five times more likely to marry outside their ethnic groups than first-generation Asian Americans.

Kitano et al. (1998) also observe that ethnicity influences interethnic marriage. Korean Americans are less likely to marry outside their group than Japanese Americans. For women, Chinese Americans and Filipino Americans are more likely to marry outside their group than Japanese Americans. Younger Asian American men are more likely to marry outside their ethnic groups than older Asian American men.

There are other factors that appear to influence Asian Americans interethnic marriage. Johnson and Ogasawara (1984) note that Asian Americans from higher socioeconomic groups marry outside their groups more than Asian Americans from lower socioeconomic groups. Sung (1990) observes that Asian American spouses in interethnic marriages in New York tend to be more educated, have higher incomes, and be older than Asian American spouses in intraethnic marriages.

Fong and Yung (1995-1996) interviewed Chinese Americans and Japanese Americans married to European Americans. They observe that acculturation to the United States is related to marrying European Americans; the more acculturated Asian Americans are, the more likely they are to marry European Americans. They also note that aversion to the Asian American patriarchy, disliking some aspects of their ethnic groups, and wanting to avoid traditional marriages like their parents lead Asian Americans to marry European Americans.

CONCLUSION

Communication is central to Asian immigrants' acculturation to the U.S. culture. It is through communication with European Americans and the use of U.S. mass media that Asian immigrants learn the rules of the U.S. culture and eventually acculturate. As Asian immigrants acculturate to the U.S. culture, they develop U.S. cultural identities.

Asian immigrants' communication with members of their ethnic groups and use of ethnic mass media plays an important role in their initial adaptation to the United States. Emphasizing ethnic communication over the long term leads to maintaining strong ethnic identities.

One indicator of Asian Americans' assimilation into the U.S. culture is interethnic marriages with European Americans. Asian American women tend to marry European Americans more than Asian American men. Japanese Americans tend to marry European Americans more than members of other Asian American ethnic groups. Generation in the United States influences Asian Americans' tendencies to marry outside their ethnic groups; the later the generation in the United States, the more likely Asian Americans are to marry outside their ethnic groups.

Appendix

Survey of Asian American Communication

$\mathcal{T}$he Survey of Asian American Communication was designed to begin to fill some of the gaps regarding data on Asian Americans' communication. The data were collected in southern California using a "snowball" sampling technique. The data are clearly not representative of all Asian Americans throughout the United States or Asian Americans in southern California. The data, nevertheless, can provide insight into similarities and differences across the various Asian American ethnic groups that have not been examined before.

My purpose in this appendix is to outline the methods used to collect the data and to explain how the variables were measured. I conclude the appendix with a brief overview of the statistical analyses that were conducted.

RESPONDENTS

Three hundred and thirty-one Asian Americans participated in this study. The respondents included only individuals who identified themselves as Asian Americans. Data were collected mainly from students at a midsize West Coast

195

university. Some students, however, were asked to have their relatives (e.g., their parents) fill out the questionnaire in order to ensure a wide variety of Asian Americans participating in the study. In addition, some questionnaires were collected at Asian American ethnic churches.

The sample consisted of 74 Chinese Americans (30 males, 44 females), 55 Japanese Americans (23 males, 32 females), 43 Korean Americans (21 males, 22 females), 74 Filipino Americans (30 males, 44 females), 49 Vietnamese Americans (14 males, 35 females), 9 from other groups (e.g., Asian Indian Americans, Cambodian Americans; 6 males, 3 females), and 27 of mixed heritage (e.g., Japanese American/European American; 6 males, 21 females). Only data from Chinese Americans, Filipino Americans, Japanese Americans, Korean Americans, and Vietnamese Americans were used in the analyses.

The sample included 131 first-generation Asian Americans, 90 second-generation Asian Americans, 52 third-generation Asian Americans, 28 fourth-generation Asian Americans, and 10 fifth-generation Asian Americans (24 did not report generation). One hundred and fifty-three of the respondents were born in the United States and 172 outside the United States (10 did not indicate where they were born). Almost half (48.3%) of those not born in the United States arrived before age 10; 14.6% arrived between ages 10 and 12. Many of those who arrived at a very young age indicated that they were second generation. (Note: 1.5 generation was not a response option.)

The average age of the sample was 26.61 ($SD = 11.75$). Eighty-four of the respondents were married, and 63 of the spouses were from the same ethnic group.

Ideally, the sample would have been larger than it is. My goal was to collect data from 100 members of each of the five groups studied. This, however, proved to be impossible.

MEASUREMENT

All measures were included in a questionnaire booklet. Only respondents 18 or over were asked to participate. Respondents were informed that participation was voluntary and that by returning a questionnaire they were giving consent to participate. The items used to measure identities and self construals were mixed together randomly in one section. The communication style items, value items, stereotype items, and expectation items were placed randomly in separate sections.

Ethnic Identities

Strength of ethnic identities was measured by adapting a scale developed by Ting-Toomey et al. (2000). The eight items used to measure ethnic identities were: "I think a lot about how my life will be affected by my ethnic group membership." "In order to learn more about my ethnic background, I have often talked to other people about my ethnic group." "I am involved with activities with my ethnic group." "I feel a strong attachment to being a member of my ethnic group." "I involve myself in causes that will help my ethnic group." "I am determined to find my ethnic identity." "I feel excitement in my own ethnic environment." and "The ethnic group I belong to is important to my sense of what kind of person I am." The scale for the items ranged from 1 (*strongly disagree*) to 7 (*strongly agree*). Combination of the items yielded a reliable scale (alpha = .85).

For several analyses, ethnic identity was divided using a median split (median = 4.38). Those respondents above the median were treated as the strong ethnic identity group, and those at the median or below were treated as the weak ethnic identity group.

Cultural Identities

Strength of cultural identities was measured by adapting a scale developed by Ting-Toomey et al. (2000). The five items measuring cultural identities were: "I generally identify strongly with the overall US culture." "It is important for me to identify with the overall US culture." "The overall US culture is an important reflection of who I am." "It is important for me to follow the overall US cultural values." and "I usually go by my values of the overall US culture." The scale for the items ranged from 1 (*strongly disagree*) to 7 (*strongly agree*). Combination of the items yielded a reliable scale (alpha = .81).

In several analyses, cultural identity was divided using a median split (median = 4.60). Those respondents above the median were treated as the strong cultural identity group, and those at the median or below were treated as the weak cultural identity group.

Identity Types

In the orthogonal model analyses, ethnic and cultural identities were treated as separate independent variables. In the typological model analyses, ethnic and cultural identities were combined to form the four types: strong cultural identities/strong ethnic identities (integration in Berry's terms), strong cultural identities/weak ethnic identities (assimilation), weak cultural identities/strong ethnic identities (separation), and weak cultural identities/weak ethnic identities (marginalization).

Individualistic Values

Individual and collectivistic values were measured using values developed by Schwartz (1992). Seven individualistic values were included: "an exciting life," "being independent," "having power," "self-cultivation," "a sense of accomplishment," "pleasure," and "social recognition." Respondents used a scale from 1 (*not at all important*) to 7 (*of supreme importance*). Combining the seven items yielded a reliable scale (alpha = .71).

Collectivistic Values

Six collectivistic values were included: "harmony with others," "being cooperative with others," "observing social rituals," "honoring parents," "being polite," and "moderation, following the middle way." The response scale was the same as for individualistic values. Combining the six values yielded a reliable scale (alpha = .70).

Independent Self Construals

The measures of the independent (the self as a separate entity) and the interdependent (the self as interdependent with other ingroup members) self construals were adapted from scales developed by Gudykunst, Matsumoto et al. (1996). Six items were used to measure independent self construals: "My personal identity is important to me." "I enjoy being unique and different from others." "I prefer to be self-reliant rather than depend on others." "I take responsibility for my own actions." "It is important for me to act as an independent person." and "I should decide my future on my own." The scale for the items ranged from 1 (*strongly disagree*) to 7 (*strongly agree*). Combining the items yielded a reliable scale (alpha = .80).

Interdependent Self Construals

Six items were used to measure interdependent self construals: "I maintain harmony in the groups of which I am a member." "I will sacrifice my self interests for the benefit of my group." "I stick with my group even through difficulties." "I respect decisions made by my group." "I respect the majority's wishes in groups of which I am a member." and "It is important to consult friends and get their ideas before making a decision." The scale for the items ranged from 1 (*strongly disagree*) to 7 (*strongly agree*). Combining the items yielded a reliable scale (alpha = .77).

Percentage of English Spoken With Family/Friends

The percentage of English used with family and friends was measured by two items: "When you communicate with your family, what percentage of your interactions take place in English?" "When you communicate with your friends, what percentage of your interactions take place in English?" The answers ranged from zero (0) to 100%. Combining the two items yielded a highly reliable scale (alpha = .94).

Ethnic Language Abilities

The ability in the ethnic language was assessed by four self-report items: "How fluent are you in speaking [understanding, writing, reading] the language associated with your ethnic background?" Respondents answered on a scale from 1 (*not at all fluent*) to 7 (*totally fluent*). Combination of the four items yielded a highly reliable scale (alpha = .93).

Shared Networks

Shared networks with other members of the ethnic group was measured using three items: "Approximately what percentage of your acquaintances [friends, close friends] are members of your ethnic group?" The answers ranged from zero (0) to 100%. Combination of the three items yielded a highly reliable scale (alpha = .88).

Relational Expectations

Relational expectations were measured using items developed by Kelley and Burgoon (1991). Five separate measures were constructed: intimacy, control, receptivity, arousal, and trust/equality. The items were preceded by the phrase "I would expect that other members of my ethnic group would . . ." at the beginning of the items and the top of each succeeding page. The response scale ranged from 1 (*not very likely*) to 7 (*very likely*).

Intimacy. Intimacy was measured using seven items: "be interested in talking to me," "establish rapport with me," "treat me like a good friend," "make me feel we are similar," "like me," "be reasonable with me," and "desire to move our conversations to deep levels." Reliability for the five items was .81.

Control. Control was measured using six items: "try to control our interactions," "act more powerful than me," "have the upper hand during our conversations," "dominate our conversations," "be in control of our relationship," and "be assertive with me." Reliability for the six items was .83.

Receptivity. Receptivity was measured using five items: "make our interactions very formal" (reversed), "keep our relationship at an impersonal level" (reversed), "be willing to listen to me," "not care what I think" (reversed), and "want to keep our conversations businesslike" (reversed). Combination of the five items yielded a reliability of .60.

Arousal. Arousal was measured using three items: "be relaxed when talking with me" (reversed), "be frustrated with me," and "be distracted by my behavior." Reliability was .70.

Trust/Equality. Trust/equality was measured by six items: "treat me as an equal," "want me to trust him or her," "establish common ground with me," "be comfortable interacting with me," "be sincere in communicating with me," and "want to cooperate with me." Reliability was .82.

Communication Styles

Measurement of communication styles was based on Norton (1983) and Gudykunst, Matsumoto et al. (1996). Ten styles were derived from Norton:

dramatic, contentious, animated, relaxed, attentive, openness, friendly, precise, nonverbal expressiveness, and communicator image. (Note: The dominant style also was measured, but the scale did not meet the minimum criteria for reliability.) Five styles were derived from Gudykunst, Matsumoto et al.: ability to infer meaning, indirect, interpersonal sensitivity, using feelings to guide behavior, and positive perceptions of silence. The response scale for all items was 1 (*strongly disagree*) to 7 (*strongly agree*).

Dramatic. Dramatic was measured by five items: "My speech tends to be very picturesque." "I frequently verbally exaggerate to emphasize a point." "I dramatize a lot." "I regularly tell jokes and stories when I communicate." and "I often physically or vocally act out what I want to communicate." Reliability was .70.

Contentious. Contentious was measured by five items: "Once I get wound up in a heated discussion, I have a hard time stopping myself." "In arguments I insist on very precise definitions." "I often insist that people present proof for what they are saying." "When I disagree with someone, I am quick to challenge them." and "I am very argumentative." Reliability was .65.

Animated. Animated was measured by five items: "I actively use facial expressions when I communicate." "I am very expressive nonverbally in social situations." "I tend to constantly gesture when I communicate." "People generally know my emotional state, even if I do not say anything." and "My eyes tend to reflect what I am feeling when I communicate." Reliability was .70.

Relaxed. Relaxed was measured by five items: "I am conscious of nervous mannerism in my speech" (reversed). "As a rule, I am very calm and collected when I talk." "Under pressure, I come across as a relaxed speaker." "The flow of my speech is affected by my nervousness" (reversed). and "I am a very relaxed communicator." Reliability was .60.

Attentive. Attentive was measured by five items: "I can always repeat to a person what was said." "I always show I am very empathic with people." "I am an extremely attentive communicator." "I like to listen very carefully to people." and "I deliberately react in a way that people know that I am listening to them." Reliability was .68.

Openness. Openness was measured by four items: "I readily reveal personal things about myself." "I am an extremely open communicator." "Usually I do not tell people very much about myself until I get to know them quite well" (reversed). and "As a rule, I generally express my feelings or emotions." Reliability was .60.

Friendly. Friendly was measured by four items: "I always prefer to be tactful." "I am an extremely friendly communicator." "Most of the time, I tend to be very encouraging to people." and "I habitually acknowledge verbally others' contributions." Reliability was .63.

Precise. Precise was measured by five items: "I try to be accurate when I communicate." "When I engage in discussion, I try to cover all possible issues." "I do not like interacting with others who do not give a firm 'yes' or 'no' response to questions." "I am a very precise communicator." and "In arguments, I insist on very precise definitions." Reliability was .63.

Nonverbal Expressiveness. Nonverbal expressiveness was measured by four items: "People always seem to know my moods from my nonverbal behavior." "People can easily read my emotional state from my facial expressions." "When I strongly feel an emotion, I show it." and "I show my anger when people make me angry." Reliability was .61.

Communicator Image. Communicator image was measured by five items: "The way I communicate influences my life positively." "I am a very good communicator." "I find it easy to communicate with strangers." "In a small group of strangers, I am a very good communicator." and "I find it easy to maintain a conversation with a member of the opposite sex whom I just met." Reliability was .77.

Inferring Meanings. Inferring meanings was measured by five items: "I catch on to what others mean even if they do not say it directly." "I am able to recognize subtle and indirect messages." "I am very good at knowing the feelings other people are experiencing." "Even if I do not receive a clear and definite response from others, I can understand what they intend." and "Usually, I can read another person 'like a book.' " Reliability was .77.

Indirect. Indirect style was measured by five items: "I am evasive when I communicate with others." "I communicate in an indirect fashion." "I am ambiguous when I communicate with others." "When pressed for an opinion, I respond with an ambiguous position." and "Others have to guess what I mean when we communicate." Reliability was .68.

Interpersonal Sensitivity. Interpersonal sensitivity was measured by five items: "I maintain harmony in my communication with others." "I qualify (e.g., use 'maybe,' 'perhaps') in my language when I communicate." "When I turn down an invitation, I make sure that the other person is not offended." "I listen carefully to people when they talk." and "If I have something negative to say to others, I will be tactful." Reliability was .62.

Using Feelings to Guide Behavior. Using feelings to guide behavior was measured by five items: "I use my feelings to determine how I should communicate." "I listen to what my 'gut' or 'heart' says in many situations." "I use my feelings to guide my behavior more than most people." "I orient to people through my emotions." and "My emotions tell me what to do in many situations." Reliability was .82.

Positive Perceptions of Silence. Positive perceptions of silence was measured by four items: "I find silence awkward in conversations with people I've just met" (reversed). "I can sit with another person, not say anything, and still be comfortable." "I feel comfortable with silences in conversations." and "I do not like conversational silences" (reversed). Reliability was .65.

Stereotypes

To assess stereotypes, respondents indicated the degree that they thought 22 adjectives were characteristic of members of their ethnic groups. The response scale ranged from 1 (*not at all characteristic*) to 7 (*very characteristic*). The adjectives were these: "intelligent," "ambitious," "compassionate," "conservative," "friendly," "aggressive," "materialistic," "industrious," "deceitful," "arrogant," "cooperative," "warm," "conventional," "quiet," "pleasure loving," "honest," "sincere," "progressive," "tradition loving," "competitive," "emotional," and "talkative."

Statistical Analyses

The data were analyzed using analyses of variance tests and correlation co-efficients. I have not presented the analysis of variance statistics in the text. Any place where I indicate that there is a difference across the five ethnic groups (or other variables), the analysis of variance test was statistically significant (e.g., differences among the five ethnic groups in their stereotypes of their own ethnic groups). When I further indicate that there are differences between specific ethnic groups (e.g., Filipino Americans see themselves as more open than Japanese Americans), follow-up t tests between the groups were statistically significant.

The associations between variables discussed in the text are based on correlation coefficients. I have not presented correlation coefficients in the text, but any association presented in the text is statistically significant. I have not, however, reported all significant correlations.

References

Abelman, N., & Lie, J. (1995). *Blue dreams: Korean Americans and the Los Angeles riots.* Cambridge, MA: Harvard University Press.

Aboud, F. (1984). Social and cognitive bases of ethnic identity consistency. *Journal of Genetic Psychology, 145*(2), 217-230.

Agbayani-Siewert, P., & Revilla, L. (1995). Filipino Americans. In P. Min (Ed.), *Asian Americans.* Thousand Oaks, CA: Sage.

Akimoto, S., & Sanbonmatsu, D. (1999). Differences in self-effacing behavior between European and Japanese Americans. *Journal of Cross-Cultural Psychology, 30,* 159-177.

Alba, R. (1990). *Ethnic identity: The transformation of white America.* New Haven, CT: Yale University Press.

Alba, R., & Nee, V. (1997). Rethinking assimilation theory for a new era of immigration. *International Migration Review, 31,* 826-874.

Ancheta, A. (1998). *Race, rights, and the Asian American experience.* New Brunswick, NJ: Rutgers University Press.

Archdeacon, T. (1983). *Becoming American.* New York: Free Press.

Arkoff, A., Meridith, G., & Iwahara, S. (1964). Male-dominated and egalitarian attitudes in Japanese, Japanese-American, and Caucasian students. *Journal of Social Psychology, 64,* 225-229.

Arkoff, A., & Weaver, H. (1966). Body image and body dissatisfaction in Japanese-Americans. *Journal of Social Psychology, 68,* 323-330.

Atkinson, D., Morton, G., & Sue, D. (1989). A minority identity development model. In D. Atkinson, G. Morton, & D. Sue (Eds.), *Counseling American minorities.* Dubuque, IA: William C. Brown.

Baldwin, L. (1984). *Patterns of adjustment: A second look at Indochinese resettlement in Orange County.* Orange, CA: Immigrant and Refugee Planning Center.

Ball-Rokeach, S., Rokeach, M., & Grube, J. (1984). *The great American values test.* New York: Free Press.

Bao, J. (1999). Chinese-Thai transmigrants. *Amerasia Journal, 25*(2), 95-115.

Barth, F. (1969). *Ethnic group and boundaries.* London: Allen & Unwin.

Befu, H. (1986). Gift giving in modernizing Japan. In T. Lebra & W. Lebra (Eds.), *Japanese culture and behavior* (Rev. ed.). Honolulu: University of Hawaii Press.

Belden, E. (1997). *Chinese American identity.* New York: Garland.

Bem, S. (1974). The measurement of psychological androgyny. *Journal of Consulting and Clinical Psychology, 42,* 155-162.

Bem, S. (1993). *The lens of gender.* New Haven, CT: Yale University Press.

Bergano, A., & Bergano-Kinney, B. (1997). Images, roles, and expectations of Filipino Americans by Filipino Americans. In M. Root (Ed.), *Filipino Americans.* Thousand Oaks, CA: Sage.

Berger, C., & Calabrese, R. (1975). Some explorations in initial interactions and beyond. *Human Communication Research, 1,* 99-112.

Berry, J. (1990). Psychology of acculturation. In J. Berman (Ed.), *Nebraska symposium on motivation* (Vol. 37). Lincoln: University of Nebraska Press.

Berry, J., Kim, U., & Boski, P. (1988). Psychological acculturation of immigrants. In Y. Y. Kim & W. B. Gudykunst (Eds.), *Cross-cultural adaptation.* Newbury Park, CA: Sage.

Bogardus, E. (1968). Comparing racial distance in Ethiopia, South Africa, and the United States. *Sociology and Social Research, 52,* 149-156.

Bonus, E. (1997). Marking and marketing "difference": Filipino oriental stores in southern California. *Positions, 5,* 643-669.

Bonus, E. (2000). *Locating Filipino Americans.* Philadelphia: Temple University Press.

Branscombe, N., & Wann, D. (1994). Collective self-esteem consequences of outgroup derogation when a valued social identity is threatened. *European Journal of Social Psychology, 24,* 641-657.

Breton, R. (1964). Institutional completeness of ethnic communities and the personal relations of immigrants. *American Journal of Sociology, 70,* 193-205.

Brewer, M. (1991). The social self. *Personality and Social Psychology Bulletin, 17,* 475-482.

Brody, J., Rimmer, T., & Trotter, E. (1999). *Media and minorities study in the Vietnamese American community in southern California.* Unpublished preliminary analyses, California State University, Fullerton.

Broom, L., & Kitsuse, J. (1955). The validation of acculturation. *American Anthropologist, 57,* 44-48.

Brown, P., & Levinson, S. (1978). Universals in language usage: Politeness phenomenon. In E. Goody (Ed.), *Questions and politeness.* Cambridge, UK: Cambridge University Press.

Burgoon, J., & Hale, J. (1988). Nonverbal expectancy violations. *Communication Monographs, 55,* 58-79.

Burgoon, J., & Walther, B. (1990). Nonverbal expectancies and the evaluative consequences of violations. *Human Communication Research, 17,* 232-265.

Burgoon, M., Dillard, J., Doran, N., & Miller, M. (1982). Cultural and situational influences on the process of persuasive strategy selection. *International Journal of Intercultural Relations, 6,* 85-99.

Cain, B., & Kiewiet, D. (1986). *Minorities in California.* Pasadena: California Institute of Technology.

Caplan, N., Whitmore, J., & Choy, M. (1989). *The boat people and achievement in America.* Ann Arbor: University of Michigan Press.

Card, J. (1985). Correspondence of data gathered from husband and wife. *Social Biology, 25*(3), 196-204.

Cha, J. (1994). Aspects of individualism-collectivism in Korea. In U. Kim, H. Triandis, C. Kagitcibasi, S. Choi, & G. Yoon (Eds.), *Individualism and collectivism.* Thousand Oaks, CA: Sage.

Chaffee, S., Nass, C., & Yang, S. (1990). The bridging role of television in immigrant political socialization. *Human Communication Research, 17,* 266-288.

Chan, K., & Lam, L. (1987). Community, kinship and family in the Chinese Vietnamese community. In K. Chan & D. Indra (Eds.), *Uprooting, loss and adaptation.* Ottawa: Canadian Public Health Association.

Chan, S. (1991). *Asian Americans: An interpretive history.* New York: Twayne.

Chang, T. (1975). The self-concept of children in ethnic groups. *Elementary School Journal, 76,* 52-58.

Chang, W. (1972). *Communication and acculturation: A case study of Korean ethnic groups in Los Angeles.* Doctoral dissertation, University of Iowa.

Chin, J. (1983). Diagnostic considerations in working with Asian Americans. *American Journal of Orthopsychiatry, 53,* 100-109.

Chinese Culture Connection. (1987). Chinese values and the search for culture-free dimensions of culture. *Journal of Cross-Cultural Psychology, 18,* 143-164.

Ching, J., McDermott, J., Fukunaga, C., Yamagida, E., Mann, E., & Waldron, J. (1995). Perceptions of family values and roles among Japanese Americans. *American Journal of Orthopsychiatry, 65,* 216-224.

Choi, S. C., Kim, U., & Choi, S. H. (1993). Indigenous analyses of collective representations: A Korean perspective. In U. Kim & J. Berry (Eds.), *Indigenous psychologies.* Newbury Park, CA: Sage.

Chung, L., & Ting-Toomey, S. (1999). Ethnic identity and relational expectations among Asian Americans. *Communication Research Reports, 16,* 157-166.

Cimmarusti, R. (1996). Exploring aspects of Filipino-American families. *Journal of Marital and Family Therapy, 22,* 205-217.

Cocroft, B., & Ting-Toomey, S. (1994). Facework in Japan and the United States. *International Journal of Intercultural Relations, 18,* 469-506.

Connor, J. (1974). Acculturation and family continuities in three generations of Japanese Americans. *Journal of Marriage and the Family, 36,* 159-165.

Connor, J. (1977). *Tradition and change in three generations of Japanese Americans.* Chicago: Nelson-Hall.

Connor, W. (1986). The impact of homelands upon diaspora. In G. Scheffer (Ed.), *Modern diasporas in international politics.* New York: St. Martins.

Cooper, C., Baker, H., Polichar, D., & Welsh, M. (1993). Values and communication of Chinese, Filipino, European, Mexican, and Vietnamese American adolescents with their family and friends. *New Directions in Child Development, 62,* 73-89.

Cordova, F. (1983). *Filipinos: Forgotten Americans.* Dubuque, IA: Kendall/Hunt.

Crocker, J., & Luhtanen, R. (1990). Collective self-esteem and ingroup bias. *Journal of Personality and Social Psychology, 58,* 60-67.

Cummings, S., & Lambert, T. (1997). Anti-Hispanic and anti-Asian sentiments among African Americans. *Social Science Quarterly, 78,* 338-353.

Cupach, W., & Imahori, T. (1993). Managing social predicaments created by others. *Western Journal of Communication, 57,* 431-444.

Daniels, R. (1972). *Concentration camps U.S.A.* New York: Holt, Reinhart & Winston.

Daniels, R., & Kitano, H. (1970). *American racism.* Englewood Cliffs, NJ: Prentice Hall.

Daniels, R., Taylor, S., & Kitano, H. (1991). *Japanese Americans: From relocation to redress.* Seattle: University of Washington Press.

Deaux, K. (1991). Social identities. In R. Curtis (Ed.), *The relational self.* New York: Guilford.

DeVos, G. (1975). Ethnic pluralism. In G. DeVos & L. Romanucci-Ross (Eds.), *Ethnic identity.* Palo Alto, CA: Mayfield.

Dinh, K., Sarason, B., & Sarason, I. (1994). Parent-child relationships in Vietnamese immigrant families. *Journal of Family Psychology, 8,* 471-488.

Dion, K., Pak, A., & Dion, K. (1990). Stereotyping physical characteristics. *Journal of Cross-Cultural Psychology, 21,* 158-179.

Do, H. (1999). *The Vietnamese Americans.* Westport, CT: Greenwood.

Doherty, R., Hatfield, E., Thompson, K., & Choo, P. (1994). Cultural and ethnic influences on love and attachment. *Personal Relationships, 1,* 391-398.

Doi, T. (1973). *The anatomy of dependence.* Tokyo: Kodansha.

Dore, R. (1958). *City life in Japan.* Berkeley: University of California Press.

Edgerton, R. (1985). *Rules, expectation, and social order.* Berkeley: University of California Press.

Edwards, J. (1985). *Language, society, and identity.* Oxford, UK: Blackwell.

Enriquez, R. (1978). Kapwa: A core concept in Filipino social psychology. *Philippine Social Sciences and Humanities Review, 42,* 100-108.

Espiritu, Y. (1992). *Asian American panethnicity.* Philadelphia: Temple University Press.

Espiritu, Y. (1995). *Filipino American lives.* Philadelphia: Temple University Press.

Fang, C., Sidanius, J., & Pratto, F. (1998). Romance across the social status continuum. *Journal of Cross-Cultural Psychology, 29,* 290-305.

Feather, N. (1990). Bridging the gap between values and actions. In E. Higgins & R. Sorrentino (Eds.), *Handbook of motivation and cognition* (Vol. 2). New York: Guilford.

Feather, N. (1995). Values, valences, and choices. *Journal of Personality and Social Psychology, 68,* 1135-1151.

Feldman, S., & Rosenthal, D. (1990). The acculturation of autonomy expectation in Chinese high schoolers residing in two Western nations. *International Journal of Psychology, 25,* 259-281.

Feldstein, S., Hennessy, B., & Bond, R. (1981). *Conversational chronography and interpersonal perception in Chinese and English dyads.* Paper presented at the American Psychological Association convention. (Cited by Welkowitz et al., 1984b)

Fong, C., & Yung, J. (1995-1996). In search of the right spouse: Interracial marriage among Chinese and Japanese Americans. *Amerasia Journal, 21*(3), 77-98.

Fong, T. (1994). *The first suburban Chinatown.* Philadelphia: Temple University Press.

Friesen, W. (1972). *Cultural differences in facial expression in a social situation.* Doctoral dissertation, University of California, San Francisco.

Frymier, A., Klopf, D., & Ishii, S. (1990). Japanese and Americans compared on the affect orientation construct. *Psychological Reports, 66,* 985-986.

Fu, X., & Heaton, T. (1997). *Interracial marriage in Hawaii, 1983-1994.* Lewiston, NY: Edwin Mellen.

Fugita, S., & O'Brien, D. (1991). *Japanese American ethnicity.* Seattle: University of Washington Press.

Fujino, D. (1992). *Extending exchange theory: Effects of ethnicity and gender on Asian American heterosexual relationships.* Doctoral dissertation, University of California, Los Angeles.

Fujino, D. (1997). The rates, patterns and reasons for forming heterosexual interracial dating relationships among Asian Americans. *Journal of Social and Personal Relationships, 14,* 809-828.

Gaetz, L., Klopf, D., & Ishii, S. (1990). *Predispositions toward verbal behavior of Japanese and Americans.* Paper presented at the Communication Association of Japan conference.

Gaines, S., Marelich, W., Bledsoe, K., Steers, W., Henderson, M., Granrose, C., Barajas, L., Hicks, D., Lyde, M., Takahashi, Y., Yum, N., Rios, D., Garcia, B., Farris, K., & Page, M. (1997). Links between race/ethnicity and cultural values as mediated by race/ethnic identity and moderated by gender. *Journal of Personality and Social Psychology, 72,* 1460-1476.

Gao, G. (1996). Self and OTHER: A Chinese perspective on interpersonal relationships. In W. B. Gudykunst, S. Ting-Toomey, & T. Nishida (Eds.), *Communication in personal relationships across cultures.* Thousand Oaks, CA: Sage.

Gao, G. (1998). "Don't take my word for it": Understanding Chinese speaking practices. *International Journal of Intercultural Relations, 22,* 163-186.

Gao, G., & Ting-Toomey, S. (1998). *Communicating effectively with the Chinese.* Thousand Oaks, CA: Sage.

Gay, G. (1985). Implications of selected models of ethnic identity development for educators. *Journal of Negro Education, 54*(1), 43-55.

Geertz, C. (1975). On the nature of anthropological understanding. *American Scientist, 63,* 47-53.

Gehrie, M. (1976). Childhood and community: On the experience of Japanese Americans in Chicago. *Ethos, 4,* 353-383.

Gilbert, G. (1951). Stereotype persistence and change among college students. *Journal of Abnormal and Social Psychology, 46,* 245-254.

Giles, H., & Coupland, N. (1991). *Language: Contexts and consequences.* Pacific Grove, CA: Brooks/Cole.

Giles, H., Coupland, N., & Wiemann, J. (1992). "Talk is cheap . . ." but "My word is my bond": Beliefs about talk. In R. Bolton & H. Kwok (Eds.), *Sociolinguistics today.* London: Routledge.

Giles, H., & Johnson, P. (1981). The role of language in ethnic group identity. In J. Turner & H. Giles (Eds.), *Intergroup behavior.* Chicago: University of Chicago Press.

Glazer, N. (1993). Is assimilation dead? *Annals of the American Society of Political and Social Science, 530,* 122-136.

Glazer, N., & Moynihan, D. (1975). *Ethnicity.* Cambridge, MA: Harvard University Press.

Glenn, E. (1983). Split household, small producer, and dual wage earner. *Journal of Marriage and the Family, 45,* 35-46.

Gordon, M. (1964). *Assimilation in American life.* Oxford, UK: Oxford University Press.

Gorer, G. (1962). Themes in Japanese culture. In B. Silberman (Ed.), *Japanese character and culture.* Tucson: University of Arizona Press.

Gotanda, P. (1991). Interview with Philip Kan Gotanda. *Los Angeles Performing Arts, 25*(1), pp. 9-11.

Grice, H. (1975). Logic and conversation. In P. Cole & J. Morgan (Eds.), *Syntax and semantics* (Vol. 3). New York: Academic Press.

Gropp, G. (1992). In Orange County's Little Saigon. *Smithsonian, 23*(5), 28-32.

Grove, K. (1991). Identity development in interracial, Asian/white late adolescents. *Journal of Youth and Adolescence, 20,* 617-628.

Gudykunst, W. B. (1995). Anxiety/uncertainty management. In R. Wiseman (Ed.), *Intercultural communication theory.* Thousand Oaks, CA: Sage.

Gudykunst, W. B. (1998). *Bridging differences* (3rd ed.). Thousand Oaks, CA: Sage.

Gudykunst, W. B., Gao, G., & Franklyn-Stokes, A. (1996). Self-monitoring in China and England. In J. Pandy, D. Sinha, & D. Bhawuk (Eds.), *Asian contributions to cross-cultural psychology.* New Delhi: Sage.

Gudykunst, W. B., Gao, G., Nishida, T., Nadamitsu, Y., & Sakai, J. (1992). Self-monitoring in Japan and the United States. In S. Iwaki, Y. Kashima, & K. Leung (Eds.), *Innovations in cross-cultural psychology.* The Hague: Zwets & Zeitlinger.

Gudykunst, W. B., & Kim, Y. Y. (1997). *Communicating with strangers* (3rd ed.). New York: McGraw-Hill.

Gudykunst, W. B., Matsumoto, Y., Ting-Toomey, S., Nishida, T., Kim, K., & Heyman, S. (1996). The influence of cultural individualism-collectivism, self construals, and individual values on communication styles across cultures. *Human Communication Research, 22,* 510-543.

Gudykunst, W. B., & Nishida, T. (1986). Attributional confidence in low-and high-context cultures. *Human Communication Research, 12,* 525-549.

Gudykunst, W. B., & Nishida, T. (1994). *Bridging Japanese/North American differences.* Newbury Park, CA: Sage.

Gudykunst, W. B., & Nishida, T. (in press). Anxiety, uncertainty, and perceived effectiveness of communication across relationships and cultures. *International Journal of Intercultural Relations.*

Gudykunst, W. B., Sodetani, L., & Sonoda, K. (1987). Uncertainty reduction in Japanese American/Caucasian relationships in Hawaii. *Western Journal of Speech Communication, 51,* 256-278.

Gudykunst, W. B., & Ting-Toomey, S. (1988). *Culture and interpersonal communication.* Newbury Park, CA: Sage.

Hall, E. (1959). *The silent language.* New York: Doubleday.

Hall, E. (1976). *Beyond culture.* New York: Doubleday.

Hall, S. (1991). The local and the global. In A. King (Ed.), *Culture, globalization, and the world system.* London: Macmillan.

Hamilton, B. (1996). Ethnicity and the family life cycle: The Chinese-American family. *Family Therapy, 23*(3), 199-212.

Hamilton, D., Sherman, S., & Ruvolo, C. (1992). Stereotyped based expectancies. In W. B. Gudykunst & Y. Y. Kim (Eds.), *Readings on communicating with strangers.* New York: McGraw-Hill. (Originally published in *Journal of Social Issues, 46*(2), 35-60)

Han, Y. (1985). Discriminant analysis of self-disclosing behavior and locus of control among Korean American and Caucasian American adolescents. *Pacific/Asian Mental Health Research Review, 4,* 20-21.

Hansen, A. (1997). Oral history, Japanese America, and the voicing of a multiplex community of memory. *Oral History Review, 24*(1), 113-122.

Hansen, A., & Mitson, B. (1974). *Voices long silent.* Fullerton: California State University, Fullerton Oral History Project.

Hansen, M. (1952). The third generation in America. *Commentary, 14,* 492-500.

Hasegawa, T., & Gudykunst, W. B. (1998). Silence in Japan and the United States. *Journal of Cross-Cultural Psychology, 29,* 668-664.

Hayano, D. (1981). Ethnic identification and disidentification. *Ethnic Groups, 3,* 157-171.

Henry, W. (1990, April 9). Beyond the melting pot. *Time,* pp. 28-31.

Heras, P., & Revilla, L. (1992). Acculturation, generational status, and family environment of Filipino Americans. *Family Therapy, 21,* 129-138.

Hill, B., Ide, S., Ikuta, S., Kawasaki, A., & Oguno, T. (1986). Universals of linguistic politeness. *Journal of Pragmatics, 10,* 347-371.

Ho, D. (1976). On the concept of face. *American Journal of Sociology, 81,* 867-884.

Hofstede, G. (1979). Value systems in forty countries. In L. Eckensberger, W. Lonner, & Y. Poortinga (Eds.), *Cross-cultural contributions to psychology.* The Hague: Zwets & Zeitlinger.

Hofstede, G. (1980). *Culture's consequences.* Beverly Hills, CA: Sage.

Hofstede, G. (1983). Dimensions of national cultures in fifty countries and three regions. In J. Deregowski, S. Dzuiraweic, & R. Annis (Eds.), *Explications in cross-cultural psychology.* The Hague: Zwets & Zeitlinger.

Hofstede, G. (1991). *Cultures and organizations.* London: McGraw-Hill.

Hofstede, G. (1998). *Masculinity and femininity.* Thousand Oaks, CA: Sage.

Hofstede, G., & Bond, M. (1984). Hofstede's culture dimensions. *Journal of Cross-Cultural Psychology, 15,* 417-433.

Holtgraves, T., & Yang, J. (1992). The interpersonal underpinnings of request strategies. *Journal of Personality and Social Psychology, 62,* 246-256.

Hong, J., & Min, P. (1999). Ethnic attachment among second generation Korean adolescents. *Amerasia Journal, 25*(1), 165-179.

Hong, L. (1982). The Korean family in Los Angeles. In E. Yu, E. Phillips, & E. Yang (Eds.), *Koreans in Los Angeles.* Los Angeles: Center for Korean American and Korean Studies, California State University, Los Angeles.

Hope, T., & Jacobson, C. (1995). Japanese American families. In C. Jacobson (Ed.), *American families.* New York: Garland.

Hraba, J., & Hoiberg, E. (1983). Origins of modern theories of ethnicity. *Sociological Quarterly, 24,* 381-391.

Hsu, F. (1971). *The challenge of the American dream: The Chinese in the United States.* Belmont, CA: Wadsworth.

Hsu, J., Tseng, W., Ashton, G., McDermott, J., & Char, W. (1985). Family interaction patterns among Japanese Americans and Caucasian families in Hawaii. *American Journal of Psychiatry, 142,* 577-581.

Hsu, T., Grant, A., & Huang, W. (1993). The influence of social networks on the acculturation behavior of foreign students. *Connections, 16*(1-2), 23-30.

Hu, H. (1944). The Chinese concept of "face." *American Anthropologist, 46,* 45-64.

Huang, L. (1981). The Chinese American family. In C. Mindel & R. Habenstein (Eds.), *Ethnic families in America.* New York: Elsevier.

Hurh, W. (1998). *The Korean Americans.* Westport, CT: Greenwood.

Hurh, W., & Kim, K. (1984). *Korean immigrants in America.* Cranbury, NJ: Associated University Press.

Hurh, W., & Kim, K. (1988). *Uprooting and adjustment: A sociological study of Korean immigrants' mental health* (Final report submitted to NIMH). Washington, DC: U.S. Department of Health and Human Services.

Hurh, W., & Kim, K. (1990). Adaptation stages and mental health of Korean male immigrants in the United States. *International Migration Review, 24,* 456-479.

Ibrahim, F., Ohnishi, H., & Sandhu, D. (1997). Asian American identity development. *Journal of Multicultural Counseling and Development, 25*(1), 34-50.

Imahori, T., & Cupach, W. (1994). A cross-cultural comparison of the interpretation and management of face. *International Journal of Intercultural Relations, 18,* 193-220.

Inglis, M., & Gudykunst, W. B. (1982). Institutional completeness and communication acculturation. *International Journal of Intercultural Relations, 6,* 251-272.

Ishiikuntz, M. (1997). Intergenerational relationships among Chinese, Japanese, and Korean Americans. *Family Relations, 46,* 23-32.

Jackson, J. (1964). The normative regulation of authoritative behavior. In W. Grove & J. Dyson (Eds.), *The making of decisions.* New York: Free Press.

Jen, G. (1997, May 23). A person is more than the sum of her social facts. *Chronicle of Higher Education,* p. B11.

References   213

Johnson, C. (1976). The principle of generation among the Japanese in Honolulu. *Ethnic Groups, 1*, 18-35.

Johnson, C. (1977). Interdependence, reciprocity, and indebtedness: An analysis of Japanese American kinship relations. *Journal of Marriage and the Family, 39*, 351-363.

Johnson, C., & Johnson, F. (1975). Interaction rules and ethnicity. *Social Forces, 54*, 452-466.

Johnson, F., & Marsella, A. (1978). Differential attitudes toward verbal behavior in students of Japanese and European ancestry. *Genetic Psychology Monographs, 97*, 43-76.

Johnson, F., Marsella, A., & Johnson, C. (1974). Social and psychological aspects of verbal behavior in Japanese Americans. *American Journal of Psychiatry, 131*, 580-583.

Johnson, R., & Ogasawara, G. (1984). Group size and group income as influences on marriage patterns in Hawaii. *Social Biology, 31*, 101-107.

Kao, E., Nagata, D., & Peterson, C. (1997). Explanatory style, family expressiveness, and self-esteem among Asian American and European American college students. *Journal of Social Psychology, 137*, 435-444.

Karlins, M., Coffman, T., & Walters, G. (1969). On the fading of social stereotypes. *Journal of Personality and Social Psychology, 13*, 1-16.

Kashima, T. (1980). Japanese American internees return. *Phylon, 41*(2), 102-115.

Katz, D., & Braly, K. (1933). Racial stereotypes of one hundred college students. *Journal of Abnormal and Social Psychology, 28*, 280-290.

Kaut, C. (1961). Utang-na-loob: A system of contractual obligations among Tagalogs. *Southwestern Journal of Anthropology, 17*, 256-272.

Kawashima, T. (1967). *Nipponjin no ho-ishiki* [The Japanese consciousness of law]. Tokyo: Iwanami.

Keesing, R. (1974). Theories of culture. *Annual Review of Anthropology, 3*, 73-97.

Keith, R., & Barranda, E. (1969). Age independence norms in American and Filipino adolescents. *Journal of Social Psychology, 78*, 285-286.

Kelley, D., & Burgoon, J. (1991). Understanding marital satisfaction and couple types as a function of relational expectations. *Human Communication Research, 18*, 40-69.

Kibria, N. (1993). *Family tightrope: The changing lives of Vietnamese Americans.* Princeton, NJ: Princeton University Press.

Kich, G. (1992). The developmental process of asserting a biracial, bicultural identity. In M. Root (Ed.), *Racially mixed people in America.* Newbury Park, CA: Sage.

Kikumura, A., & Kitano, H. (1973). Interracial marriage: A picture of the Japanese Americans. *Journal of Social Issues, 29*(2), 67-81.

Kikumura, A., & Kitano, H. (1981). The Japanese American family. In C. Mindel & R. Habenstein (Eds.), *Ethnic families in America.* New York: Elsevier.

Kim, B. (1980). *The Korean American child at school and at home.* Washington, DC: Department of Health, Education, and Welfare.

Kim, J. (1980). Explaining acculturation in a communication framework. *Communication Monographs, 47*, 155-179.

Kim, J., Lee, B., & Jeong, W. (1982). *Uses of mass media in acculturation.* Paper presented at the Association for Education in Journalism convention.

Kim, L., & Kim, G. (1998). Searching for and defining a Korean American identity in a multicultural society. In Y. Song & A. Moon (Eds.), *Korean American women.* Westport, CT: Praeger.

Kim, M. S. (1994). Cross-cultural comparisons of the perceived importance of conversational constraints. *Human Communication Research, 21,* 128-151.

Kim, M. S., & Hunter, J. (1995). *A test of an ethno-cultural model of conflict styles.* Paper presented at the Speech Communication Association convention.

Kim, M. S., & Kitani, K. (1998). Conflict management styles of Asian- and Caucasian-Americans in romantic relationships in Hawaii. *Journal of Asian Pacific Communication, 8,* 51-68.

Kim, M. S., & Sharkey, W. (1995). Independent and interdependent construals of self. *Communication Quarterly, 43,* 20-38.

Kim, M. S., Sharkey, W., & Singelis, T. (1994). The relationship between individuals' self construals and perceived importance of interactive constraints. *International Journal of Intercultural Relations, 18,* 117-140.

Kim, M. S., & Wilson, S. (1994). A cross-cultural comparison of implicit theories of requesting. *Communication Monographs, 61,* 210-235.

Kim, Y. Y. (1977a). Communication patterns of foreign immigrants in the process of acculturation. *Human Communication Research, 4,* 66-77.

Kim, Y. Y. (1977b). Interethnic and intraethnic communication. *International and Intercultural Communication Annual, 4,* 53-68.

Kim, Y. Y. (1978a). A communication approach to the acculturation process. *International Journal of Intercultural Relations, 2,* 197-224.

Kim, Y. Y. (1978b). *Acculturation and patterns of interpersonal communication relationships: A study of Japanese, Mexican, and Korean communities in Chicago.* Paper presented at the Speech Communication Association convention.

Kim, Y. Y. (1979a). Toward an interactive theory of communication acculturation. In D. Nimmo (Ed.), *Communication yearbook 3.* New Brunswick, NJ: Transaction.

Kim, Y. Y. (1979b). *Dynamics of intrapersonal and interpersonal communication: A study of Indochinese refugees in the initial phase of acculturation.* Paper presented at the Speech Communication Association convention.

Kim, Y. Y. (1988). *Communication and cross-cultural adaptation.* Clevendon, UK: Multilingual Matters.

Kim, Y. Y. (1989). Personal, social, and economic adaptation. In D. Haines (Ed.), *Refugees as immigrants.* Totowa, NJ: Rowman & Littlefield.

Kim, Y. Y. (1990). Communication and adaptation: The case of Asian Pacific refugees in the U.S. *Journal of Asian Pacific Communication, 1,* 191-207.

Kim, Y. Y. (in press). *Becoming intercultural: An integrative theory of communication and cross-cultural adaptation.* Thousand Oaks, CA: Sage.

King, R. (1997). Multiraciality reigns supreme. *Amerasia Journal, 23*(1), 113-129.

Kinkead, G. (1992). *Chinatown.* New York: Harper.

Kinloch, G. (1973). Race, socio-economic status, and social distance in Hawaii. *Sociology and Social Research, 57,* 156-167.

Kitano, H. (1976). *Japanese Americans* (2nd ed.). Englewood Cliffs, NJ: Prentice Hall.

Kitano, H. (1989). A model for counseling Asian Americans. In P. Pedersen, J. Draguns, W. Lonner, & J. Trimble (Eds.), *Counseling across cultures* (3rd ed.). Honolulu: University of Hawaii Press.

Kitano, H. (1993a). Japanese American values and communication patterns. In W. B. Gudykunst (Ed.), *Communication in the United States and Japan.* Albany: State University of New York Press.

Kitano, H. (1993b). *Generations and identity: The Japanese Americans.* Needham, MA: Ginn Press.

Kitano, H., & Chai, L. (1982). Korean interracial marriage. *Marriage and Family Review, 5*(1), 75-78.

Kitano, H., & Daniels, R. (1995). *Asian Americans* (2nd ed.). Englewood Cliffs, NJ: Prentice Hall.

Kitano, H., Fujino, D., & Sato, J. (1998). Interracial marriages. In L. Lee & N. Zane (Eds.), *Handbook of Asian American psychology.* Thousand Oaks, CA: Sage.

Kitano, H., & Yeung, W. (1982). Chinese interracial marriage. *Marriage and Family Review, 5*(1), 35-48.

Kitano, H., Yeung, W., Chai, L., & Hatanaka, H. (1984). Asian American interracial marriage. *Journal of Marriage and the Family, 46,* 179-190.

Kitayama, S., Markus, H., Matsumoto, H., & Norasalekunkit, V. (1997). Individualistic and collectivistic processes in the construction of the self. *Journal of Personality and Social Psychology, 72,* 1245-1267.

Kuo, E. (1974). The family and bilingual socialization. *Journal of Social Psychology, 92,* 181-191.

Kwan, K., & Sodowsky, G. (1997). Internal and external ethnic identity and their correlates. *Journal of Multicultural Counseling and Development, 25*(1), 51-67.

Kwong, P. (1987). *The new Chinatown.* New York: Noonday.

Lam, L. (1980). The role of ethnic media for immigrants. *Canadian Ethnic Studies, 12*(1), 74-92.

Lay, C., & Verkuyten, M. (1999). Ethnic identity and its relation to personal self-esteem. *Journal of Social Psychology, 139,* 288-299.

Lebra, T. (1974). Reciprocity and the asymmetrical principle. In T. Lebra & W. Lebra (Eds.), *Japanese culture and behavior.* Honolulu: University of Hawaii Press.

Lebra, T. (1976). *Japanese patterns of behavior.* Honolulu: University of Hawaii Press.

Lebra, T. (1987). The cultural significance of silence in Japanese communication. *Multilingua, 6,* 343-357.

Lee, D. (1975). *Acculturation of Korean residents in Georgia.* San Francisco: R and E Research Associates.

Lee, H. (1982). Korean American voluntary associations. In E. Yu, E. Phillips, & E. Yang (Eds.), *Koreans in Los Angeles.* Los Angeles: Center for Korean American and Korean Studies, California State University, Los Angeles.

Lee, J. (1998). *Dynamics of ethnic identity.* New York: Garland.

Lee, K., & Levenson, R. (1992). *Ethnic similarities in emotional reactivity to unanticipated startle.* Paper presented at the Society for Psychophysiological Research convention. (Cited by Tsai & Levenson, 1997)

Lee, R. (1999). *Orientals: Asian Americans in popular culture.* Philadelphia: Temple University Press.

Lee, S. (1996). Perceptions of panethnicity among Asian American high school students. *Amerasia Journal, 22*(2), 109-125.

Lee, S., & Yamanaka, K. (1990). Patterns of Asian intermarriage and marital assimilation. *Journal of Comparative Family Studies, 21,* 287-305.

Levine, G., & Rhodes, C. (1981). *The Japanese American community.* New York: Praeger.

Li, W. (1999). Building ethnoburbia. *Journal of Asian American Studies, 2,* 1-28.

Liem, N. (1980). *Vietnamese intercultural communication.* Paper presented at the International Communication Association convention.

Liem, R. (1997). Shame and guilt among first-and second-generation Asian Americans and European Americans. *Journal of Cross-Cultural Psychology, 28,* 365-392.

Light, I., & Bonacich, E. (1988). *Immigrant entrepreneurs.* Berkeley: University of California Press.

Lim, J. (1998). *Reconstructing Chinatown.* Minneapolis: University of Minnesota Press.

Lim, T. S., & Choi, S. H. (1996). Interpersonal relationships in Korea. In W. B. Gudykunst, S. Ting-Toomey, & T. Nishida (Eds.), *Communication in personal relationships across cultures.* Thousand Oaks, CA: Sage.

Lindgren, H., & Yu, R. (1975). Cross-cultural insight and empathy among Chinese immigrants to the U.S. *Journal of Social Psychology, 96,* 305-306.

Lippman, W. (1922). *Public opinion.* New York: Macmillan.

Liu, J., Campbell, S., & Condie, H. (1995). Ethnocentrism in dating preferences for an American sample. *European Journal of Social Psychology, 25,* 95-115.

Loo, C. (1998). *Chinese Americans.* Thousand Oaks, CA: Sage.

Lott, J. (1998). *Asian Americans: From racial category to multiple identities.* Walnut Creek, CA: Altamira.

Lowe, L. (1991). Heterogeneity, hybridity, multiplicity. *Diaspora, 1,* 24-44.

Luhtanen, R., & Crocker, J. (1992). A collective self-esteem scale. *Personality and Social Psychology Bulletin, 18,* 302-318.

Lyman, S. (1968). Contrasts in the community organization of Chinese and Japanese in North America. *Canadian Review of Sociology and Anthropology, 5,* 51-67.

Lyman, S. (1971). Generation and character. In A. Tachiki, E. Wong, & F. Odo (Eds.), *Roots: An Asian American reader.* Los Angeles: UCLA Asian American Studies Center.

Lyman, S. (1986). *Chinatown and Little Tokyo.* Millwood, NY: Associated Faculty Press.

Lyman, S. (1988). On *Nisei* interpersonal style. *Amerasia Journal, 14*(2), 105-108.

Lynch, F. (1973). Social acceptance reconsidered. In F. Lynch & A. de Guzman (Eds.), *Four readings on Philippine values* (4th ed.). Quezon City: Atenes de Manila University Press.

Marchetti, G. (1993). *Romance and the "yellow peril."* Berkeley: University of California Press.

Mare, L. (1990). *Ma* and Japan. *Southern Communication Journal, 55,* 319-328.

Markus, H., & Kitayama, S. (1991). Culture and the self. *Psychological Bulletin, 98,* 224-253.

Mass, A. (1992). Interracial Japanese Americans. In M. Root (Ed.), *Racially mixed people in America.* Newbury Park, CA: Sage.

Masuda, M., Matsumoto, G., & Meridith, G. (1970). Ethnic identity in three generations of Japanese Americans. *Journal of Social Psychology, 81,* 199-207.

Mataragon, R. (1988). *Pakikiramdam* in Filipino social interactions. In P. Paranjpe, D. Ho, & R. Ruben (Eds.), *Asian contributions to psychology.* New York: Praeger.

Matsumoto, G., Meridith, G., & Masuda, M. (1970). Ethnic identification: Honolulu and Seattle Japanese-Americans. *Journal of Cross-Cultural Psychology, 1,* 63-76.

Maykovich, M. (1971). White-yellow stereotypes. *Pacific Sociological Review, 14,* 447-467.

McDermott, J., Char, W., Robbillard, A., Hsu, J., Tseng, W., & Ashton, G. (1983). Cultural variations in family attitudes and their implications for therapy. *Journal of the Academy of Child Psychiatry, 22,* 454-458.

McNaughton, W. (1974). *The Confucian vision.* Ann Arbor: University of Michigan Press.

McQueen, M. (1991, May 17). Voters' responses to poll disclose chasm between attitudes of Blacks and Whites. *Wall Street Journal,* p. A16.

Meridith, G. (1966). *Amae* and acculturation among Japanese-American college students in Hawaii. *Journal of Social Psychology, 70,* 171-180.

Meridith, G. (1967). Ethnic identity scale. *Pacific Speech Quarterly, 2,* 57-67.

Meridith, G. (1969). Sex temperament among Japanese-American college students in Hawaii. *Journal of Social Psychology, 77,* 149-156.

Miller, G., & Steinberg, M. (1975). *Between people.* Chicago: Science Research Associates.

Miller, M., Reynolds, R., & Cambra, R. (1982). *The selection of persuasive strategies in multicultural groups.* Paper presented at the Speech Communication Association convention.

Miller, M., Reynolds, R., & Cambra, R. (1987). The influence of gender and culture on language intensity. *Communication Monographs, 54,* 101-105.

Min, P. (1993). Korean immigrants in Los Angeles. In I. Light & P. Bhachu (Eds.), *Immigration and entrepreneurship.* New Brunswick, NJ: Transaction Press.

Min, P. (Ed.). (1995). *Asian Americans.* Thousand Oaks, CA: Sage.

Min, P. (1996). *Caught in the middle: Korean communities in New York and Los Angeles.* Berkeley: University of California Press.

Min, P. (1998). *Changes and conflicts: Korean immigrant families in New York.* Boston: Allyn & Bacon.

Min, P., & Kim, R. (Eds.). (1999). *Struggle for ethnic identity.* Walnut Creek, CA: Altamira.

Miyamoto, S. F. (1984). *Social solidarity among the Japanese in Seattle* (3rd ed.). Seattle: University of Washington Press.

Miyamoto, S. F. (1986). Problems of interpersonal style among the *Nisei. Amerasia Journal, 13*(2), 29-45.

Miyamoto, S. F. (1988). Miyamoto reply to Sanford Lyman. *Amerasia Journal, 14*(2), 109-113.

Mizutani, O., & Mizutani, N. (1987). *How to be polite in Japanese.* Tokyo: Japan Times.

Montero, D. (1980). *Japanese Americans.* Boulder, CO: Westview.

Moon, A., & Song, Y. (1998). Ethnic identities reflected in value orientations of two generations of Korean women. In Y. Song & A. Moon (Eds.), *Korean American women.* Westport, CT: Praeger.

Moore, M. (1999). Value structures and priorities of three generations of Japanese Americans. *Sociological Spectrum, 19,* 119-132.

Morisaki, S., & Gudykunst, W. B. (1994). Face in Japan and the United States. In S. Ting-Toomey (Ed.), *The challenge of facework.* Albany: State University of New York Press.

Morrison, T. (1992). *Playing in the dark.* Cambridge, MA: Harvard University Press.

Murphy-Shigematsu, S. (1987). *The voices of Amerasians.* Doctoral dissertation, Harvard University.

Nagata, D. (1993). *Legacy of silence.* New York: Plenum.

Nagata, G. (1969). *A statistical approach to the study of acculturation of an ethnic group based on communication oriented variables: The case of Japanese Americans in Chicago.* Doctoral dissertation, University of Illinois, Urbana.

Nakamura, H. (1964). *Ways of thinking of Eastern peoples.* Honolulu: East-West Center Press.

Nakamura, H. (1968). Basic features of the legal, political, and economic thought of Japanese. In C. Moore (Ed.), *The Japanese mind.* Honolulu: East-West Center Press.

Nakane, C. (1970). *Japanese society.* Berkeley: University of California Press.

Nakashima, C. (1988). Research notes on Nikkei Happa identity. In G. Okohiro, S. Hune, A. Hansen, & J. Liu (Eds.), *Reflections on shattered windows.* Pullman: Washington State University Press.

Nathan, J., Marsella, A., Horvath, A., & Coolidge, F. (1999). The concepts of individual, self, and group in Japanese national, Japanese-American, and European-American samples. *International Journal of Intercultural Relations, 23,* 711-726.

Newton, B., Buck, E., Kunimura, D., Colfer, C., & Scholsberg, D. (1988). Ethnic identity among Japanese-Americans in Hawaii. *International Journal of Intercultural Relations, 12,* 305-315.

Ng, F. (Ed.). (1998a). *Asian American family life and community.* New York: Garland.

Ng, F. (Ed.). (1998b). *The history and immigration of Asian Americans.* New York: Garland.

Ng, F. (Ed.). (1998c). *The Taiwanese Americans.* Westport, CT: Greenwood.

Nguyen, H., Messe, L. & Stollak, G. (1999). Toward a more complex understanding of acculturation and adjustment. *Journal of Cross-Cultural Psychology, 30,* 5-31.

Nicassio, P. (1985). The psychological adjustment of Southeast Asian refugees. *Journal of Cross-Cultural Psychology, 16,* 153-173.

Nishi, S. (1995). Japanese Americans. In P. Min (Ed.), *Asian Americans.* Thousand Oaks, CA: Sage.

Norton, R. (1978). Foundations of a communicator style construct. *Human Communication Research, 4,* 99-112.

Norton, R. (1983). *Communicator style.* Beverly Hills, CA: Sage.

Novak, M. (1971). *The rise of the unmeltable ethnics.* New York: Macmillan.

O'Brien, D., & Fugita, S. (1983). Generational differences in Japanese Americans' perceptions and feelings about social relationships between themselves and Caucasian Americans. In W. McCready (Ed.), *Culture, ethnicity, and identity.* New York: Academic Press.

O'Brien, D., & Fugita, S. (1991). *The Japanese American experience.* Bloomington: Indiana University Press.

Oetting, E., & Beauvais, F. (1990-1991). Orthogonal cultural identification theory. *International Journal of the Addictions, 25,* 655-685.

Ogawa, D. (1971). *From Japs to Japanese.* Berkeley, CA: McCutchan.

Ogawa, N., & Gudykunst, W. B. (1999). Politeness rules in Japan and the United States. *Intercultural Communication Studies, 9*(1), 47-68.

Okabe, K. (1987). Indirect speech acts of Japanese. In D. Kincaid (Ed.), *Communication theory: Eastern and Western perspectives.* New York: Academic Press.

Okabe, R. (1983). Cultural assumptions of East and West: Japan and the United States. In W. B. Gudykunst (Ed.), *Intercultural communication theory.* Beverly Hills, CA: Sage.

Okamura, J. (1998). *Imagining the Filipino American diaspora.* New York: Garland.

Olsen, M. (1978). *The process of social organization* (2nd ed.). New York: Holt, Reinhart & Winston.

Omi, M., & Winant, H. (1994). *Racial formation in the United States.* New York: Routledge.

Ong, A. (1996). Cultural citizenship as subject making. *Current Anthropology, 37,* 737-762.

Osajima, K. (1988). Asian Americans as the model minority. In G. Okihiro, S. Hune, A. Hansen, & J. Lui (Eds.), *Reflections on shattered windows.* Pullman: Washington State University Press.

Osajima, K. (1989). *Internalized racism and the educational experience of Asian American college students.* Paper presented at the Association for Asian American Studies convention. (Cited by O'Brien & Fugita, 1991)

Padilla, A., Wagatsuma, Y., & Lindholm, K. (1985). Acculturation and personality as predictors of stress in Japanese and Japanese-Americans. *Journal of Social Psychology, 125,* 295-305.

Palinkas, L. (1982). Ethnic identity and mental health. *Journal of Psychoanalytic Anthropology, 5,* 235-258.

Park, K. (1999). "I really do feel I'm 1.5!" The construction of self and community by young Korean Americans. *Amerasia Journal, 25*(1), 139-164.

Park, R. (1930). Assimilation. *Encyclopedia of the Social Sciences, 2,* 282.

Park, R. (1950). Our racial frontier in the Pacific. In R. Park (Ed.), *Race and culture.* New York: Free Press.

Parreñas, R. (1998). "White trash" meets the "little brown monkeys." *Amerasia Journal, 24*(2), 115-134.

Parsons, T. (1951). *The social system.* Glencoe, IL: Free Press.

Phinney, J. (1989). Stages of ethnic identity development in minority group adolescents. *Journal of Early Adolescence, 9,* 34-49.

Phinney, J. S. (1990). Ethnic identity in adolescents and adults. *Psychological Bulletin, 108,* 499-514.

Phinney, J. (1991). Ethnic identity and self-esteem. *Hispanic Journal of Behavioral Science, 13,* 193-208.

Phinney, J. S. (1992). The multiplegroup ethnic identity measure. *Journal of Adolescent Research, 7*(2), 156-176.

Phinney, J. (1993). A three-stage model of ethnic identity development in adolescence. In M. Bernal & G. Knight (Eds.), *Ethnic identity.* New York: Cambridge University Press.

Pido, A. (1986). *The Pilipinos in America.* Staten Island, NY: Center for Migration Studies.

Pittinsky, T., Shih, M., & Ambady, N. (1999). Identity adaptiveness. *Journal of Social Issues, 55*(3), 503-518.

Portes, A. (Ed.). (1994). The new second generation [Special Issue]. *International Migration Review, 28*(4).

Portes, A., & Rumbaut, R. (1990). *Immigrant America.* Berkeley: University of California Press.

Posadas, B. (1999). *The Filipino Americans.* Westport, CT: Greenwood.

Revilla, L. (1989). Dating and marriage preferences among Filipino Americans. *Journal of the Asian American Psychological Association, 13,* 72-79.

Revilla, L. (1997). Filipino American identity. In M. Root (Ed.), *Filipino Americans.* Thousand Oaks, CA: Sage.

Rhee, E., Uleman, J., & Lee, H. (1996). Variations in collectivism and individualism by ingroup and culture. *Journal of Personality and Social Psychology, 71,* 1037-1054.

Rhee, E., Uleman, J., Lee, H., & Roman, R. (1995). Spontaneous self-descriptions and ethnic identities in individualistic and collectivistic cultures. *Journal of Personality and Social Psychology, 69,* 142-152.

Roloff, M. (1987). Communication and conflict. In C. Berger & S. Chaffee (Eds.), *Handbook of communication science.* Newbury Park, CA: Sage.

Roosens, E. (1989). *Creating ethnicity.* Newbury Park, CA: Sage.

Root, M. (1990). Resolving "other" status. In L. Brown & M. Root (Eds.), *Diversity and complexity in feminist therapy.* New York: Hayworth.

Root, M. (Ed.). (1992a). *Racially mixed people in America.* Newbury Park, CA: Sage.

Root, M. (1992b). Within, between, and beyond race. In M. Root (Ed.), *Racially mixed people in America*. Newbury Park: Sage.

Root, M. (1998). Multiracial Asian Americans. In L. Lee & N. Zane (Eds.), *Handbook of Asian American psychology*. Thousand Oaks, CA: Sage.

Rosenthal, D., & Feldman, S. (1992). The nature and stability of ethnic identity in Chinese youth. *Journal of Cross-Cultural Psychology, 23*, 19-31.

Rotter, J. (1966). Generalized expectancies for internal versus external control of reinforcement. *Psychological Monographs, 80*(1), 1-28.

Rumbaut, R. (1995). Vietnamese, Laotian, and Cambodian Americans. In P. Min (Ed.), *Asian Americans*. Thousand Oaks, CA: Sage.

Rutledge, P. (1992). *The Vietnamese experience in America*. Bloomington: Indiana University Press.

Samter, W., Whaley, B., Mortenson, S., & Burlson, B. (1997). Ethnicity and emotional support in same-sex friendships. *Personal Relationships, 4*, 413-430.

Schlesinger, A. (1991). *The disuniting of America*. Knoxville, TN: Whittle Communications.

Schwartz, S. (1990). Individualism-collectivism. *Journal of Cross-Cultural Psychology, 21*, 139-157.

Schwartz, S. (1992). Universals in the content and structure of values. In M. Zanna (Ed.), *Advances in experimental social psychology* (Vol. 25). New York: Academic Press.

Sharkey, W., & Singelis, T. (1993). *Embarrassability and relational orientation*. Paper presented at the International Network on Personal Relationships convention.

Shibutani, T., & Kwan, K. (1965). *Ethnic stratification*. New York: Macmillan.

Shinagawa, L. (1996). The impact of immigration on the demography of Asian Pacific Americans. In B. Hing & R. Lee (Eds.), *Reframing the immigration debate*. Los Angeles: UCLA Asian American Studies Center.

Shinagawa, L., & Pang, G. (1988). Intraethnic, interethnic, and interracial marriage among Asian Americans in California. *Berkeley Journal of Sociology, 33*, 95-114.

Shinagawa, L., & Pang, G. (1996). Asian American panethnicity and intermarriage. *Amerasia Journal, 22*(2), 127-152.

Shon, S., & Ja, D. (1982). Asian families. In M. McGoldrick, J. Pearce, & J. Giordano (Eds.), *Ethnicity and family therapy*. New York: Guilford.

Simon, R. (1993). Old minorities, new immigrants. *Annals of the American Society of Political and Social Science, 530*, 61-73.

Sinclair, S., Sidanius, J., & Levin, S. (1998). The interface between ethnic and social system attachment. *Journal of Social Issues, 54*(4), 741-758.

Singelis, T., & Brown, W. (1995). Culture, self, and collectivist communication. *Human Communication Research, 21*, 354-389.

Singelis, T., & Sharkey, W. (1995). Culture, self construal, and embarrassability. *Journal of Cross-Cultural Psychology, 26*, 622-644.

Smith, K. (1983). Social comparison processes and dynamic conservativism in intergroup relations. *Research in Organizational Behavior, 5*, 199-233.

Smith, R. (1983). *Japanese society.* Cambridge, UK: Cambridge University Press.

Snyder, M., & Haugen, J. (1995). Why does behavioral confirmation occur? *Personality and Social Psychology Bulletin, 21,* 526-537.

Sodowsky, G., Kwan, K. L., & Pannu, R. (1995). Ethnic identity of Asians in the United States. In J. Ponterotto, J. Casas, L. Suzuki, & C. Alexander (Eds.), *Handbook of multicultural counseling.* Thousand Oaks, CA: Sage.

Song, Y. (1996). *Battered women in Korean immigrant families.* New York: Garland.

Sorrentino, R., & Short, J. (1986). Uncertainty orientation, motivation, and cognition. In R. Sorrentino & E. Higgins (Eds.), *Handbook of motivation and cognition.* New York: Guilford.

Spencer, M., & Markstrom-Adams, C. (1990). Identity processes among racial and ethnic minority children in America. *Child Development, 61,* 290-310.

Spickard, P. (1989). *Mixed blood: Intermarriage and ethnic identity in twentieth-century America.* Madison: University of Wisconsin Press.

Stephan, C. (1991). Ethnic identity among mixed-heritage people in Hawaii. *Symbolic Interactionism, 14,* 261-277.

Stephan, C. (1992). Mixed-heritage individuals: Ethnic identity and trait characteristics. In M. Root (Ed.), *Racially mixed people in America.* Newbury Park, CA: Sage.

Stephan, W., & Stephan, C. (1985). Intergroup anxiety. *Journal of Social Issues, 41*(3), 157-166.

Strobel, L. (1996). "Born-again Filipino": Filipino American identity and Asian panethnicity. *Amerasia Journal, 22*(2), 31-53.

Stryker, S. (1987). Identity theory. In K. Yardley & T. Honess (Eds.), *Self and identity.* Chichester, UK: Wiley.

Sue, D., Mak, W., & Sue, D. W. (1998). Ethnic identity. In L. Lee & N. Zane (Eds.), *Handbook of Asian American psychology.* Thousand Oaks, CA: Sage.

Sue, D. W., & Sue, D. (1990). *Counseling the culturally different.* New York: Wiley.

Sue, S., & Sue, D. W. (1971). Chinese American personality and mental health. *Amerasia Journal, 1*(1), 36-49.

Sue, S., & Morishima, J. (1982). *The mental health of Asian Americans.* San Francisco: Jossey-Bass.

Sung, B. (1990). Chinese American intermarriage. *Journal of Comparative Family Studies, 21,* 337-352.

Tajfel, H. (1978). Social identity, social categorization, and social comparisons. In H. Tajfel (Ed.), *Differentiation between social groups.* London: Academic Press.

Takahashi, J. (1997). *Nisei, Sansei.* Philadelphia: Temple University Press.

Takahashi, L. (1985). *Studying the Sansei generation.* Unpublished independent study project, UCLA. (Cited by Kitano & Daniels, 1995)

Takaki, R. (1989). *Strangers from a different shore.* New York: Penguin.

Takezawa, Y. (1995). *Breaking the silence.* Ithaca, NY: Cornell University Press.

Tam, V., & Detzner, D. (1995). Grandparents as a family resource in Chinese American families. In H. McCubbin, E. Thompson, A. Thompson, & J. Froner (Eds.), *Resil-

iency in ethnic minority families. Madison: University of Wisconsin Center for Excellence in Family Studies.

Tamura, E. (1994). *Americanization, acculturation, and ethnic identity.* Urbana: University of Illinois Press.

Tateishi, J. (1984). *And justice for all.* New York: Random House.

Tchen, J. (1999). *New York before Chinatown.* Baltimore: Johns Hopkins University Press.

Teske, R., & Nelson, B. (1974). Acculturation and assimilation. *American Anthropologist, 76,* 351-367.

Thornton, M. (1992). Is multiracial status unique? In M. Root (Ed.), *Racially mixed people in America.* Newbury Park, CA: Sage.

Thornton, M. (1996). Hidden agendas, identity theories, and multiracial people. In M. Root (Ed.), *The multiracial experience.* Thousand Oaks, CA: Sage.

Ting-Toomey, S. (1981). Ethnic identity and close friendship in Chinese American college students. *International Journal of Intercultural Relations, 5,* 383-406.

Ting-Toomey, S. (1985). Toward a theory of conflict and culture. In W. Gudykunst, L. Stewart, & S. Ting-Toomey (Eds.), *Communication, culture, and organizational processes.* Beverly Hills, CA: Sage.

Ting-Toomey, S. (1988). A face negotiation theory. In Y. Kim & W. Gudykunst (Eds.), *Theories in intercultural communication.* Newbury Park, CA: Sage.

Ting-Toomey, S. (1994). Managing conflict in intimate intercultural relationships. In D. Cahn (Ed.), *Intimate conflict in personal relationships.* Hillsdale, NJ: Erlbaum.

Ting-Toomey, S., Yee-Yung, K., Shapiro, R., Garcia, W., Wright, T., & Oetzel, J. (2000). Ethnic/cultural identity salience and conflict styles in four U.S. ethnic groups. *International Journal of Intercultural Relations, 24,* 47-82.

Tran, T. (1988). The Vietnamese American family. In C. Mindel, R. Habenstein, & R. Wright (Eds.), *Ethnic families in America* (3rd ed.). New York: Elsevier.

Triandis, H. C. (1988). Collectivism vs. individualism. In G. Verma & C. Bagley (Eds.), *Cross-cultural studies of personality, attitudes, and cognition.* London: Macmillan.

Triandis, H. C. (1989). The self and social behavior in differing social contexts. *Psychological Review, 96,* 506-517.

Triandis, H. C. (1995). *Individualism & collectivism.* Boulder, CO: Westview.

Triandis, H. C., Bontempo, R., Villareal, M., Asai, M., & Lucca, N. (1988). Individualism-collectivism: Cross-cultural studies of self-ingroup relations. *Journal of Personality and Social Psychology, 54,* 323-338.

Triandis, H. C., Leung, K., Villareal, M., & Clack, F. (1985). Allocentric versus idiocentric tendencies. *Journal of Research in Personality, 19,* 395-415.

Tsai, J., & Levenson, R. (1997). Cultural influences on emotional responding. *Journal of Cross-Cultural Psychology, 28,* 600-625.

Tsai, J., Levenson, R., & Carstensen, L. (1992). *Physiological and subjective responses of Chinese Americans and European Americans to emotional films.* Paper presented at the Society for Psychophysiological Research convention. (Cited by Tsai & Levenson, 1997)

Tse, L. (1999). Finding a place to be: Ethnic identity explorations of Asian Americans. *Adolescence, 34,* 121-138.

Tsui, P., & Schultz, G. (1988). Ethnic factors in group processes. *American Journal of Orthopsychiatry, 132,* 378-384.

Tuan, M. (1998). *Forever foreigners or honorary whites?* New Brunswick, NJ: Rutgers University Press.

Turner, J. (1987). *Rediscovering the social group.* Oxford, UK: Blackwell.

Turner, R. (1987). Articulating self and social structure. In K. Yardley & T. Honess (Eds.), *Self and society.* Chichester, UK: Wiley.

Uba, L. (1994). *Asian Americans.* New York: Guilford.

U.S. Bureau of the Census. (1993). *1990 census of the population, Asian and Pacific Islanders of the United States* (CP-3-5). Washington, DC: Government Printing Office.

U.S. Bureau of the Census. (1998). [Index of population]. See the World Wide Web: http://www.census.gov/population

U.S. Commission on Civil Rights. (1986). *Recent activities against citizens of Asian descent.* Washington, DC: Government Printing Office.

U.S. Commission on Civil Rights. (1992). *Civil rights issues facing Asian Americans in the 1990s.* Washington, DC: Government Printing Office.

Wei, W. (1993). *The Asian American movement.* Philadelphia: Temple University Press.

Weiss, M. (1970). Selective acculturation and the dating process. *Journal of Marriage and the Family, 32,* 273-278.

Welkowitz, J., Bond, R., & Feldstein, S. (1984a). Conversational time patterns of Japanese-American adults and children in same and mixed gender dyads. *Journal of Language and Social Psychology, 3,* 127-138.

Welkowitz, J., Bond, R., & Feldstein, S. (1984b). Conversational time patterns of Hawaiian children as a function of ethnicity and gender. *Language and Speech, 27,* 173-191.

White, M. (1993). *The material child: Coming of age in Japan and the United States.* New York: Basic Books.

Wiemann, J., Chen, V., & Giles, H. (1986). *Beliefs about talk and silence in a cultural context.* Paper presented at the Speech Communication Association convention.

Wierzbica, A. (1991). Japanese key words and cultural values. *Language in Society, 20,* 333-385.

Wink, P. (1997). Beyond ethnic differences. *Journal of Social Issues, 53*(2), 329-350.

Wong, H. (1985). Asian and Pacific Americans. In L. Snowden (Ed.), *Reaching the unserved.* Beverly Hills, CA: Sage.

Wong, M. (1995). Chinese Americans. In P. Min (Ed.), *Asian Americans.* Thousand Oaks, CA: Sage.

Wooden, W., Leon, J., & Tashima, E. (1988). Ethnic identity among Sansei and Yonsei church-affiliated youth in Los Angeles and Honolulu. *Psychological Reports, 62,* 268-270.

Wu, D., & Foster, B. (1982). Conclusion. In D. Wu (Ed.), *Ethnicity and interpersonal interaction*. Singapore: Maruzen.

Xing, J. (1998). *Asian Americans through the lens*. Walnut Creek, CA: Altamira.

Yamaguchi, S., (1994). Collectivism among the Japanese. In U. Kim, H. Triandis, C. Kagitcibasi, S. Choi, & G. Yoon (Eds.), *Individualism and collectivism*. Thousand Oaks, CA: Sage.

Yamaguchi, S., Kuhlman, D., & Sugimori, S. (1995). Personality correlates of allocentric tendencies in individualistic and collectivistic cultures. *Journal of Cross-Cultural Psychology, 26,* 645-657.

Yamamoto, T. (1999). *Masking selves, making subjects: Japanese American women, identity, and the body*. Berkeley: University of California Press.

Yanagisako, S. (1985). *Transforming the past traditions and kinship among Japanese Americans*. Stanford, CA: Stanford University Press.

Yang, P. (1999). Sojourners or settlers. *Journal of Asian American Studies, 2,* 61-91.

Yang, S. (1988). *The role of mass media in immigrants' political socialization: A study of Korean immigrants in northern California*. Doctoral dissertation, Stanford University.

Yee, B., Huang, L., & Lew, A. (1998). Families: Life-span socialization in a cultural context. In L. Lee & N. Zane (Eds.), *Handbook of Asian American psychology*. Thousand Oaks, CA: Sage.

Yee-Jung, K., & Ting-Toomey, S. (1996). *Strength of ethnic identity and interpersonal conflict styles among Asian Americans*. Paper presented at the Theory and Research on Communication and Culture conference, California State University, Fullerton.

Yeh, C., & Huang, K. (1996). The collective nature of ethnic identity development among Asian American college students. *Adolescence, 31,* 645-661.

Yik, M., Bond, M., & Paulhus, D. (1998). Do Chinese self-enhance or self-efface? *Personality and Social Psychology Bulletin, 24,* 399-406.

Ying, Y., & Lee, P. (1999). The development of ethnic identity in Asian American adolescents. *American Journal of Orthopsychiatry, 69*(2), 194-208.

Yinger, M. (1994). *Ethnicity*. Albany: State University of New York Press.

Yu, K., & Kim, L. (1983). The growth and development of Korean American children. In G. Powell (Ed.), *The psychosocial development of minority group children*. New York: Brunner/Mazel.

Yu, Y. (1995). Patterns of work and family: An analysis of Chinese American family since the 1920s. In C. Jacobson (Ed.), *American families*. New York: Garland.

Yum, J. O. (1982). Communication diversity and information acquisition among Korean immigrants in Hawaii. *Human Communication Research, 8,* 154-169.

Yum, J. O. (1983). Social network patterns of five ethnic groups in Hawaii. In R. Bostrom (Ed.), *Communication yearbook 7*. Beverly Hills, CA: Sage.

Yum, J. O. (1987). The practice of *uye-ri* in interpersonal relationships in Korea. In D. Kincaid (Ed.), *Communication theory: Eastern and Western perspectives*. New York: Academic Press.

Yum, J. O. (1988a). Locus of control and communication patterns of immigrants. In Y. Kim & W. Gudykunst (Eds.), *Cross-cultural adaptation*. Newbury Park, CA: Sage.

Yum, J. O. (1988b). The impact of Confucianism on interpersonal relationships and communication patterns in East Asia. *Communication Monographs, 55,* 374-388.

Yum, J. O., & Wang, G. (1983). Interethnic perception and the communication behavior among five ethnic groups in Hawaii. *International Journal of Intercultural Relations, 7,* 285-308.

Zhou, M., & Bankston, C. (1998). *Growing up American*. New York: Russell Sage.

Index

Abelman, N., 78
Aboud, F., 92
Acculturation, 119, 170, 171, 172
    Asian American communication and,
        170, 192
    Berry's model, 108-109
    definition, 171
    English competency and, 177
    See also Acculturation process; Assimila-
        tion; Communication acculturation,
        Kim's theory of; Integration;
        Marginalization; Separation; Typo-
        logical models of identities
Acculturation process, 170-174
    adaptation process, 170-171
    as two-way, 173
Achievement, 28
    serving individualistic interests, 29
Adaptation predisposition, 182
Agbayani-Siewert, P., 54, 72, 73, 75, 76
Akimoto, S., 161
Alba, R., 105, 172, 174
Alien Land Acts of 1913-1920, 55
Allocentric individuals, 26, 51
Allocentrism, 26, 37
    versus idiocentrism, 85
Ambady, N., 95
Amerasians, 97-98
Ancheta, A., 2, 8
Anti-Asian prejudice/discrimination, 186
    anti-Chinese, 54-55
    anti-Filipino, 72

anti-Japanese, 55
Anxiety/uncertainty management, 164-165
    by cultural identity, 168
    by ethnic identity, 167
    by ethnicity, 166
    strength of cultural identities and, 165
Archdeacon, T., 59
Arkoff, A., 71, 110
Asai, M., 26
Ashton, G., 70
Asian American ethnic groups, U.S., 1-2. See
        also specific Asian American groups
Asian American immigration patterns, 58.
        See also specific Asian American
        groups
Asian American movement, 100-102,
        173-174
    antiwar movement and, 101
    community activists, 100
    student activists, 100
    See also Asian Americans for Action;
        Asian Americans for a Fair Media
Asian American population statistics, 1, 58.
        See also specific Asian American
        groups
Asian Americans for Action, 101
Asian Americans for a Fair Media, 101
Asian Indian Americans, 1, 2
Assimilation, 17, 109, 114, 115, 174, 193
    as one-way process, 173
    attitude receptional, 172
    behavioral, 172

behavior receptional, 172
  civic, 172
  cultural, 172
  definition, 171
  identification, 172
  Kitano's typological model and, 108
  marital, 187
  structural, 172
  subprocesses, 172, 187
  versus pluralism, 171-174
  See also Acculturation; Melting pot meta-
    phor
Atkinson, D., 110, 130

Baker, H., 63, 75, 83
Baldwin, L., 97, 186
Ball-Rokeach, S., 28
Bankston, C., 81, 82, 84, 124, 127
Bao, J., 98
Barajas, L., 85
Barranda, E., 76
Barth, F., 91
Beauvais, F., 106, 109
Befu, H., 39
Belden, E., 96, 129
Bem, S., 46
Benevolence, 28, 37
  serving collective interests, 29
Bergano, A., 73
Bergano-Kinney, B., 73
Berger, C., 164
Berry, J., 108, 112, 115, 198
Bledsoe, K., 85
Bogardus, E., 143
Bonacich, E., 78
Bond, M., 19, 41, 161
Bond, R., 154
Bontempo, R., 26
Bonus, E., 74
Boski, P., 108
Braly, K., 141
Branscombe, N., 99
Breton, R., 183, 184
Brewer, M., 93
Brody, J., 82, 97, 125, 180
Broom, L., 184
Brown, P., 159
Brown, W., 30, 36

Buck, E., 119, 126
Burgoon, J., 132, 133, 200
Burgoon, M., 166
Burlson, B., 153

Cain, B., 185
Calabrese, R., 164
Cambra, R., 166
Campbell, S., 187
Caplan, N., 83
Card, J., 76
Carstensen, L., 152
Cha, J., 23, 24
Chaffee, S., 181
Chai, L., 188, 190
Chan, K., 183
Chan, S., 53, 88
Chang, T., 110
Chang, W., 181
Char, W., 70
Chen, V., 151, 152
Chin, J., 95
Chinatowns, 61, 96, 100
  Chicago, 61
  Los Angeles, 61
  Monterey Park (CA), 61
  New York, 61
  San Francisco, 61, 124
  See also Ethnoburbs
Chinese American families, 62-63
  child control through guilt, 63
  child control through shame, 63
  conformity in, 63
  Confucianism values and, 62
  dating issues, 63
  filial piety, 62
  grandparents, 62
  indirect communication, 63
  living in/near Chinatowns, 62-63
  living in suburbs, 63
  restrained communication, 63
  See also Chinese Americans
Chinese American Museum (New York), 101
Chinese Americans, ix, x, 1, 2, 13, 53, 59-63,
    85, 89, 98, 129
  beliefs about talk, 151-152
  cultural identity, 98
  cultural variation, 18

English conversations, 125
ethnic identity, 97, 98
generation and language usage, 123,
    126-127
idiocentric tendencies, 85
institutions, 61-62
interethnic dating, 189
interethnic marriage, 190, 191, 192
language usage and, 125
panethnic identity, 105
population statistics, 58, 59, 60, 61
research on, 14
susceptibility to embarrassment, 136
See also Chinatowns; Chinese American
    families; Chinese cultural concepts;
    Chinese culture; Chinese immigration
Chinese cultural concepts:
    bao, 40
    bu fu hori wang, 23
    gan qing, 23
    han xu, 23
    rong ren, 23
    sui he, 23
    ti hui, 23
    ting hui, 50
    tuan jie, 23
    xiao, 40
    yi zai yan wai, 23
    zuo mo, 23
    zuo ren, 23
    See also Chinese culture
Chinese culture:
    collectivism, 22-23
    concept of self, 22-23
    Confucianism and, 49-50
    power distance in, 43
    uncertainty avoidance in, 40
Chinese Culture Connection, 47, 48, 49
Chinese-English bilinguals, 124
Chinese Exclusion Act, 54-55, 59, 60
    repeal of, 56, 60
Chinese immigration, 54-55, 59
    paper sons, 60
    patterns, 59-61
    quotas, 56, 60
    war brides, 56
Ching, J., 71
Choi, S. C., 23
Choi, S. H., 23, 24

Choo, P., 85, 153
Choy, M., 83
Chung, L., 109, 116, 133
Cimmarusti, R., 75, 88
Civil Liberties Act of 1988, 66
Clack, F., 35
Cocroft, B., 160
Coffman, T., 141
Colfer, C., 119, 126
Collective self-esteem:
    components, 99-100
    ethnic identity and, 95, 99-100
    group memberships, 100
    membership, 99
    private, 99
    public, 99
Collectivist culture:
    Asian American, 6, 8, 12, 18, 35, 51
    communication, 37
    group goals in, 19
    groups over individuals in, 18
    importance of ingroup in, 19-20
    indirect communication in, 7, 36
    individual level, 37
    ingroups over individuals in, 20
    major characteristics, 37
    members' self view, 7, 13
    predicting others' behavior, 18
    sensitive communication, 36
    See also High-context communication;
        Individualism-collectivism
Collectivistic values, 112
Commission on Wartime Relocation and In-
    ternment 1982 report, 66
Communication, Asian American, 3-4, 13
    Asian American networks and, 13
    connections to other Asian Americans, 13
    content of ethnic/cultural identities and,
        8, 12-13
    culture and, 4-7
    ethnic enclaves and, 13
    ethnicity and, 7-8
    generation in United States and, 9
    immigrant versus nonimmigrants and, 9
    language abilities and, 9-10
    strength of cultural identities and, 8,
        10-12
    strength of ethnic identities and, 8, 10-12,
        168

See also specific Asian American groups;
Communication acculturation, Kim's
theory of; Individualism-collectivism
Communication acculturation, Kim's theory
of, 174-175
adaptation predisposition, 182
host environment conditions, 182-187
personal communication, 175-177
social communication, 177-182
Communication channels, 4
Communication expectations:
conversational constraints, 136-137
for silence, 138
nature of, 132
politeness rules, 137-138
relational, 133-134
violations of, 134-136
See also Stereotypes
Communication rules, 6
Communication styles, 147-149
Asian American, 155-158
by cultural identity, 157
by ethnic identity, 157
by ethnicity, 156
Chinese American, 149, 151-152
conversational time patterns, 154-155
emotional 152-154
high-context, 137, 148, 149, 156, 168
individual preferences, 168
Japanese American, 149-151
low-context, 137, 148, 149, 156, 158, 168
U.S., 147
Components model of identities, 106-107,
111
activating ethnic identities, 107
adopting ethnic identities, 107
affective component, 106
behavioral component, 106
cognitive component, 106
consciousness of ethnicity, 107
Condie, H., 187
Conflict sources, 162
Conflict styles, 148, 162-164
Asian American, 163-164
expressive, 162
implications of cross-cultural studies,
162-163
individualistic versus collectivistic cultures, 162-164

instrumental, 162
mediators, 163
nonconfrontational, 163
nonforce styles, 164
Conformity, 28, 37
serving collective interests, 29
Confucian dynamism, 49
moral discipline and, 49
values, 48
See also Confucianism
Confucianism, 18, 43, 47-50
as context-centered philosophy, 49
as situation-centered philosophy, 49
communication function in, 49
cultural-level, 47-49
culture-specific, 49-50
four tenants of, 48
i, 48, 49
influence on behavior, 49
jen, 48-49
li, 48, 49
right conduct, 48-49
shu, 49
ting hui, 50
wu lun, 48, 49
See also Confucian dynamism; Cultural
variability dimensions, Confucian
Connor, J., 70, 118, 119
Connor, W., 74
Conversational constraints, 136-137
concern for avoiding hurting other's feelings, 136
concern for avoiding negative evaluations, 136
concern for clarity, 136
interactive, 136
Conversational maxims, 32-34
manner, 32
quality, 32, 33
quantity, 32, 34
relevancy, 32, 33
Conversational time patterns, 154-155
Coolidge, F., 85
Cooper, C., 63, 75, 83
Cordova, F., 54, 73
Coupland, N., 122, 151, 99
Crocker, J., 99
Cultural identities, 11, 88, 108, 116, 117,
129, 168, 179

content of and communication, 12-13
for Asian Americans, 92
strength of and communication, 10-12, 90
Cultural individualism-collectivism
influence of on communication, 27
Cultural variability, 12, 14, 17-18. *See also*
Cultural variability dimensions, Confucian; Cultural variability dimensions, Hofstede's; Self construals
Cultural variability dimensions, Confucian,
48-49. *See also* Confucian dynamism;
Confucianism
Cultural variability dimensions, Hofstede's,
18, 36-47. *See also* Masculinity-femininity; Power distance; Uncertainty
avoidance
Culture:
definition of, 5
mass media and, 6
parents and, 6
peers and, 6
religious institutions and, 6
subdivisions, 5-6
teachers and, 6
See also Culture, Asian American communication and; Subculture; Television
Culture, Asian American communication
and, 4-7
Culture-general information, 18
Culture-specific information, 18
Cummings, S., 185
Cupach, W., 160

Daniels, R., 1, 53, 59, 60, 65, 66, 68, 78, 79,
88, 169
Deaux, K., 10, 11
Decoding, 3-4
Deculturation, 171
Detzner, D., 62
Developmental models of identities, 106,
110-111
caveats, 111
conformity stage, 110
dissonance stage, 110
integrative awareness stage, 110, 111
introspection stage, 110, 111
resistance and immersion stage, 110-111

DeVos, G., 91, 122
Dillard, J., 166
Dinh, K., 83, 84
Dion, K., 142
Direct communication, 32
Displaced Person Act of 1948, 56
Do, H., 80
Doherty, R., 85, 153
Doi, T., 22
Doran, N., 166
Dore, R., 39

Edgerton, R., 39
Edwards, J., 122
Embarrassment, 135, 136
ethnic differences in susceptibility to, 136
Emergency Detention Act, 57
Emotional communication, Asian Americans', 152-154
Encoded messages, 3
Encoding, 3, 4
Enculturation, 170. *See also* Acculturation
process
Enriquez, R., 24
Espiritu, Y., 8, 73, 88, 102, 103, 105
Ethnic exclusivity, 109, 133
Ethnic groups:
primary ingredients, 91
Ethnic identities, 10, 88, 116, 117, 129, 169,
179, 180
birthplace and, 97
changing, 99
collective self-esteem and, 95
communities and, 96-97
content of and communication, 12-13
ethnicity and, 97
for Asian Americans, 92-97
generation in United States and, 117-121
importance of, 93, 96
language usage and, 113-114, 121-126
self esteem-and, 95
shared networks and, 114
simultaneous, 99
situation-specific, 99
strength of and communication, 10-12, 89
See also Models of ethnic/cultural identities; Panethnic identities; Panethnicity
Ethnicity, 4, 7-8, 91-92

as racialized, 117
development of awareness of, 92
importance of, 92
versus race, 8, 90
See also specific Asian American groups
Ethnic polarization, 173
Ethnic pride, 109, 133
Ethnic slurs, 104
Ethnoburbs, 61

Face, 159. See also Face negotiation
Face negotiation, 148, 159-162
fear of loss of, 160-161
high face concerns, 160
implications of cross-cultural studies,
159-161
indirect, 160
politeness, 159, 160
remediation, 160
self-effacement, 161-162
Fang, C., 190
Farris, K., 85
Feather, N., 28
Feldman, S., 63, 118, 127, 129
Feldstein, S., 154
Filipino American families, 75-76
controlling children through guilt, 75
controlling children through shame, 75
emphasis on etiquette, 75
family cohesion, 75
loyalty in, 75
problems, 76
smooth interpersonal relationships in, 75
solidarity in, 75
strain on, 76
See also Filipino Americans
Filipino American Historical Society (Seattle), 102
Filipino Americans, ix, x, 1, 2, 11, 13, 53,
71-73, 85, 89, 129, 204
cultural identity, 98
cultural variability, 18
differentiation by language, 74
differentiation by place of origin, 74
enclaves, 74
English conversations, 125
ethnic identity, 97, 98
fraternal organizations, 73

generation and language usage, 123,
124-125
institutions, 73-74
interethnic dating, 187-188
interethnic marriage, 190, 191, 192
internal locus of control, 176
language usage and, 125
neighborhoods, 73
panethnic identity, 104-105
research on, 14
self-perceptions, 147
shops, 74
susceptibility to embarrassment, 136
Filipino cultural concepts, 24-25
amor proprio, 75
hiya, 25, 74, 75
kapwa, 24
pakikiramdam, 25
pakikisama, 75
utang na loob, 40, 75
See also Filipino culture
Filipino culture:
collectivism, 24-25
masculine, 47
power distance in, 43, 51
uncertainty avoidance in, 40, 41
vertical/collectivistic, 21
Filipino immigration, 54, 55
patterns, 71-73
pensionados, 71
quotas, 56
war brides, 56
See also Manila men
Fong, C., 192
Fong, T., 61
Foster, B., 90, 91, 93, 122
Franklyn-Stokes, A., 26
Friesen, W., 152
Frymier, A., 35
Fu, X., 191
Fugita, S., 67, 118, 119, 185
Fujino, D., 188, 189, 190, 191, 192
Fukunaga, C., 71

Gaetz, L., 35
Gaines, S., 85
Gao, G., 22, 23, 26, 35, 40, 50
Garcia, B., 85

Garcia, W., 109, 116, 130, 163, 197
Gay, G., 92
Geary Act of 1892, 55
Geertz, C., 30
Gehrie, M., 180
Generation in United States:
    Asian American communication and, 9,
        169
    ethnic identities and, 117-121
    first generation Asian Americans, 9, 123
    language usage and, 123, 126-129
    post-second generation Asian Americans,
        9, 123
    second generation Asian Americans, 9,
        123
    See also specific Asian American groups;
        Japanese Americans, generations of;
        Korean Americans, generations of;
        Third generation return hypothesis
Gilbert, G., 141
Giles, H., 91, 93, 122, 151, 152
Glazer, N., 172, 173
Glenn, E., 62
Gordon, M., 7, 90, 172, 187
Gorer, G., 45
Gotanda, P., 96
Granrose, C., 85
Grant, A., 179
Grice, H., 32, 33, 34
Gropp, G., 81
Grove, K., 99
Grube, J., 28
Gudykunst, W. B., 3, 15, 18, 26, 27, 30, 32,
        33, 34, 35, 36, 37, 40, 42, 43, 44, 46,
        47, 51, 85, 92, 113, 129, 137, 138,
        139, 155, 156, 158, 159, 164, 165,
        166, 168, 178, 179, 181, 184, 198,
        200, 201
Guilt:
    as violation of expectations, 134, 135

Hale, J., 132
Hall, E., 4, 31, 33, 35, 149
Hall, S., 94
Hamilton, B., 62, 88
Hamilton, D., 139, 140
Han, Y., 79
Hansen, A., 65, 88, 118

Hansen, M., 119, 126
Hasegawa, T., 34, 138
Hatanaka, H., 188, 190
Hatfield, E., 85, 153
Haugen, J., 140
Hayano, D., 95
Heaton, T., 191
Hedonism, 28, 37, 120
    serving individualistic interests, 29
Henderson, M., 85
Hennessy, B., 154
Henry, W., 172
Heras, P., 75, 88
Heyman, S., 30, 36, 85, 113, 155, 156, 158,
        168, 198, 200, 201
Hicks, D., 85
High-context communication, 31, 32, 33, 34,
        36, 137, 148, 149, 156, 168
    ambiguous, 35
    indirect, 35
    individualism-collectivism and, 35-36,
        168
    reserved, 35
    sensitive, 35
High-context communicators, 34
Hill, B., 137
Hmong Americans, 2
Ho, D., 159
Hofstede, G., 18, 19, 33, 36, 37, 38, 41, 42,
        44, 45, 45, 46, 47, 48
Hoiberg, E., 173
Holtgraves, T., 159, 160
Hong, J., 121, 124
Hong, L., 79
Hope, T., 69, 88
Horizontal cultures, 20
    collectivist, 20
    individualistic, 21
    versus vertical cultures, 20-21
Horvath, A., 85
Host environment conditions, 182-187
    European Americans' attitudes toward
        immigrants, 183, 184-186
    institutional completeness or ethnic com-
        munities, 183-184
    interaction potential, 182-183
    modes of incorporation immigrants, 183,
        186-187
Hraba, J., 173

Hsu, F., 62
Hsu, J., 70
Hsu, T., 179
Hu, H., 159
Huang, K., 95, 127, 160
Huang, L., 53, 62, 88
Huang, W., 179
Hunter, J., 164
Hurh, W., 78, 79, 88, 183

Ibrahim, F., 110, 130
Ide, S., 137
Identities:
    age and, 10
    gender and, 10
    hierarchical arrangements, 10
    human, 10
    integrating, 11
    master, 10
    personal, 10
    social, 10, 11
    See also Cultural identities; Ethnic identities; Panethnic identities
Identity politics, 93
Idiocentric individuals, 26
Idiocentrism, 26, 37, 153
    in Chinese Americans, 85
    in Japanese Americans, 85
    versus allocentrism, 85
Ikuta, S., 137
Imahori, T., 160
Immigrants, modes of incorporating, 186-187
    ethnic communities, 186
    government policies, 186
    Korean immigrants, 186-187
    societal reception, 186
    Vietnamese immigrants, 186
Immigration Act of 1924, 56, 57, 77
    quotas, 56
Immigration and Naturalization Act of 1965,
    1, 57, 60, 64, 68, 72, 77, 169
    revisions, 57
Immigration legislation, federal, 54. See also
    specific legislation
Immigration patterns, general Asian American, 53-59
Indirect communication, 32

Individualism-collectivism, 6-7, 12, 14,
    18-19, 31, 47
    across ethnic groups, 85-87
    cultural-level, 19-21
    culture-specific aspects of, 21-25
    mediating factors on communication behavior and, 25-31
    socialization, 26
    See also Cultural individualism-collectivism; High-context communication;
    Low-context communication
Individualistic cultures:
    communication, 37
    direct communication in, 7, 32
    importance of ingroup in, 19-20
    individual level, 37
    individuals' goals in, 19
    individuals over groups in, 18
    major characteristics, 37
    members' view of self, 6-7, 12
    predicting others' behavior, 18
    U.S. as, 6, 12
    See also Low-context communication
Individualistic values, 28-29, 112. See also
    specific value domains
Inglis, M., 178, 179, 181, 184
Ingroups, 7, 31
    Chinese, 23
    family as, 20
    family as in Philippines, 24
    Filipino, 24
    harmony, 32
    importance of, 19-20
    Japanese, 20, 21
    Korean, 23, 24
Integration, 108, 114, 115
Interethnic dating, 187-189
    by Asian American women, 188-189
    stereotyping and, 188
Interethnic marriage, 190-192, 193
    by Asian American women, 190, 193
    by ethnic group, 190, 191
    ethnicity and, 192
    generation in United States and, 192, 193
    interpersonal panethnicity and, 105
    legality of, 190
Interethnic relations, assimilation view of,
    172
    challenge to, 172-173

Internment camps, World War II American, 65
Intraethnic dating partners, 133
Ishii, S., 35
Ishiikuntz, M., 63, 88
Iwahara, S., 71

Ja, D., 160
Jackson, J., 132
Jacobson, C., 69, 88
Japan Association of America, 64
Japanese American Assistance League, 68
Japanese American Citizens League, 64, 67
  1972 convention, 65
Japanese American families, 69-71
  ethic of collective obligations, 69
  family cooperation, 71
  family harmony, 71
  hierarchical status, 71
  positive interactions, 71
  role differentiation, 71
  See also Japanese Americans; Japanese
    Americans, generations of
Japanese American National Museum (Los
    Angeles), 101-102
Japanese Americans, ix, x, 1, 2, 8, 11, 13, 19,
    53, 63-71, 85, 89, 129, 180, 204
  as Buddhists, 67
  conversational time patterns, 154-155
  cultural identity, 98
  cultural variability, 18
  English conversations, 125
  ethnic identity, 97, 98
  ethnicity, 7-8
  ethnic organizations, 67
  idiocentric tendencies, 85
  in Gardena, CA, 67
  institutions, 66-69
  interethnic dating, 189
  interethnic marriage, 190, 191, 192, 193
  internal locus of control, 176
  internment and redress, 64-66
  language usage and, 125
  panethnic identity, 105
  population statistics, 58, 63, 64, 67
  relocation of, 56
  research on, 14
  self-perceptions, 147

  social distance, 143
  susceptibility to embarrassment, 136
  See also Japanese American families;
    Japanese Americans, generations of
Japanese Americans, generations of:
  Gosei, 68
  Issei, 67, 68, 69, 70, 118, 119, 120, 180,
    181
  language usage and, 123, 126
  Nisei, 65, 66, 67, 68, 69-70, 118, 119,
    120, 141, 150, 151, 180, 181, 185
  Sansei, 65, 67, 68, 70, 95, 118, 119, 141,
    150, 151, 180, 181, 185, 187, 191
  Shin Nisei, 120
  Yonsie, 68, 141, 150
Japanese cultural concepts:
  amae, 18, 22, 68
  bun, 50
  enryo, 18, 22, 68, 150-151
  giri, 39-40
  honne, 22
  on, 39, 40
  ittaikan, 21
  kodomo no tame ni, 68
  shikataganai, 68
  soto, 21
  tatemae, 22
  uchi, 21
  wa, 18, 21-22
  See also Japanese culture
Japanese culture:
  collectivism, 21-22, 35
  Confucianism and, 50
  horizontal/collectivistic, 20-21
  masculine culture, 47
  masculinity-femininity in, 45-46
  power distance in, 43
  teen relationships, 45
  uncertainty avoidance in, 38-40, 41
Japanese immigration, 55
  gentleman's agreement, 55, 63-64
  patterns, 63-64
  quotas, 57
  war brides, 56,
Japantowns, 66-67
  San Francisco, 66
  Seattle, 66
  See also Little Tokyo (Los Angeles)
Jen, G., 93

Jeong, W., 179
Johnson, C., 70, 95, 149, 150, 151
Johnson, F., 70, 149, 150, 151
Johnson, P., 91, 93
Johnson, R., 187, 190, 192

Kao, E., 152
Karlins, M., 141
Kashima, T., 65
Katz, D., 141
Kaut, C., 40
Kawasaki, A., 137
Kawashima, T., 21
Keesing, R., 5
Keith, R., 76
Kelley, D., 133, 200
Kibria, N., 83
Kich, G., 99, 110, 130
Kiewiet, D., 185
Kikumura, A., 69, 190
Kim, B., 79
Kim, G., 108, 130
Kim, J., 179
Kim, K., 30, 36, 78, 79, 85, 113, 155, 156, 158, 168, 183, 198, 200, 201
Kim, L., 79, 108, 130
Kim, M. S., 35, 36, 85, 86, 136, 137, 164
Kim, R., 96, 129
Kim, U., 23, 108
Kim, Y. Y., 92, 171, 174, 175, 176, 177, 178, 179, 180, 181, 182, 183, 184
King, R., 69
Kinkead, G., 61, 88
Kinloch, G., 144
Kitani, K., 85, 86, 164
Kitano, H., 1, 53, 59, 60, 65, 66, 68, 69, 70, 78, 79, 88, 106, 108, 111, 118, 119, 126, 130, 149, 150, 151, 163, 169, 188, 190, 191, 192
Kitayama, S., 13, 30, 31, 112, 161
Kitsuse, J., 184
Klopf, D., 35
Korean American families, 78-80
  adolescents, 79-80
  clear tasks/roles, 78-79
  language usage, 79
  marriage, 79

Korean Americans, ix, x, 1, 2, 13, 19, 53, 76-80, 85, 89, 129, 175-176, 180, 182, 183-184
  churches and, 78
  cultural identity, 98
  cultural variability, 18
  culture and, 78
  English conversations, 125
  ethnic identity, 97, 98
  in ethnic neighborhoods, 77
  institutions, 77-78
  interethnic marriage, 190, 191, 192
  internal locus of control, 176
  Los Angeles riot of 1992 and, 77, 78, 120-121
  maintaining ethnic attachments, 78
  population statistics, 58, 76, 77
  research on, 14
  self-perceptions, 147
  small businesses and, 77, 78
  susceptibility to embarrassment, 136
  See also Korean American families; Korean cultural concepts; Korean culture; Korean immigration
Korean Americans, generations of:
  differences among, 120-121
  language usage and, 123, 124, 125
  mothers and adolescent daughters, 121
  1.5 generation, 121
  second generation, 121
Korean cultural concepts, 23-24
  bunsu, 24
  cheong, 23
  ch'ung-hyo, 24
  noon-chi, 24
  uichi, 23
  uye-ri, 40
  ye, 24
  See also Korean culture
Korean culture:
  collectivism, 23-24, 35
  feminine, 47
  power distance in, 43
  uncertainty avoidance in, 40, 41
  vertical/collectivistic, 21
Korean immigration, 55, 57
  patterns, 76-77
  picture brides, 77
  war brides, 77

Koreatowns, 77-78
 Chicago, 77
 Los Angeles, 77-78
 New York, 77
Kuhlman, D., 28
Kunimura, D., 119, 126
Kuo, E., 123
Kwan, K., 102, 161
Kwan, K. L., 110
Kwong, P., 61, 88

Lam, L., 182, 183
Lambert, T., 185
Language:
 emotional component of ethnic identity, 122
 ethnic group membership, 122
 to categorize ethnic groups, 122
 to facilitate group cohesion, 122
 to mark ethnic group boundaries, 121
Language abilities, Asian American, 9-10
Languages, 3
Language usage, ethnic identities and, 113-114, 121-126
Laotian Americans, 2
Lay, C., 95
Lebra, T., 21, 22, 34, 39, 45, 50, 59
Lee, B., 179
Lee, D., 79
Lee, H., 78, 85, 123
Lee, K., 152
Lee, P., 110, 130
Lee, R., 54, 55, 57, 60, 94, 101, 130
Lee, S., 103, 104, 190
Leon, J., 118, 119
Leung, K., 35
Levenson, R., 152, 153
Levin, S., 92
Levine, G., 119
Levinson, S., 159
Lew, A., 53, 88
Li, W., 61
Lie, J., 78
Liem, R., 50, 134, 135, 136
Light, I., 78
Lim, J., 61, 88
Lim, T. S., 24
Lindgren, H., 179

Lindholm, K., 119
Lippman, W., 138
Little Saigon (Los Angeles), 81-82, 97, 186
Little Tokyo (Los Angeles), 67
Liu, J., 187
Loo, C., 124
Lott, J., 98, 130
Loving v. Virginia, 190
Low-context communication, 31, 32, 36, 137, 148, 149, 156, 158, 168
 consistent with one's feelings, 35
 conversational maxims, 32-34
 explicit, 35
 direct, 35
 individualism-collectivism and, 35-36, 168
 openness, 33, 35, 36
 preciseness, 34, 35, 36
 silence, 34
Lowe, L., 7
Lucca, N., 26
Luhtanen, R., 99
Lyde, M., 85
Lyman, S., 67, 118, 149
Lynch, F., 25

Magnuson Act, 56
Mak, W., 105, 110
Manila men, 1, 43, 54, 71
Mann, E., 71
Marchetti, G., 101, 130
Mare, L., 34
Marelich, W., 85
Marginalization, 109, 114, 115
Markstrom-Adams, C., 99
Markus, H., 13, 30, 31, 112, 161
Marsella, A., 70, 85, 149, 150
Masculinity-femininity, 18, 36, 44-47, 51
 cultural, 44-45
 culture-specific, 45-46
 individual-level, 46-47
Mass, A., 99
Mass communication, 181-182, 192
 Asian immigrant's acculturation and, 181
 ethnic media, 181, 192
 host mass media, 181
 reading ethnic newspapers, 181-182
 U.S. newspapers, 181

U.S. television, 181
Masuda, M., 95, 119, 120, 126
Mataragon, R., 25
Matsumoto, G., 95, 119, 120, 126
Matsumoto, H., 161
Matsumoto, Y., 30, 36, 85, 113, 155, 156, 158, 168, 198, 200, 201
Maykovich, M., 141
McCarran-Walter Act of 1952, 57, 64
McDermott, J., 70, 71
McNaughton, W., 49
McQueen, M., 185
Melting pot metaphor, 172
Meridith, G., 71, 95, 119, 120, 126, 154
Messe, L., 179
Miller, G., 165
Miller, M., 166
Min, P., 77, 78, 79, 88, 96, 120, 121, 124, 129
Mitson, B., 65, 88
Mitsuye Endo v. United States, 65
Mixed-heritage Asian Americans, 90
    Chinese Thais, 97, 98
    ethnic identities of, 91, 97-99
    identity issues, 98
    Japanese Peruvians, 97
    See also Amerasians
Miyamoto, S. F., 66, 69, 88, 149, 150, 151
Mizutani, N., 22
Mizutani, O., 22
Model minorities, 57
Models of ethnic/cultural identities, 105-106
    comparing, 111-117
    individualistic versus collectivistic tendencies, 112-113
    language usage, 113-114
    shared networks, 114
    testing, 114-117
    See also Components model of identities; Developmental models of identities; Orthogonal model of identities; Typological models of identities
Montero, D., 119
Moon, A., 121
Moore, M., 119
Morisaki, S., 159
Morishima, J., 95
Morrison, T., 94, 172
Mortenson, S., 153

Morton, G., 110, 130
Moynihan, D., 172, 173
Multiplegroup ethnic identity measure, 111
Murphy-Shigematsu, S., 99

Nadamitsu, Y., 26, 35
Nagata, D., 15, 65, 88, 95, 181, 187, 191
Nakamura, H., 21, 47
Nakane, C., 20, 50, 69
Nakashima, C., 99
Nass, C., 181
Nathan, J., 85
Nee, V., 172
Nelson, B., 173
Newton, B., 119, 126
New York Chinatown History Project, 101
Ng, F., 53, 61, 62, 88
Nguyen, H., 179
Nicassio, P., 177
Nishi, S., 64, 151
Nishida, T., 18, 26, 30, 34, 35, 36, 85, 113, 155, 156, 158, 165, 168, 198, 200, 201
Norasalekunkit, V., 161
Norms/rules, 6
    Asian collectivistic, 25
    predicting behavior based on, 168
    U.S. individualistic, 25
Norton, R., 33, 147, 155, 156, 200
Novak, M., 172

O'Brien, D., 67, 118, 119, 185
Oetting, E., 106, 109
Oetzel, J., 109, 116, 130, 163, 197
Ogasawara, G., 187, 190, 192
Ogawa, D., 142, 143
Ogawa, N., 137, 139
Oguno, T., 137
Ohnishi, H., 110, 130
Okabe, K., 32, 33
Okabe, R., 34
Okamura, J., 74
Olsen, M., 6, 162
Omi, M., 90
Ong, A., 94
Open communicators, 33
Openness, 33, 182

Orthogonal model of identities, 106,
109-110, 112, 113, 129
cultural identity salience, 109
ethnic identity salience, 109
language usage and, 113-114
shared networks and, 114
social psychology and, 109-110
testing, 116-117
See also Ethnic exclusivity; Ethnic pride
Osajima, K., 57, 180
Ozawa, Takeo, 55-56

Pacific Islanders, 2
Padilla, A., 119
Page, M., 85
Page Act of 1870, 54
Pak, A., 142
Palinkas, L., 95
Panethnic identities, 11, 90, 92, 93, 103-105,
129.
See also Panethnicity
Panethnicity, 8, 90, 102-103
Asian American, 100-105
individual, 103
interethnic marriages and, 105
panethnic entrepreneurs and, 103
panethnic organizations and, 103
survival of Asian American, 103
See also Asian American movement;
Panethnic identities
Pang, G., 105, 188, 190
Pannu, R., 110
Park, K., 121
Park, R., 171, 172
Parrenas, R., 72
Parsons, T., 20
Paulhus, D., 161
Personal communication, 175-177
affective orientations, 175, 176
behavioral skills, 175, 176-177
cognitive abilities, 175-176
Personality orientations, 26-28, 85. *See also*
Allocentrism; Idiocentrism
Persuasive strategies, 148, 165-167
definition, 165
gender and, 166-167
individualistic cultures versus
collectivistic cultures, 165-167

liking, 166
positive altercasting, 166
positive expertise, 166
positive self-feeling, 166
positive self-esteem, 166
pregiving, 166
strategies of promise, 166
Peterson, C., 152
Phinney, J., 106, 107, 110, 130
Phinney, J. S., 106, 111
Pido, A., 24, 43, 73, 74, 76
Pittinsky. T., 95
Pluralism, 174
in United States, 173
versus assimilation, 171-174
See also Tossed salad metaphor
Polichar, D., 63, 75, 83
Politeness rules, 137-138, 139
Politeness theory, 159
Portes, A., 120, 130, 186
Posadas, B., 73, 88
Power, 28, 37, 120
serving individualistic interests, 29
Power distance, 18, 36, 41-44, 47, 51, 167
cultural, 41-42
culture-specific, 43
definition, 41
egalitarianism and, 43
individual-level, 43
variations in, 167
Pratto, F., 190

Race:
versus ethnicity, 90
Refugee Relief Acts:
of 1957, 60
of 1953, 57
Relational expectations:
across ethnic groups, 133-134
arousal, 133, 135
by ethnicity, 135
by strength of cultural identities, 135
by strength of ethnic identities, 135
control, 133, 135
for dating relationships, 133
intimacy, 133, 134, 135
predictive, 133
prescriptive, 133

receptivity, 133, 135
trust/equality, 133, 134, 135
violations of, 134-136
Resilience, 182
Revilla, L., 54, 72, 73, 75, 76, 88, 124, 125, 187
Reynolds, R., 166
Rhee, E., 85, 123
Rhodes, C., 119
Rimmer, T., 82, 97, 125, 180
Rios, D., 85
Robbillard, A., 70
Rokeach, M., 28
Roloff, M., 162
Roosens, E., 7, 92
Root, M., 97, 98, 99, 130
Rosenthal, D., 63, 118, 127, 129
Rotter, J., 176
Rumbaut, R., 80, 81, 186
Rutledge, P., 25, 40, 46, 82, 83, 84
Ruvolo, C., 139, 140

Sakai, J., 26, 35
Samter, W., 153
Sanbonmatsu, D., 161, 162
Sandhu, D., 110, 130
Sarason, B., 83, 84
Sarason, I., 83, 84
Sato, J., 190, 191, 192
Schlesinger, A., 173
Scholsberg, D., 119, 126
Schultz, G., 62
Schwartz, S., 28, 29, 112, 198
Scott Act of 1888, 60
Security, 28
    serving mixed interests, 29
Self construals, 30-31
    Chinese other-oriented, 22-23
    communication style predictors, 168
    independent, 30, 31, 36, 37, 86, 112, 136, 137, 158, 168
    independent versus interdependent, 85-86
    individualists' independent, 12
    interdependent, 13, 30, 31, 36, 37, 51, 86, 112-113, 135, 136, 137, 158, 168
Self-direction, 28, 37
    serving individualistic interests, 29
Separation, 109, 114, 115

Shame:
    as violation of expectation, 134-136
Shapiro, R., 109, 116, 130, 163, 197
Shared networks, ethnic identities and, 114, 129
Sharkey, W., 36, 85, 86, 136, 137
Sherman, S., 139, 140
Shibutani, T., 102
Shih, M., 95
Shinagawa, L., 105, 188, 190
Shon, S., 160
Shootoku, Prince, 21
Short, J., 40
Sidanius, J., 92, 190
Silence:
    expectations for, 138
    Japanese use of, 34
Simon, R., 185
Sinclair, S., 92
Singelis, T., 30, 36, 85, 86, 136, 137
Smith, K., 93
Smith, R., 22, 40
Snyder, M., 140
Social amnesia, 65
Social communication, 177-182
    Asian immigrants' self-images, 178
    differences across Asian American ethnic groups, 180
    ethnic communication, 179
    interpersonal communication, 178-181
    involvement in U.S. culture, 179
    length of stay in United States, 178
    mass communication, 181-182
Social distance, 143-144
Social identities, 92-97
    negotiating, 94
    See also Cultural identities; Ethnic identities
Social influence, communication and, 165
Sodetani, L., 129
Sodowsky, G., 110, 161
Song, Y., 79, 121
Sonoda, K., 129
Sorrentino, R., 40
Spencer, M., 99
Spickard, P., 187, 190
Spirituality, 28
    serving mixed interests, 29
Steers, W., 85

Steinberg, M., 165
Stephan, C., 99, 164
Stephan, W., 164
Stereotypes, 138-147
  affective, 138
  cognitive, 138
  create expectations, 139-140
  European Americans' of Japanese Americans, 141-142, 143
  Japanese of Japanese Americans, 141
  of Americans, 141
  of Asian American ethnic groups, 144-147
  of Chinese, 141
  of Japanese, 141
  self-fulfilling prophecies, 140, 142-143
Stereotyping, 104
  interethnic dating and, 188
  See also Stereotypes
Stimulation, 28, 37
  serving individualistic interests, 29
Stollak, G., 179
Strobel, L., 104, 105
Stryker, S., 10
Subcultures, 5-6
  occupational, 6
  regional, 6
  social, 6
Sue, D., 105, 106, 110, 111, 130
Sue, D. W., 105, 106, 108, 110, 111, 130
Sue, S., 95, 106, 108, 111
Sugimori, S., 28
Sung, B., 190, 192
Survey of Asian American Communication, x, 14, 86, 97, 112, 114, 117, 121, 125, 126, 131, 133, 134, 144, 147, 149, 155, 165, 195-204
  measurement of collectivistic values, 198
  measurement of communication styles, 200-201
  measurement of cultural identities, 197
  measurement of English spoken with family/friends, 199
  measurement of ethnic identities, 197
  measurement of ethnic language abilities, 199
  measurement of identity types, 197-198
  measurement of independent self construals, 198

measurement of individualistic values, 198
measurement of interdependent self construals, 199
measurement of relational expectations, 200
measurement of shared networks, 199
measurement of stereotypes, 203
respondents, 195-196
statistical analyses, 204
Symbols, 3

Tajfel, H., 92, 99
Takahashi, J., 120
Takahashi, Y., 85
Takaki, R., 53, 88
Takeo Ozawa v. the United States, 56
Takezawa, Y., 65, 66, 88, 174
Tam, V., 62
Tamura, E., 151
Tashima, E., 118, 119
Tateishi, J., 65, 88
Taylor, S., 65, 88
Tchen, J., 61, 88
Television:
  learning cultural norms/rules from, 6
  See also Mass communication
Teske, R., 173
Thai Americans, 2
Third generation return hypothesis, 118, 126
Thompson, K., 85, 153
Thornton, M., 98, 99, 130
Ting-Toomey, S., 30, 32, 33, 36, 50, 85, 109, 113, 116, 118, 130, 133, 155, 156, 158, 159, 160, 162, 163, 166, 168, 197, 198, 200, 201
Tossed salad metaphor, 173
Tradition, 28, 37
  serving collective interests, 29
Tran, T., 83
Triandis, H. C., 12, 18, 19, 20, 26, 30, 35, 112
Trotter, E., 82, 97, 125, 180
Tsai, J., 152, 153
Tse, L., 110, 130
Tseng, W., 70
Tsui, P., 62
Tuan, M., 93, 95, 96, 105, 188

Turner, J., 10
Turner, R., 109
Tydings-McDuffe Act of 1934, 56, 72
Typological models of identities, 106,
    107-109, 112, 113, 117
    Asian Americans, 108
    assimilation in, 108
    dominant groups, 108
    high assimilation/high-ethnic identities,
        108
    high assimilation/low-ethnic identities,
        108
    language usage and, 114
    low assimilation/high-ethnic identities,
        108
    low assimilation/low-ethnic identities,
        108
    marginal Asian Americans, 108
    shared networks and, 114
    subordinate groups, 108
    testing, 115-116
    traditional Asian Americans, 108
    See also Acculturation; Assimilation

U.S. Bureau of the Census, 1, 58, 122, 123,
    124
U.S. Commission on Civil Rights, 186
U.S. Supreme Court, 190
Uba, L., 63, 75, 83, 107, 117, 119
Uleman, J., 85, 123
Uncertainty avoidance, 18, 36, 37-41, 47, 51
    cultural, 37-38
    culture-specific, 38-40
    individual-level, 40-41
Universalism, 28
    serving mixed interests, 29

Verkuyten, M., 95
Versailles Village (New Orleans), 81
Vertical cultures, 20
    collectivistic, 21
    individualistic, 21
    versus horizontal cultures, 20-21
Vietnamese American families, 82-84
    acculturation and family relationships,
        83, 84
    age roles, 82

dating practices, 84
decision making, 83
family first principal, 84
male-headed, 82
nonnuclear members in, 83
parent-child conflicts, 83
role conflicts, 84
sex roles, 82
work, 83, 84
See also Vietnamese Americans
Vietnamese Americans, ix, x, 1, 2, 8, 13, 53,
    80-84, 85, 89, 129
as refugees, 80-81
cultural identity, 98
cultural variability, 18
English conversations, 125-126
ethnic enclaves, 81
ethnic identity, 97, 98
generation and language usage, 123, 124
institutions, 81-82
interaction patterns of, 180
interethnic marriage, 190, 191
language usage and, 125
population centers, 81
population statistics, 58, 80-81
research on, 14
self-perceptions, 147
See also Little Saigon (Los Angeles);
    Versailles Village (New Orleans)
Vietnamese cultural concepts:
    ho, 25
    nha, 25
    See also Vietnamese culture
Vietnamese culture:
    collectivism, 25
    Confucianism and, 50
    masculinity-femininity in, 46
    power distance in, 43
    uncertainty avoidance in, 40
Vietnamese immigration, 57
    patterns, 80-81
Villareal, M., 26, 35

Wagatsuma, Y., 119
Waldron, J., 71
Walters, G., 141
Walther, B., 133
Wang, G., 142

Wann, D., 99
War Brides Act of 1945, 56
Weaver, H., 110
Weber, ?., 47
Wei, W., 100, 101, 102, 173
Weiss, M., 188
Welkowitz, J., 154
Welsh, M., 63, 75, 83
Whaley, B., 153
White, M., 45
Whitmore, J., 83
Wiemann, J., 151, 152
Wierzbica, A., 21, 22, 39
Wilson, S., 35
Winant, H., 90
Wink, P., 86
Wong, H., 94
Wong, M., 60, 62, 63
Wooden, W., 118, 119
Wright, T., 109, 116, 130, 163, 197
Wu, D., 90, 91, 93, 122

Xing, J., 101, 130

Yamagida, E., 71

Yamaguchi, S., 28
Yamamoto, T., 96, 129
Yamanaka, K., 190
Yanagisako, S., 69
Yang, J., 159, 160
Yang, P., 61
Yang, S., 179, 181
Yee, B., 53, 88
Yee-Jung, K., 109
Yee-Yung, K., 109, 116, 130, 163, 197
Yeh, C., 95, 127, 160
Yeung, W., 188, 190
Yik, M., 161
Ying, Y., 110, 130
Yinger, M., 91
Yu, K., 79
Yu, R., 179
Yu, Y., 62, 88
Yum, J. O., 32, 33, 40, 48, 49, 142, 176, 177, 180, 181
Yum, N., 85
Yung, J., 192

Zhou, M., 81, 82, 84, 124, 127

About the Author

William B. Gudykunst is Professor of Speech Communication and a member of the Asian American Studies Program Council at California State University, Fullerton. His work focuses on developing a theory of interpersonal and intergroup effectiveness that can be applied to improving the quality of communication, and on explaining similarities and differences in communication across cultures and ethnic groups. He is the author of *Bridging Differences* and co-author of *Culture and Interpersonal Communication, Communicating With Strangers, Bridging Japanese/North American Differences,* and *Building Bridges,* among others. He has edited or co-edited numerous books, including *Communication in Japan and the United States, Handbook of International and Intercultural Communication, Theories of Intercultural Communication,* and *Communication in Personal Relationships Across Cultures,* among others. He is the editor of *Communication Yearbook* and a Fellow of the International Communication Association.